In this book, Christopher Allen provides a fascinating account of the political, social, and intellectual influences on the development of evidence law during the Victorian period. He sets out to challenge the traditional view of the significance of Jeremy Bentham's critique of the state of contemporary evidence law, and shows how statutory reforms were achieved for reasons that had little to do with Bentham's radical programme and how evidence law was developed by common law judges in a way diametrically opposed to that advocated by Bentham. Dr Allen's meticulous account provides a wealth of detail about the functioning of courts in Victorian England and will appeal to everyone interested in the English legal system during this period.

CHRISTOPHER ALLEN is a senior lecturer in law at the Inns of Court School of Law, London.

CAMBRIDGE STUDIES
IN ENGLISH LEGAL HISTORY

THE LAW OF EVIDENCE IN
VICTORIAN ENGLAND

CAMBRIDGE STUDIES
IN ENGLISH LEGAL HISTORY

Edited by
J. H. BAKER
Fellow of St Catherine's College, Cambridge

Recent series titles include

Sir William Scott, Lord Stowell
Judge of the High Court of Admiralty 1798–1828
HENRY J. BOURGUIGNON

Sir Henry Maine
A Study in Victorian Jurisprudence
R. C. J. COCKS

Roman canon law in Reformation England
R. H. HELMHOLZ

Fundamental authority in late Medieval English law
NORMAN DOE

Law, Politics and the Church of England
The Career of Stephen Lushington 1782–1873
S. M. WADDAMS

The early history of the law of bills and notes
A study of the origins of Anglo-American commercial law
JAMES STEVEN ROGERS

THE LAW OF
EVIDENCE IN
VICTORIAN ENGLAND

C. J. W. ALLEN

Senior Lecturer in Law, Inns of Court School of Law, London

CAMBRIDGE
UNIVERSITY PRESS

PUBLISHED BY THE PRESS SYNDICATE OF THE UNIVERSITY OF CAMBRIDGE
The Pitt Building, Trumpington Street, Cambridge CB2 1RP,
United Kingdom

CAMBRIDGE UNIVERSITY PRESS
The Edinburgh Building, Cambridge, CB2 2RU, United Kingdom
40 West 20th Street, New York, NY 10011-4211, USA
10 Stamford Road, Oakleigh, Melbourne 3166, Australia

First published 1997

Printed in the United Kingdom at the University Press, Cambridge

Typeset in Imprint 10/12

A catalogue record for this book is available from the British Library

Library of Congress Cataloguing in Publication data
Allen, C. J. W. (Christopher J. W.), 1944–
The law of evidence in Victorian England / C. J. W. Allen.
p.   cm. – (Cambridge studies in English legal history)
Includes bibliographical references and index.
ISBN 0 521 58418 3
1. Evidence (Law) – Great Britain – History.   I. Title.   II. Series.
KD7499.A83   1997
347.42'06 – dc21   96–49926   CIP

ISBN 0 521 58418 3   hardback

PO 1315
G.2-98

CE

To Richard Lander
1937–1992

CONTENTS

ACKNOWLEDGEMENTS

This book developed from research that I originally undertook as a part-time graduate student at University College London. Neither the book nor the thesis on which it is based would have appeared without William Twining's inspiration and encouragement. He first revived my interest in legal theory and history in LLM seminars and afterwards supervised my PhD thesis. To him I owe a substantial debt of gratitude. I am grateful also to the examiners of my thesis, William Cornish and Andrew Lewis, for their advice and help. Ian Dennis, Richard Friedman, Stephen Guest, John Langbein and Philip Schofield read drafts of my work at various stages, and I have benefited greatly from their advice and encouragement. Parts of chapter 3 first appeared in an article published in 1995 in the *Journal of Legal History*, and I am grateful to the publishers for permitting me to reproduce that material here. My thanks are also due to the staffs of the British Library, the Senate House Library of London University, the D. M. S. Watson Library of University College London, and the libraries of the Inner and Middle Temple and of Lincoln's and Gray's Inns. Finally, I am grateful to John Baker, the editor of this series, for the interest which he has shown in my work, and to Christopher Hart at the Cambridge University Press for all his help in the production of this book.

ABBREVIATIONS

Brougham MSS	The Manuscripts of Lord Brougham in University College London
Parl. Deb.	*Parliamentary Debates*
PP	*Parliamentary Papers*
UCL	The Manuscripts of Jeremy Bentham in University College London (followed by box and page numbers)
Works	*The Works of Jeremy Bentham, published under the Superintendance of his Executor, John Bowring*, 11 vols. (Edinburgh, 1838–43)

ENGLISH LAW REPORTS

A & E	Adolphus, John Leycester, and Thomas Flower Ellis, *Reports of Cases ... in the Court of King's Bench*, 12 vols. (London, 1834–40)
Atk	Atkyns, John Tracy, *Reports of Cases ... in the High Court of Chancery in the time of Lord Chancellor Hardwicke*, 3rd edn, by Francis Williams Sanders, 3 vols. (London, 1794)
B & Ad	Barnewall, Richard Vaughan, and John Leycester Adolphus, *Reports of Cases ... in the Court of King's Bench*, 5 vols. (London, 1831–5)
B & Ald	Barnewall, Richard Vaughan, and Edward Hall Alderson, *Reports of Cases ... in the Court of King's Bench*, 5 vols. (London, 1818–22)

B&S	Best, William Mawdesley, and George James Phillip Smith, *Reports of Cases . . . in the Court of Queen's Bench and the Court of Exchequer Chamber on Appeal from the Court of Queen's Bench*, 10 vols. (London, 1862–71)
Beav	Beavan, Charles, *Reports of Cases in Chancery*, 36 vols. (London, 1840–69)
Bing	Bingham, Peregrine, *Reports of Cases . . . in the Court of Common Pleas and Other Courts*, 10 vols. (London, 1824–34)
Bing NC	Bingham, Peregrine, *New Cases . . . in the Court of Common Pleas and Other Courts*, 6 vols. (London, 1835–41)
Brod & B	Broderip, William John, and Peregrine Bingham, *Reports of Cases . . . in the Court of Common Pleas and Other Courts*, 3 vols. (London, 1820–2)
Camp	Campbell, John, *Reports of Cases . . . at Nisi Prius, in the Courts of King's Bench and Common Pleas and on the Home Circuit*, 4 vols. (London, 1812–16)
Car & Kir	Carrington, F. A., and A. V. Kirwan, *Reports of Cases . . . at Nisi Prius*, 3 vols. (London, 1845–52)
Car & P	Carrington, F. A., and J. Payne, *Reports of Cases . . . at Nisi Prius*, 9 vols. (London, 1825–41)
CB	Manning, James, T. C. Granger, and John Scott, *Common Bench Reports. Cases . . . in the Court of Common Pleas and in the Exchequer Chamber*, 18 vols. (London, 1846–56)
C&J	Crompton, Charles, and John Jervis, *Reports of Cases . . . in the Courts of Exchequer and Exchequer Chamber*, 2 vols. (London, 1832–3)
Cowp	Cowper, Henry, *Reports of Cases . . . in the Court of King's Bench from . . . 1774 to . . . 1778*, 2nd edn, 2 vols. (London, 1800)

Cox CC	Cox, Edward William, *et al.* (eds.), *Reports of Cases in Criminal Law*, 31 vols. (London, 1846–1948)
Cr App R	*Criminal Appeal Reports* (London, 1908–)
Cr M & R	Crompton, Charles, R. Meeson and H. Roscoe, *Reports of Cases . . . in the Courts of Exchequer and Exchequer Chamber*, 2 vols. (London, 1835–6)
De G F & J	De Gex, J. P., F. Fisher and H. Cadman Jones, *Reports of Cases Heard and Determined by the Lord Chancellor and the Court of Appeal in Chancery*, 4 vols. (London, 1861–70)
Dougl	Douglas, Sylvester, *Reports of Cases . . . in the Court of King's Bench, in the Nineteenth, Twentieth, and Twenty First Years of the Reign of George III*, 4th edn, by W. Frere and H. Roscoe, 4 vols. (London, 1813–31)
East	East, Edward Hyde, *Reports of Cases . . . in the Court of King's Bench*, 16 vols. (London, 1801–14)
Esp	Espinasse, Isaac, *Reports of Cases . . . at Nisi Prius, in the Court of King's Bench and Common Pleas from . . . 1793 to . . . 1796*, 6 vols. (London, 1801–7)
Exch	Welsby, W. N., E. T. Hurlstone, and J. Gordon, *The Exchequer Reports. Reports of Cases . . . in the Courts of Exchequer and Exchequer Chamber*, 11 vols. (London, 1849–56)
Fitzg	Fitz-Gibbons, John, *The Reports of Several Cases . . . in the Court of King's Bench* (London, 1732)
Holt	Holt, Francis Ludlow, *Reports of Cases . . . at Nisi Prius.* (London, 1818)
JP	*The Justice of the Peace* (London, 1837–)
LJMC	*The Law Journal Reports, Magistrates' Cases, New Series* (London, 1831–96)
LR	*The Law Reports* (London, 1866–)

LT	*The Law Times Reports* (London, 1859–1947)
LTOS	*The Law Times Reports, Old Series* (London, 1843–59)
Leach	Leach, Thomas, *Cases in Crown Law*, 4th edn, 2 vols. (London, 1815)
Lewin	Lewin, Sir Gregory A., *A Report of Cases Determined on the Crown Side on the Northern Circuit*, 2 vols. (London, 1834–9)
Lofft	Lofft, Capel, *Reports of Cases . . . in the Court of King's Bench*. (Dublin, 1790)
Mac & G	Macnaghten, Steuart, and Alexander Gordon, *Cases in the High Court of Chancery*, 3 vols. (London, 1850–2)
Mod	*Modern Reports: or Select Cases Adjudged in the Courts of King's Bench, Chancery, Common Pleas and Exchequer from the Restoration of Charles the Second to the Twenty Eighth Year of George the Second*, 12 vols., 5th edn, by Thomas Leach (London, 1793–6)
PD	*The Law Reports, Probate, Divorce and Admiralty Division* (London, 1875–90)
Peake	Peake, Thomas, *Cases Determined at Nisi Prius*, 3rd edn (London, 1820)
Peake Add Cas	Peake, Thomas, *Additional Cases* (London, 1829)
P Wms	Williams, William Peere, *Reports of Cases . . . in the High Court of Chancery, and of some Special Cases Adjudged in the Court of King's Bench*, 4th edn, by Samuel Compton Cox, 3 vols. (London, 1826)
QB	Adolphus, John Leycester, and Thomas Flower Ellis, *Queen's Bench Reports*, 18 vols. (London, 1843–52)
Rob Ecc	Robertson, J. E. P., *Reports of Cases . . . in the Ecclesiastical Courts*, 2 vols. (London, 1850–3)
Russ	Russell, James, *Reports of Cases . . . in the*

	High Court of Chancery, 5 vols. (London, 1827–9)
Russ & Ry	Russell, William Oldnall and Edward Ryan, *Crown Cases*. (London, 1825)
Ry & Mood	Ryan, Edward, and William Moody, *Reports of Cases Determined at Nisi Prius*. (London, 1827)
Salk	Salkeld, William, *Reports of Cases Adjudged in the Court of King's Bench; with some Special Cases in the Courts of Chancery, Common Pleas and Exchequer*, 6th edn, by William David Evans, 3 vols. (London, 1795)
Stark	Starkie, Thomas, *Reports of Cases . . . at Nisi Prius, in the Courts of King's Bench and Common Pleas, and on the Circuit*, 3 vols. (London, 1817–20)
TLR	*The Times Law Reports* (London, 1884–1952)
TR	Durnford, Charles and Edward Hyde East, *Term Reports in the Court of King's Bench*, 8 vols. (London, 1817)
Taunt	Taunton, William Pyle, *Reports of Cases . . . in the Court of Common Pleas, and other Courts*, 8 vols. (London, 1810–23)
Vent	*The Reports of Sir Peyton Ventris* (London, 1726)
Wils KB	Wilson, George, *Reports of Cases . . . in the King's Courts at Westminster*, 3rd edn, 3 vols. (London, 1799)
WN	*Weekly Notes* (London, 1866–1952)
WR	*Weekly Reporter* (London, 1853–1906)

1

INTRODUCTION

In their Report of 1852–3 the Common Law Commissioners remarked that it was 'painful to contemplate the amount of injustice which must have taken place under the exclusive system of the English law'.[1] They referred to what any observer in the middle of the nineteenth century would have recognised as the outstanding feature of the English law of evidence as it operated in the superior courts of common law: the extent to which it prevented potential witnesses from giving testimony. Persons who might have been able to give useful evidence could be barred in a variety of circumstances. A witness with criminal convictions might be excluded, as might one who was unable for reasons of conscience to take a Christian oath. Those accused in criminal proceedings could not go into the witness box in their own defence. Persons, including the parties and their spouses, who had any pecuniary interest in the outcome of a civil action were not allowed to testify in that action. By 1852, the abolition of these restrictions had just begun, and it took until the end of the century to finish the job.

By the middle of the nineteenth century, English evidence law was becoming exclusive in another way. An observer might have reckoned that once a suitably disinterested witness had been found who was conventionally religious and without criminal convictions, that person would be allowed to testify without further restraint. But for several decades judicial decisions had been developing restrictions on what even a competent witness could say in court. Evidence of questionable reliability, which would

---

[1] *Second Report of H. M. Commissioners for Inquiring into the Process, Practice, and System of Pleading in the Superior Courts of Common Law* PP 1852–3 [1626] XL, 11.

have been heard for what it was worth a century earlier, was frequently excluded. This feature of evidence law was to become even more pronounced and would not retreat until the second half of the twentieth century.

The increasing restrictions on competent witnesses were reflected in the professional literature. For much of the eighteenth century there was no serious rival to a small work on evidence written by Sir Jeffrey Gilbert,[2] and posthumously published in 1754. Just over half of this book dealt with what we would now recognise as principles or rules of evidence law, and of this part by far the larger portion was devoted to the evidence of written instruments such as deeds, affidavits, writs, and even Acts of Parliament. The remainder of the work was a digest, which contained information about what it was proper or improper to prove in relation to the various issues that might be pleaded in particular actions. For example, pages were devoted to the learning on such pleas as *non est factum* and *non assumpsit*, and of not guilty in ejectment, trespass, and trover. In effect, this amounted to a miscellany of substantive law.[3] By the 1850s Gilbert's work had been superseded by new treatises, of which the most popular were written by Peake, Phillipps, Starkie, and Best.[4] All these writers, save Best, began by producing a work that was, like Gilbert's, to a large extent a digest of substantive law. Peake's work never changed this pattern but ultimately Phillipps and Starkie shed their digests in order to concentrate on providing an adequate account of a rapidly developing subject.[5]

A visit to the courts presided over by the common law judges

---

[2] Sir Jeffrey Gilbert (1674–1726) held judicial appointments in Ireland and then, from 1722, was a Baron of the English Court of Exchequer, becoming Chief Baron in 1725. The treatises that appeared under his name were all published posthumously, that on evidence being first published in Dublin in 1754. The last edition, by J. Sedgwick, was published in London in 1801. See the entry by John H. Langbein in A. W. B. Simpson, ed., *Biographical Dictionary of the Common Law* (London, 1984), p. 206; William Twining, 'The Rationalist Tradition of Evidence Scholarship', in *Rethinking Evidence* (Evanston, Ill., 1994), pp. 35–8.

[3] See, e.g., in the discussion of assault, the well-known example of the man who lays his hand on his sword, declaring that were it not assize time he would tell the plaintiff more of his mind (Sir Jeffrey Gilbert, *Law of Evidence*, 3rd edn (London, 1769), p. 256).

[4] See ch. 2, pp. 14–25, and Twining, *Rethinking Evidence*, pp. 42, 45–7, 48–9.

[5] See, e.g., the advertisement in the 4th edition of Thomas Starkie's *A Practical Treatise* (London, 1853).

in the 1850s would have revealed a procedural formality that had developed alongside the formal rules of evidence and was particularly marked in criminal trials. Defendants in criminal trials in both the eighteenth and nineteenth centuries were incompetent as witnesses in their own defence. But an eighteenth-century defendant, particularly one in the first half of that century, could still take an active part in the proceedings, and was expected to do so.

The presence of counsel on both sides was unusual for much of the eighteenth century, and consequently the judge had far more control over the proceedings than when he shared control with other professional lawyers: he would intervene frequently to examine prosecution witnesses and the accused; he could talk informally with jurors during the course of the trial; he could advise them on the verdict that should be returned, discuss the grounds of the verdict with them after it had been given, and, if need be, require them to deliberate further. This close contact between judge and jury meant that there was little need for the judge to become concerned with formal directions designed to protect the defendant, or to worry about the quality of evidence admitted. If the jury appeared to be going astray, the judge could correct them. However, by the middle of the nineteenth century this atmosphere of informality had been absent for some decades. For reasons that are discussed in chapter 5, by that time counsel was playing a larger part in criminal trials, with the judge taking a more passive role, and the defendant having scarcely any part to play at all. But, because there was less opportunity for ad hoc guidance, greater care had to be taken to exclude evidence that jurors might not be able to assess accurately. Whether evidence was admissible at all and, if admissible, what should be said about it in the summing up were questions that began to assume some importance. In criminal trials, because of the absence of an effective appellate system, this area of law remained in an embryonic state. In the civil courts, where there was for a time a surfeit of appellate courts,[6] the opportunity nevertheless existed for the growth of a new body of rules dealing with these questions.

While the common law courts were building up new evidential

---

[6] A. H. Manchester, *A Modern Legal History of England and Wales 1750–1950* (London, 1980), pp. 171–7.

barriers, Parliament was breaking down the old ones: from the 1850s onwards we can see the gradual collapse of the old restrictions based on competency. What brought about these changes? One question that has to be considered is whether there was a sharp division between lawyers and politicians. Was the victory for evidence law reform in Parliament counterbalanced by the victory in the courts of an essentially conservative profession? We cannot progress far with questions such as this without taking into account the figure of Jeremy Bentham and the tradition concerning the influence that he had on the evidence reforms of the nineteenth century.[7]

In 1861, Maine wrote of 'Bentham's immense influence in England during the past thirty years',[8] and twenty years later expressed the opinion that Bentham and his supporters had 'suggested and moulded the entire legislation of the fifty years just expired'.[9] 'Bentham's immense influence' soon became a commonplace, as can be seen from a students' handbook published in 1875, which Dicey acknowledged as an influence on his own writings. In this work, Wilson wrote:

Generally speaking, legislation has in all countries been directed rather at symptoms than at causes, and has been quite as likely as not to open a new sore while closing an old one. That the legislation of this century has been in some degree an exception, that amidst all its shortcomings and inconsistencies there is traceable something which is not mere quackery, something like a clear perception of the true conditions of health in the body politic, is due mainly to the presence of one new element – to the faithful labours, prolonged over more than half a century, of one man who dared to sit still and think, while others were acting at random, who dared to believe that law is capable of scientific treatment. What Socrates did for

---

[7] On Bentham generally see Elie Halévy, *The Growth of Philosophic Radicalism*, trans. Mary Morris (London, 1928); Ross Harrison, *Bentham* (London, 1983); John Dinwiddy, *Bentham* (Oxford, 1989). On Bentham and evidence law, see William Twining, *Theories of Evidence: Bentham and Wigmore* (London, 1985).

[8] Sir Henry Sumner Maine, *Ancient Law*, new edn, with notes by Sir Frederick Pollock (1861, London, 1930), p. 90.

[9] Sir Henry Sumner Maine, 'Radicalism Old and New', *St James's Gazette*, 25 January 1881, quoted in William Thomas, *The Philosophic Radicals: Nine Studies in Theory and Practice 1817–1841* (Oxford, 1979), p. 6.

moral philosophy, what Adam Smith did for political economy, that Bentham did, so far as England is concerned, for jurisprudence.[10]

Similar claims were made in entries in the *Encyclopaedia Britannica* and *Dictionary of National Biography*.[11]

It was in this intellectual context that Dicey wrote *Lectures on the Relation between Law and Public Opinion in England during the Nineteenth Century*. In this work he argued that from about 1825 onwards the teaching of Bentham had found ready acceptance among 'thoughtful Englishmen' because 'when it became obvious to men of common sense and of public spirit that the law required thoroughgoing amendment, the reformers of the day felt the need of an ideal and of a programme'.[12] But Dicey weakened his argument and created problems of falsifiability by the broad interpretation he put on 'Benthamism' and 'Benthamite doctrine'. His contention was that, although the men who had guided the course of legislation 'were in many instances not avowed Benthamites', and 'some of them would have certainly repudiated the name of utilitarians', nevertheless they

were all at bottom individualists. They were all, consciously or unconsciously, profoundly influenced by utilitarian ideas ... they were

[10] Sir Roland K. Wilson, *The History of Modern English Law* (London, 1875), pp. 278–9. The book was one of a series entitled 'Historical Handbooks' under the general editorship of Oscar Browning. Dicey acknowledged Wilson's work as an influence on his own writings: see the preface to the first edition of A. V. Dicey, *Lectures on the Relation between Law and Public Opinion in England during the Nineteenth Century* (London, 1905).

[11] *Encyclopaedia Britannica* 9th edn, s.v. 'Bentham, Jeremy', by T. E. Holland; *Dictionary of National Biography*, s.v. 'Bentham, Jeremy', by Sir John MacDonnell. The latter article referred to 'the abolition of arbitrary rules excluding from the cognisance of juries facts material for them to know', and to the passing of legislation whereby 'the legislature approached step by step towards [Bentham's] principle that no class of witnesses should be incompetent and no species of evidence excluded, but that every fact relevant to the inquiry should be admitted for what it is worth'. According to MacDonnell, while zealous disciples of great ability such as Brougham, Romilly, Horner, and Macintosh had assisted the work of legal reform, the originating spirit had been that of Bentham. For a similar approach see John Forrest Dillon, 'Bentham's Influence in the Reforms of the Nineteenth Century', in *Select Essays in Anglo-American Legal History*, compiled and edited by a committee of the Association of American Law Schools (Cambridge, 1907), vol. I, pp. 492–515.

[12] Dicey, *Law and Public Opinion*, 2nd edn (London, 1914), p. 168. In this he followed Maine, who had been of the opinion that the secret of 'Bentham's immense influence' had been his success in placing before the nation 'a distinct object to aim at in the pursuit of improvement' (Maine, *Ancient Law*, 1930 edn, p. 90).

utilitarians, but they accepted not the rigid dogmas of utilitarianism, but that Benthamism of common sense which, under the name of liberalism, was to be for thirty or forty years a main factor in the development of English law.[13]

The extent of Bentham's role was allowed to go unrevised by Holdsworth, who endorsed and explained a famous observation of Brougham in these words:

Bentham was the first English lawyer to think out a comprehensive set of philosophical principles upon which reforms in the law ought to be made. In the light of these principles he devoted his long life to the production of detailed programmes of reform in the subject matter of the law, in the form of its statement, in the machinery of its enforcement, in the institutions of the state; and he insisted on the duty of the Legislature to make all these reforms by direct legislation. It is for these reasons that Brougham could truly say that 'the age of law reform and the age of Jeremy Bentham are one and the same'.[14]

This left open the extent to which Bentham's work had affected particular reforms in the law, but elsewhere Holdsworth stated that in the period 1833–75 the legislative changes in the law of evidence, 'though not extensive, were almost as important, as those made in the law of civil procedure and pleading, *for, as we have seen, Bentham had paid as much attention to evidence as to procedure and pleading*'. The words emphasised show that Holdsworth assumed a connection between Bentham's writings on procedure and evidence and the enactment of reforming legislation. In another passage, after stating that some of Bentham's best work had been done on evidence, Holdsworth continued, 'and *as a result of it* important changes in the law had been made by the Legislature'.[15]

---

[13] Dicey, *Law and Public Opinion*, 2nd edn, pp. 169–70; see also p. 177. Dicey extended still further the scope for Benthamism by suggesting that it possessed a latent 'despotic or authoritative element', and that between 1868 and 1900 changes took place that brought this into prominence. He concluded that 'English collectivists' had 'inherited from their utilitarian predecessors a legislative doctrine, a legislative instrument, and a legislative tendency pre-eminently suited for the carrying out of socialistic experiments' (ibid., pp. 308, 310).

[14] Sir William Holdsworth, *A History of English Law*, (London, 1922–66) vol. XIII, p. 42; H. Brougham, *Speeches of Henry Lord Brougham upon Questions Relating to Public Rights, Duties & Interests; with Historical Introductions, and a Critical Dissertation upon the Eloquence of the Ancients* (Edinburgh, 1838), vol. II, pp. 287–8.

[15] Holdsworth, *History of English Law*, vol. XV, pp. 138, 307 (my emphases).

Similarly, in a collection of essays published in 1948, Keeton and Marshall attributed to the cogency of Bentham's arguments the progressive abandonment of the 'best evidence rule', and claimed that his work had been 'directly responsible for the removal of disabilities due to the form of the oath'.[16]

The extent of Bentham's influence was vigorously questioned in the context of administrative reform in the debate on the 'Victorian revolution in government'.[17] Despite the scepticism generated by this debate, as late as 1982 Hart maintained the traditional view of Bentham's influence on nineteenth-century law reform when he alleged that 'Bentham's attack inspired the great statutory reforms of the law of evidence of 1843, 1851, and 1898'.[18] More recently, Landsman claimed that

Bentham's ideas had a profound impact on the development of the rules of evidence. His work significantly advanced the process that led to the rejection of virtually all competency exclusions.[19]

Thus the story of evidence law in the nineteenth century has traditionally been that of one man and the legislation that his writings inspired. I shall argue that this is a misleading story and that there is another that is both more complex and more reliable. In this story Bentham has a part to play, but it is not the only, nor even the leading, part. No consideration of Bentham's role can

---

[16] G. W. Keeton and O. R. Marshall, 'Bentham's Influence on the Law of Evidence', in G. W. Keeton and G. Schwartzenberger, eds., *Jeremy Bentham and the Law* (London, 1948), pp. 86, 88.

[17] On this debate, and for references to earlier contributions to it, see generally Stephen Conway, 'Bentham and the Nineteenth-Century Revolution in Government', in Richard Bellamy, ed., *Victorian Liberalism: Nineteenth-Century Political Thought and Practice* (London, 1990), pp. 71–90.

[18] H. L. A. Hart, 'The Demystification of the Law', in *Essays on Bentham: Studies in Jurisprudence and Political Theory* (Oxford, 1982), p. 31. This essay was first published in 1973 but appeared substantially unchanged in Hart's 1982 collection.

[19] Stephan Landsman, 'From Gilbert to Bentham: the Reconceptualization of Evidence Theory', *Wayne Law Review* 36 (1990), 1149–86. See also Robert Stewart, *Henry Brougham 1778–1868: His Public Career* (London, 1986), p. 234. For a more cautious assessment, see Dinwiddy, *Bentham*, p. 117; David Lieberman, *The Province of Legislation Determined: Legal Theory in Eighteenth-Century Britain* (Cambridge, 1989), pp. 3–4, 122–44, 179–98. In a radical criticism, T. S. Midgley has argued that whatever influence Bentham had was solely on a tradition of legal historiography, and not on the upsurge of legal reform in the nineteenth century (T. S. Midgley, 'The Role of Legal History', *British Journal of Law and Society* 2 (1975), 153, 158).

begin, however, without some introduction to his ideas on adjective law, and it is necessary to turn now to this subject.[20]

BENTHAM ON ADJECTIVE LAW

In Bentham's view, the proper end of substantive law was 'the
creation and preservation of the greatest happiness of the greatest
number'. The proper end of adjective law, including the law of
evidence, was to give effect to substantive law. But law of all kinds
had been diverted to serve various 'sinister interests'. Bentham
believed that legislation, instead of being designed to secure the
greatest happiness of the greatest number, was designed to secure
the creation and preservation of the greatest quantity of happiness
to those few persons who had the powers of government, and to
their connections. Further, judges had made their own sinister
interests the actual direct ends of their exercise of judicial
authority. Other members of 'the governing body' had jumped on
the bandwagon and as 'sinecurists or over-paid placemen, or
holders of needless places' had been allowed to share in the 'fruits
of scientifically and diligently cultivated delay, vexation and
expense'. In pursuit of their true object the judges had to maintain
some appearance of justice, but it was for this reason alone that
any justice was to be found at all. Most affected by the sinister
interests of the judiciary had been procedural law, and within that
branch it was evidence law that had suffered most.

Any legislator, Bentham argued, had duties in relation to
evidence. In the first place he had a duty to ensure, so far as
possible, that there was sufficient evidence to support every right
and duty that might be litigated. The results of litigation should
not depend on the hazard of being able to find, after the event,
adequate oral testimony to support the right or duty in question.
A system of 'pre-appointed' evidence should be developed, by

---

[20] Bentham's main writings on procedure and evidence are to be found in the
following works, which are indicated by short title and date of printing: *Scotch
Reform* (1807), *Introductory View of the Rationale of Evidence* (1812), *Swear Not
At All* (1813), *A Treatise on Judicial Evidence* (1825), *Rationale of Judicial
Evidence* (1827), *Principles of Judicial Procedure* (1843). For fuller bibliographies
see Halévy, *Growth of Philosophic Radicalism* and Harrison, *Bentham*.

which rights and duties could be recorded before any question of their being litigated arose.

Secondly, the legislator should ensure that no evidence was excluded, except where this was required to avoid preponderant delay, vexation, and expense.[21] Bentham envisaged a utilitarian calculation. There might be circumstances in which the harm from delay, vexation, or expense would be greater if a party were permitted to adduce a particular item of evidence than if the evidence were excluded. But apart from this consideration, nothing justified exclusion. In particular, evidence should not be excluded simply because too much weight might be attached to it. The legislator, instead of using exclusion to reduce the risk of misdecision, should provide guidelines to assist triers of facts in assessing the materials presented to them.

In Bentham's eyes, the exclusion of evidence was not just an error; it was a fundamental part of a corrupt system of judicial procedure. It was the judges who had developed adjective law, and the system which had emerged was one in which suitors paid fees for items of judicial labour. This was the worst of all possible developments. While a legislator operated by way of rules laid down in advance, judges laid down no such rules. What was thought right, or was pretended to be thought right, was done to suit each occasion. It was left to suitors to frame whatever rules for guidance that they could from their observation of what judges did. In this way there developed what Bentham called the 'technical' system of procedure.[22] Bentham argued further that, because of the system for paying judges, the very people who were responsible for developing adjective law had a personal interest in making it as obscure as possible. For this reason he referred to the system then in existence as the 'fee-gathering' system.

Bentham looked for an alternative model of procedure and found one in the institution of the family. The way in which facts were inquired into and justice administered within the family

---

[21] Bentham used 'vexation' to refer to any evil produced by the law but not directly intended. He compared vexation to punishment, the latter being directly intended (*Rationale of Judicial Evidence* in *Works*, vol. VII, p. 345).

[22] From the Greek *technē*, meaning skill, or art. Because there were no rules laid down 'in determinate words', whatever rules there might be could not be understood, or guessed at, without art (*Rationale of Judicial Evidence* in *Works*, vol. VII, p. 197).

Bentham called the 'natural' or 'domestic' mode of procedure. A domestic tribunal operated without forms or rules, but, according to Bentham, had no fewer safeguards against misdecision than the technical system. Indeed, the technical system was more likely to lead to misdecision through its exclusion of relevant evidence in an inquiry. There was no witness of whom it could be said with certainty that his testimony would be untrue throughout, so as to justify a judge in refusing to hear it. Nor was there any kind of interest that would inevitably overpower a witness so as to make it certain that his testimony was bound to be untrue.[23]

BENTHAM AND INFLUENCE

A classic example of law reform inspired by Bentham is to be found, not in England, but in the North American state of Maine. John Appleton, a justice of the supreme court from 1852 until 1862 and then Chief Justice until his retirement in 1883, was an enthusiastic follower of Bentham and a supporter of evidence law reform. He wrote a number of articles in legal periodicals on the subject, and in 1860 published them in a collection entitled *The Rules of Evidence Stated and Discussed*.[24]

In the preface he acknowledged that he had read with great interest 'the masterly work of Bentham on the subject of Evidence'. He continued: 'But as that is not readily accessible, and is so voluminous, it occurred to me, that a careful examination of the more important rules of law, as to the admission and exclusion of evidence ... would not be without interest to the legal profession and would be of utility to the public.' He was careful to emphasise that he regarded his task as one of spelling out Bentham's ideas and their implications. 'In what I have done, I have only endeavored to apply the reasoning and principles of Bentham, of which I have made free use, to the law as found in the treatises of jurisconsults and the decisions of the courts.'[25]

Appleton was not content merely with writing. He campaigned,

---

[23] *Introductory View of the Rationale of Evidence*, in *Works*, vol. VI, pp. 5–14; *Rationale of Judicial Evidence* in *Works*, vol. VII, pp. 197–9.

[24] John Appleton, *The Rules of Evidence Stated and Discussed* (Philadelphia, Penn., 1860).

[25] Ibid., pp. iii–iv.

using the authority of his judicial position, for legislation that would bring into effect some of the changes advocated by Bentham, and was the prime mover behind the adoption in 1856 of legislation that extended competency to the parties in civil suits. But Appleton's most significant achievement was to secure for defendants in criminal trials the right to testify on their own behalf. As a result of a campaign which relied heavily on Bentham's arguments, in 1864 Maine became the first common law jurisdiction in the world to allow this.[26]

Such an obvious example of Bentham's influence on particular law reforms is lacking in England, though something like Appleton's enthusiasm for Bentham can be found in the support for reform that came from Brougham and Denman.[27] But to take the case of Appleton as an exclusive model for the operation of Bentham's influence would be to neglect the many possibilities of indirect influence exerted by his ideas. An analysis that took these possibilities into account was adopted in the context of the debate over the Victorian revolution in government by S. E. Finer. He suggested that Bentham's influence operated through a complex process of absorption and interpretation by others involving three elements.

Finer called the first of these 'irradiation', which was 'the process by which small knots of Benthamites attracted into their salons, their committees and their associations a much wider circle of men whom they infected with some at least of their enthusiasms'. The second element of 'suscitation' was 'the process of arranging public inquiries or the press or both together in such a way as to create a favourable public opinion, of a temporary kind, amid influential groups in the country'. Finer called the third element 'permeation', which was 'the process of securing official employment of oneself and thereafter using this position' to promote Benthamite policies by further irradiation and suscitation.[28]

Finer's categories suggest a more organised campaign in the

[26] David M. Gold, *The Shaping of Nineteenth-Century Law: John Appleton and Responsible Individualism* (New York, 1990), pp. 59–61, 168.

[27] See chs. 3 and 4.

[28] S. E. Finer, 'The Transmission of Benthamite Ideas 1820–50', in Gillian Sutherland, ed., *Studies in the Growth of Nineteenth-Century Government* (London, 1972), p. 13.

field of government than existed in that of law reform. Among law reformers there were those, including Denman and Brougham, who set out to place some of Bentham's views before the public in a more readily digestible form, such as articles in the *Westminster Review* or *Law Magazine*. Writers of this kind, though they may in some respects have been critical, had been persuaded by at least some of Bentham's arguments. Occasionally, persons speaking or writing in favour of reforms mentioned the name of Bentham in that connection, and a similar presumption may be made about them. But references to Bentham of this kind were unusual.

Far more frequently we find persons who advocated evidence law reform using arguments that Bentham had used, but without acknowledging Bentham as their source. Caution is necessary in such cases. Bentham's arguments were not by any means all original, and the fact that a Member of Parliament used an argument which Bentham also had used does not show that he followed Bentham in using it. For example, one of the arguments used by Bentham against the employment of oaths in judicial proceedings was that it led to a double standard of truth. This was an argument used later in debates on the requirement that all testimony should be on oath.[29] Yet the argument had been familiar to Shakespeare, as we can tell from the objection made by Brutus when Cassius proposes that the conspirators should bind themselves by an oath.[30] It should also be remembered that there was a tradition of conservative utilitarianism, represented, for example, in the writings of Paley.[31] Even where we find an argument that looks as if it is a utilitarian one, it does not follow that the person adopting it was influenced by the radical utilitarianism of Bentham.[32]

However, the question of Bentham's influence is a lively one only in relation to the statutory reforms. There were other devel-

---

[29] See ch. 3.   [30] *Julius Caesar* 2. 1. 129–40.
[31] See, e.g. William Paley, *The Principles of Moral and Political Philosophy* (London, 1785, and subsequent edns).
[32] It might be tempting to suggest that there were reformers who had been deeply influenced by Bentham's writings but who, for diplomatic reasons, encouraged reforms without relying on the radical arguments that would have established a link between themselves and Bentham. But I have found no evidence that this was so, and the theory obviously presents problems of falsifiability. Cf. the criticism of 'ad hoc hypotheses' in Colin Howson and Peter Urbach, *Scientific Reasoning: The Bayesian Approach* (La Salle, Ill., 1989), pp. 106–8.

opments taking place in the common law of evidence that have been generally ignored in accounts of nineteenth-century evidence law. Historically, the common law had from time to time been a creative instrument of reform. How far was it creative in this period in relation to this subject?

2

COMMON LAW DEVELOPMENTS

The main problem presented by the development of evidence case
law in the nineteenth century is how to account for the exclusionary, rule-based system that began to govern testimony given
in court, and that was in marked contrast to the moves made in
Parliament to abolish the old exclusionary rules about competency
of witnesses. Treatise writers, law reporters, and judges were all
involved. To some extent, it is artificial to consider their contributions separately; each group affected, and was in turn affected by,
the others. But for the purposes of this discussion it is convenient
to deal with treatise writers separately from law reporters and
judges.

TREATISE WRITERS

For much of this period treatises were written solely for practitioners; there was no formal system of legal education to create a
student market.[1] But in one respect the requirements of practitioners were the same as those of the student market that began
to develop towards the end of the nineteenth century: both practitioners and students needed a method of organisation that
would, so far as possible, provide coherence and unity grounded
in a set of general principles from which a body of particular rules
could be deduced.[2]

---

[1] W. R. Cornish and G. de N. Clark, *Law and Society in England 1750–1950*
(London, 1989) pp. 105–7; William Twining, '1836 and All That: Laws in the
University of London 1836–1986', in B. Hepple, ed., *Current Legal Problems
1987* (London, 1987), pp. 261, 262–6.
[2] A. W. B. Simpson, 'The Rise and Fall of the Legal Treatise: Legal Principles and
the Forms of Legal Literature', *University of Chicago Law Review* 48 (1981), 632,
665–6; David Sugarman, 'Legal Theory, the Common Law Mind and the

14

How influential were the attempts of nineteenth-century writers on evidence to rationalise their subject? The fact that the treatises were a commercial success tells us nothing certain about the use made of their contents. Then, as now, books might be purchased more from a sense of duty or a desire for display than from any other motive. Nevertheless, it is probable that treatise writers did help to form evidence law. Treatises, even if not directly cited to a court, were an obvious source of material for legal argument,[3] and occasional references in law reports suggest that they were used in this way. For example, in *Nelson* v. *Whittall* (1817)[4] Bayley J referred critically to Phillipps's *Treatise* and its treatment of proof in an action on a promissory note. In *Batthews* v. *Galindo* (1828)[5] Best CJ stated that he regarded Phillipps's *Treatise* as 'proof of the understanding of Westminster Hall' on the question of whether the evidence of a mistress was on the same footing as that of a wife with regard to admissibility. In *Chapple* v. *Durston* (1830)[6] Vaughan B referred to a suggestion in Starkie's 'valuable, practical treatise on the law of evidence' on a point concerning the statute of limitations. A review of the first edition of Best's *Treatise* referred to the fact that his earlier work on presumptions had been 'favourably noticed by the Bench'.[7]

These nineteenth-century treatises differed from most earlier legal writings. According to older tradition, the common law was derived from both legal and non-legal sources. For example, there were principles of nature and reason – morality and logic – which were part of the common law and enabled it to operate as an instrument of reform. Bacon suggested that the more subtle and abstruse rules of law were to be 'gathered from the harmony of laws and decided cases', and were in fact 'the general dictates of reason, which run through the different matters of law, and act as its ballast'.[8] Coke praised judge-made law as the accumulation and

Making of the Textbook Tradition', in William Twining, ed., *Legal Theory and Common Law* (Oxford, 1986), pp. 26–61. Cf. review of the 6th edn of Henry Roscoe's *Digest of the Law of Evidence*: 'Text books should be expositions of principles, not strings of cases. No cases should be cited but those which establish or modify the law as it is' (*Law Magazine* 2 (NS) (1844), 201).
[3] J. S. Mill, 'Austin on Jurisprudence', in J. M. Robson, ed., *Collected Works of John Stuart Mill* (Toronto, 1963–91), vol. XXI, p. 171.
[4] 1 B & Ald 19, 21.   [5] 4 Bing 610, 614.   [6] 1 C & J 10.
[7] *Law Magazine* 11 (NS) (1849), 201.
[8] *De Augmentis Scientarum*, in J. Spedding, R. Ellis, and D. Heath, eds., *The Works of Francis Bacon* (London, 1857–74), vol. V, pp. 105–6.

refinement of experience.[9] Blackstone saw the common law as having undergone a continuous process of change. Not all customs had been accepted as part of the law. The decisions of the courts provided the chief evidence of those that had, but judges' opinions were not the same thing as the law itself: a previous judicial opinion might be contrary to reason, and thus not law. But courts could also decide new cases where no previous decisions were in point. Such cases were determined according to 'reason and convenience, adapted to the circumstances of the time'.[10] Mansfield was another judge who emphasised the ability of the common law to respond to changing social conditions. In his view, '*quicquid agunt homines* is the business of Courts, and as the usages of society alter, the law must adapt itself to the various situations of mankind'. According to Mansfield, 'precedent, though it be evidence of law, is not law in itself; much less the whole of the law'. The law did not consist in particular cases, but in general principles that ran through the cases and governed the decision of them.[11] These beliefs led to widespread criticism within the legal profession when Blackstone's *Commentaries* first appeared, because their author was thought to have distorted the law by attempting to reduce it to a system of general rules.[12] By contrast, the nineteenth-century profession willingly adopted treatises that increasingly presented law as a system of rules, derived by the writer from judicial decisions.

The beginnings of this development in evidence law can be seen

[9] Pocock concluded that in the course of time the term 'custom' came to mean 'time and experience' or 'time and reason' (J. G. A. Pocock, *The Ancient Constitution and the Feudal Law: a Study of English Historical Thought in the Seventeenth Century* (Cambridge, reissued 1987), p. 272). This emphasis on the refinement of experience suggests a law in constant change and adaptation. In fact, common lawyers came to believe that the law, and constitutional law in particular, had always been the same. The idea of custom was ambiguous: it could suggest something in a process of constant adaptation, or something that had survived unchanged from time immemorial (ibid., pp. 35–7).

[10] William Blackstone, *Commentaries on the Laws of England*, ed. Edward Christian, 15th edn (London, 1809), vol. II, p. 385; David Lieberman, *The Province of Legislation Determined: Legal Theory in Eighteenth-Century Britain* (Cambridge, 1989), pp. 43–6, 84–6.

[11] *Barwell* v. *Brooks* (1784) 3 Dougl 371, 373; *Jones* v. *Randall* (1774) Lofft 383, 385; *Rust* v. *Cooper* (1774) 2 Cowp 629, 632.

[12] Michael Lobban, *The Common Law and English Jurisprudence 1760–1850* (Oxford, 1991), pp. 2–15, 47–79. See also Gerald J. Postema, *Bentham and the Common Law Tradition* (Oxford, 1986), ch. 1; Lieberman, *Province of Legislation Determined*, pp. 71–4, 89–93, 96–8, 123.

in an appendix to W. D. Evans's translation, published in 1806, of Pothier's treatise on the law of obligations. Evans saw the manifestation of truth and the exclusion of falsehood as the two aims of any system of evidence. But he thought that full attainment of these aims was often impossible because 'the latitude which is requisite for the one is inconsistent with the caution which is too often necessary for securing the other'.[13] Evans acknowledged that whatever rule might be established in general for the purpose of securing these respective advantages would frequently be defective or erroneous in its particular application. Nevertheless, he believed that to avoid deception and error it was necessary to accept evidence with some caution: in particular, by adopting rules of authenticity that would wholly exclude the admission of less authentic testimony, such as that of interested persons. 'By this exclusion truth is often frustrated, as in the general reception of evidence it is often disguised and perverted; but in both cases, the general principle of conduct is to provide for the greatest promotion and preservation of it upon the whole.' For example, in private conversation a hearsay might carry full conviction; but to admit it in the administration of justice 'would be productive of very considerable error and inconvenience'. To admit hearsay evidence would involve a misplaced reliance on the truthfulness, accuracy, and completeness of each person through whom the information had been transmitted. The sanction of an oath would be absent, and the testimony could not be properly tested under cross-examination.[14]

Evans's choice of subject matter and emphasis were very much in the tradition reflected in Gilbert's earlier work. Like Gilbert, he saw the 'best evidence rule' as the foundation on which all evidence law rested.[15] Evans, too, thought written evidence more significant because it was less likely than oral evidence to be mis-

[13] R. J. Pothier, *A Treatise on the Law of Obligations, or Contracts. Translated from the French, with an Introduction, Appendix, and Notes, Illustrative of the English Law on the Subject by William David Evans, Esq. Barrister at Law* (London, 1806), vol. II, p. 141.
[14] Ibid., pp. 239, 283–4.
[15] 'The first therefore and most signal Rule, in Relation to Evidence, is this, That a Man must have the utmost Evidence the Nature of the Fact is capable of . . .' (Sir Jeffrey Gilbert, *Law of Evidence*, 3rd edn (London, 1769), p. 4). Cf. John Locke, *An Essay Concerning Human Understanding*, P. H. Nidditch, ed., (Oxford, 1975), bk. IV, ch. 11, sect. 10, p. 636. See also Steven Shapin, *A Social History of Truth: Civility and Science in Seventeenth-Century England* (Chicago, Ill., 1994), ch. 5.

constructed or misrepresented. Indeed, Evans criticised English courts for tending to receive a mass of testimony at considerable expense when the proceedings might have been curtailed by concentrating on those facts likely to be decisive of the cause.[16] The increasing emphasis on exclusionary rules of evidence that appears in treatises published in the second quarter of the nineteenth century has to be seen against the background of Bentham's writings on evidence, of which three main works were published in the 1820s. In 1823 the *Traité des preuves judiciaires* was published in Paris. An English translation was published in serial form in the *Law Journal* in the following year, and as a complete work in 1825. In 1827 there appeared the *Rationale of Judicial Evidence*.[17] These works, like Bentham's other writings on adjective law, repeatedly emphasised two themes that had the capacity to affect the future development of evidence law. The first was his criticism of judge-made law; the second, his criticism of exclusionary rules of evidence.[18]

[16] Pothier, *Treatise*, trans. Evans, vol. II, pp. 223–5. William Twining's discussion of Evans suggests that he differed significantly from Gilbert in his treatment of the 'best evidence rule' (William Twining, 'The Rationalist Tradition of Evidence Scholarship', in *Rethinking Evidence: Exploratory Essays* (Oxford, 1990), p. 44). In fact, Evans stated that 'the greater part of the particular system which is established respecting the law of evidence, may be regarded as an amplification and exposition of this general rule' (Pothier, *Treatise*, trans. Evans, vol. II, p. 148). And, like Evans, Gilbert recognised that there could be flexibility in the operation of the rule, so that if a party offered the best evidence that they could, that might be enough. If, e.g., a witness fell sick by the way, their deposition might be used, 'for in this Case, the deposition is the best Evidence that possibly can be had, and that answers what the Law requires'. A similar principle applied where a witness had died, or could not be found after a search. (Gilbert, *Evidence*, (1769), pp. 61–2). See also J. B. Thayer, *A Preliminary Treatise on Evidence at the Common Law* (Boston, Mass., 1898), pp. 490–1; Dale A. Nance, 'The Best Evidence Principle', *Iowa Law Review* 73 (1988), 227–97.

[17] *Traité des preuves judiciaires, ouvrage extrait des MSS de M. Jeremie Bentham, jurisconsulte anglais, par Et. Dumont*, 2 vols. (Paris, 1823); *A Treatise on Judicial Evidence, Extracted from the MSS of Jeremy Bentham by M. Dumont, Translated into English* (London, 1825); *Rationale of Judicial Evidence, Specially Applied to English Practice, from the MSS of Jeremy Bentham*, 5 vols. (London, 1827). Of Dumont's *Traité*, A. D. E. Lewis has written: 'Although based exclusively on Bentham's manuscripts and by general scholarly consent faithful to Bentham's thought, this work is essentially Dumont's, not least in the clarity of its exposition' (A. D. E. Lewis, 'Bentham's View of the Right to Silence', in Roger Rideout and Bob Hepple, eds., *Current Legal Problems 1990*, (London, 1990), p. 138).

[18] See, generally, William Twining, *Theories of Evidence: Bentham and Wigmore*

Bentham's concern to keep the judge from usurping the function of the legislator was based on the belief that any resulting short-term gain would be outweighed by the threat to the expectations of litigants that such a power would present.[19] Admittedly, the legislature was equally capable of defeating litigants' expectations. But what made intervention by the judiciary so undesirable was the fact that judges, unlike the legislature, were unable to take the wide view of both law and human activities needed for intervention to be effective. This argument was diametrically opposed to earlier legal opinion. Lawyers in the seventeenth and eighteenth centuries had preferred common law to statute as an instrument of reform because it had been thought that statutes gave rise to greater uncertainty than common law, and were unable to deal as efficiently with the variety of situations giving rise to legal disputes.[20] But so radical was the law reform that Bentham advocated that it could be achieved only as a result of long-term planning. Judicial reform was inappropriate because of its piecemeal, blinkered nature. Another of Bentham's objections was that judges who made new common law rules were in effect legislating retrospectively, while attempting to conceal what they were doing by the fiction that their new rules were implicit in existing law. Governing Bentham's criticism of judge-made law was his belief in the need to distinguish carefully between the functions of the legislature and those of the judiciary, and to avoid usurpation by judges of the legislative function, not least because of his deep distrust of the 'sinister interest' of 'Judge & Co'.[21]

Bentham was particularly critical of the use of precedent as a source of law. Even if the original decision had been right, to make

(London, 1985), ch. 2; Postema, *Bentham and the Common Law Tradition*, chs. 5–8.

[19] UCL 63:49, quoted by Postema, *Bentham and the Common Law Tradition*, p. 193.

[20] Pocock, *The Ancient Constitution and the Feudal Law*, p. 34; Donald R. Kelley, 'History, English Law and the Renaissance', *Past and Present* 65 (1974), 35; Barbara Shapiro, 'Law Reform in Seventeenth Century England', *American Journal of Legal History* 19 (1975), 298; Shapiro, 'Sir Francis Bacon and the Mid-Seventeenth Century Movement for Law Reform', *American Journal of Legal History*, 24 (1980), 337; Lieberman, *Province of Legislation Determined*, p. 102.

[21] In some of his early writings Bentham tried to set out principles to which the existing common law system should conform, but by 1774–5 he had concluded that the common law system could not stand (Postema, *Bentham and the Common Law Tradition*, p. 197 *et seq.*).

it a precedent did injustice, because it meant following something
designed to meet the different needs of an earlier time. Worse still,
the practice of following precedents substituted 'mechanical judicature' for 'mental judicature': reasoning was displaced by imitation. On Bentham's analysis, the common law suffered from a
deep internal contradiction: it could not satisfactorily reconcile the
conflicting demands of general security, in the sense of predict-
ability of outcomes, with the need for flexibility in adjudication.
Therefore it was compelled to swing between arbitrariness and
rigidity, condemned alike for judicial manipulation and mindless
imitation.[22]

The immediate aim of legal procedure was, for Bentham, to
achieve rectitude of decision. Facts had to be reliably determined,
so that the substantive law could be correctly applied. The system
of procedure best adapted to achieve rectitude of decision was the
Natural System,[23] which had no place for rules of evidence. Thus
in a chapter in the *Rationale of Judicial Evidence*, entitled 'On the
Probative Force of Circumstantial Evidence', Bentham wrote:

*What ought to be done, and what avoided, in estimating the probative force of
circumstantial evidence?*

On this as on every other part of the field of evidence, rules capable of
rendering right decisions secure, are what the nature of things denies. To
the establishment of rules by which misdecision is rendered more
probable than it would otherwise be, the nature of man is prone. To put
the legislator and the judge upon their guard against such rashness, is all
that the industry of the free inquirer can do in favour of the ends of
justice.[24]

In the preface to the first edition of Starkie's *Treatise*, which
appeared in 1824, the author acknowledged that exclusionary rules
might not always be satisfactory, but he asserted that there were
arguments in their support. It was

essential in practice to guard and limit the reception of evidence by
certain definite and positive rules. Nature has no limits; but every system
of the positive law must, on grounds of policy, prescribe artificial
boundaries, even in its application to a subject which from its independent
nature least of all admits of such restraint. These, however, are necessarily
for the most part of a negative description, the effect of which is to

---

[22] Jeremy Bentham, *Rationale of Judicial Evidence* in *Works*, vol. VII, pp. 308–9.
    See also Postema, *Bentham and the Common Law Tradition*, pp. 284–5.
[23] See ch. 1, n. 23 and accompanying text.
[24] *Rationale of Judicial Evidence* in *Works*, vol. VII, p. 64.

exclude evidence in particular cases, and under special circumstances, on general grounds of utility and convenience; yet even here so difficult is it to prescribe limits on such a subject, without the hazard of committing injustice, that rules, the general policy of which is obvious, are by no means favoured.

In a justification of evidential presumptions of law, Starkie described them as 'nothing more than technical and positive rules, which are wholly independent of the principles of evidence, and whose only foundation is their general utility and convenience'. He continued:

To go farther, and by any positive and arbitrary rules to annex to particular evidence any technical and artificial force which it does not naturally possess, or to abridge and limit its proper and natural efficacy, must in all cases, where the object is simply the attainment of truth, not only be inconsistent and absurd in a scientific view, but what is worse would frequently be productive of absolute injustice. To admit every light which reason and experience can supply for the discovery of truth, and to reject that only which serves not to guide, but to bewilder and mislead, are the great principles which ought to pervade every system of evidence. It may safely be laid down as an universal position, that the less the process of inquiry is fettered by rules and restraints, founded on extraneous and collateral considerations of policy and convenience, the more certain and efficacious will it be in its operation.[25]

It is possible that Starkie had read a copy of the *Traité*, which had been published in Paris the previous year. If he had not read that work, he might have read the serialised translation in 1824 or Denman's review of the *Traité*, which appeared in the *Edinburgh Review* in the same year.[26] But Starkie did not refer to Bentham, and his justification of exclusionary rules may have been intended as no more than appropriate comment, just as some justification had seemed appropriate to Evans when he published his appendix to Pothier in 1806.[27] Why there should be rules that compelled exclusion, rather than a discretion to exclude, did not appear in Starkie's preface. In a later section of the *Treatise*, dealing with the rule against hearsay, there appeared another attempt to justify rules of exclusion and an elaboration of the classes of evidence that ought to be excluded. Starkie made three points in favour of this exclusionary rule. First, hearsay was obviously inferior as a source of information, even for the common purposes of daily intercourse

---

[25] Starkie, *Treatise* (1824), vol. I, pp. iii–iv.
[26] *Edinburgh Review* 40 (1824), 169–207.   [27] See n. 14 and text.

in society. Secondly, it could not be subjected to the ordinary tests
of oath and cross-examination which the law had provided to
ascertain truth. Thirdly, Starkie argued that although in the
common course of life such evidence was frequently acted on,
those circumstances generally lacked any considerable temptation
to deceive. It was otherwise in a legal investigation, which
involved the highest and dearest interests of the parties concerned.

But Starkie had not as yet come to grips with the main criticism
of the rule excluding hearsay. Even assuming the truth of the
propositions already set out, why was hearsay evidence not at least
admissible? The answer he gave was that 'the law must proceed by
general and by certain rules'. If hearsay were to be admitted in
cases where it was likely to be reliable, it would have to be
admitted in all cases. 'The consequence would be to let in
numberless wanton, careless, and unfounded assertions, unworthy
of the least regard.' And although

one who had been long enured to judicial habits might be able to assign to
such evidence just so much, and no greater credit than it deserved, yet,
upon the minds of a jury unskilled in the nature of judicial proofs,
evidence of this kind would frequently make an erroneous impression.[28]

Starkie's argument rested on two assumptions. The first was
that the law of evidence, as much as any other part of the law, was
a system of rules. Certainty required that the rules should be
adhered to, without any judicial discretion to dispense with them.
The second was that juries needed to be protected from hearing
evidence that was particularly difficult to assess or was for some
other reason liable to mislead.

Shortly after the appearance of the first edition of Starkie's
Treatise, Bentham's arguments were given renewed publicity, first
by the publication of the English translation of *Traité des preuves
judiciaires* in 1825 and then by the publication of the *Rationale of
Judicial Evidence* in 1827.[29] It may, therefore, have been in
response to Bentham's criticisms, though again Bentham was not
referred to, that the second edition of Starkie's work, published in
1833, provided a fuller discussion of exclusionary rules. Starkie
began with the observation that '[t]he means which the law
employs for investigating the truth of a past transaction are those
which are resorted to by mankind for similar, but extrajudicial

28 Starkie, *Treatise* (1824), vol. I, pp. 43–6.   29 See n. 17.

purposes'. The law, however, could interfere with the ordinary processes of inquiry,

in order to provide more certain tests of truth than can be provided, or indeed than are necessary, in the ordinary course of affairs, and thereby to exclude all weaker evidence to which such tests are inapplicable, and which, if generally admitted, would be more likely to mislead than to answer the purposes of truth.[30]

There are two arguments here, and Starkie proceeded to spell them out. One is the familiar argument from the preface to the first edition and from the later discussion about hearsay: evidence is excluded that would injure the cause of truth by its tendency to distract or mislead the jury. The other argument is hinted at in the discussion in the first edition on hearsay, where Starkie had made the point that, although in everyday life hearsay was frequently acted upon, circumstances were different in court, where the temptation to deceive was greater because of the interests at stake. In the second edition Starkie elaborated this point by arguing that the law adopted principles of exclusion to aid the natural powers of decision of the jury. Superior tests of truth were required because the evidence on which an individual in everyday transactions might safely rely could not, without such further security, be safely relied on, or even admitted, in judicial investigations. In the ordinary business of life there were not so many temptations or opportunities to practise deceit as in legal investigations, where property, reputation, liberty, and even life were frequently at stake. In everyday life, each individual was able to use their own discretion to decide whom to deal with and trust.

[H]e has not only the sanction of general reputation and character for the confidence which he reposes, but slight circumstances, and even vague reports, are sufficient to awaken his suspicion and distrust, and place him on his guard; and where doubt has been excited, he may suspend his judgment till by extended and repeated inquiries doubt is removed. In judicial inquiries it is far otherwise; the character of a witness cannot easily be subjected to minute investigation, the nature of the proceeding usually excludes the benefit which might result from an extended and protracted inquiry, and a jury are under the necessity of forming their conclusions on a very limited and imperfect knowledge of the real characters of the witnesses on whose testimony they are called on to decide.[31]

[30] Starkie, *Treatise* (1833), vol. I, pp. 11–15.   [31] Ibid.

Another writer who shared Starkie's concern to justify the law
was Best. For him, judicial evidence was 'for the most part
nothing more than natural evidence restrained or modified by
rules of positive law'. He accepted that a general rule of exclusion
might in particular instances exclude the truth and so work
injustice; but he thought that 'the mischief is immeasurably
compensated by a stability which the general operation of the rule
confers on the rights of men, and the feeling of security generated
in their minds by the conviction that they can be divested of them
only by the authority of the law, and not at the pleasure of a
tribunal'.[32]

The textbook writers not only justified exclusionary rules of
evidence, but acknowledged and approved of judicial development
of evidence law. For example, Phillipps and Amos stated that the
law of evidence in operation in 1838 had been almost entirely
created since the time of Salkeld, Lord Raymond, and Strange.[33]
In 1849, Best referred to Lord Kenyon's observation[34] that 'the
rules of evidence have been matured by the wisdom of ages, and
are now revered from their *antiquity* and the good sense in which
they are founded'; but Best added that this was 'not the general
opinion of the present day, in which our system of judicial
evidence is commonly spoken of as something altogether modern'.
Best clearly saw this modern development as an improvement on
earlier, less rigorous, practice. According to him, although the
'law of evidence' was the creation of comparatively modern times,
most of the leading principles on which it was founded had been
known and admitted from earliest times. The 'germs of our law of
evidence' were traceable in the proceedings of our ancestors, who
had not, however, 'reduced its principles into a system, or vested
them with the obligatory force essential to the steady and impartial
administration of justice'. In most cases, Best stated, these principles had been merely discretionary. Thus ancient lawyers had been
aware of the weakness of hearsay evidence but had not thought
themselves bound to reject it absolutely, and quite often had used
it to introduce, explain, or corroborate more regular proof.[35]

---

[32] Best, *Treatise* (1849), p. 31.
[33] Phillipps and Amos, *Treatise* (1838), vol. I, p. 335. The period referred to began
     shortly after 1688 and ended during the reign of George II.
[34] In *R* v. *Inhabitants of Eriswell* (1790) 3 TR 707, 721.
[35] Best, *Treatise* (1849), pp. 117–18, 125–9.

By the time the second edition of Taylor's *Treatise* was published in 1855, evidence law was clearly perceived as a system of rules developed by judges. The author noted that the table of cases in that edition referred to at least 1,300 more decisions than had been noticed in the first, and that 'a vast number of decisions, which either overrule, qualify, illustrate, or confirm the fluctuating doctrines of the common law' had been embodied in the text.[36]

LAW REPORTERS AND JUDGES

Wigmore described how, in the period after 1830, 'the established principles began to be developed into rules and precedents of minutiae relatively innumerable in comparison with what had gone before'. He attributed this to the increase of printed reports of nisi prius rulings, which he described as the cause 'and afterwards the self-multiplying effect of the detailed development of the rules of evidence'. Before this, practice had varied from circuit to circuit, and had 'rested largely in the memory of the experienced leaders of the trial bar and in the momentary discretion of the judges'. Until the multiplication of nisi prius reports there had been neither fixity nor tangible authority. Later, there was 'a sudden precipitation of all that had hitherto been suspended in solution', assisted and emphasised by the appearance of such treatises as those of Starkie and Phillipps.[37] But, as John Langbein has made clear, it is unlikely that writers would have been at pains to produce law reports and treatises unless they had thought that there was a market for them. Furthermore, why should they have thought that a market existed unless there had been a change in the conception of case law? Three factors suggest that there was such a change.

In the first place, during the nineteenth century judges and lawyers came to see case law as rules made by the courts. For example, in 1863, on the first reading of a bill for the revision of statute law, Lord Westbury stated:

---

[36] Taylor, *Treatise* (1855), vol. I, pp. xi–xii.
[37] J. H. Wigmore, *A Treatise on the System of Evidence in Trials at Common Law*, ed. Peter Tillers, (Boston, Mass., 1983), vol. I, pp. 609–10.

But a judicial opinion is also a legislative enactment. It decides a particular case, and it sets a precedent for all future cases. Therefore the Judges become legislators – legislators *ex arbitrio*.[38]

Once lawyers had begun to think of case law as a set of rules, it became natural to want to define the rules with as much clarity as possible, and so a strict conception of binding authority was encouraged.[39]

The second factor was the criticism of Bentham and Austin. Both attacked the fiction that the common law was common custom and was not made but declared from time to time by the judges. By the 1860s, Bentham's expression 'judge-made law' had become a popular term in newspaper discussions.[40] Finally, institutional changes in the 1830s helped develop a setting in which 'judge-made-law' could flourish. In the late 1820s, professional judges came to dominate judicial decisions of the House of Lords, and in 1830 the existing system of civil appeals was simplified by the creation of a single court of Exchequer Chamber, uniformly superior to each of the common law courts, and intermediate between these and the House of Lords.[41]

It might be thought that the increase of legal representation in criminal trials during the century encouraged the growth of a rule-based system of criminal evidence through the taking of technical points at trial about admissibility. But, in fact, the development of rules of criminal, as opposed to civil, evidence did not proceed very far during the nineteenth century, because the criminal courts lacked an effective appellate structure, such as that gained by the civil courts in the 1830s. This gap seems to have been recognised by the judges, who tried to use their system of informal consultation to settle disputed questions of law.[42] Even in the

---

[38] *Parl. Deb.*, 3rd series, clxxi, 782.
[39] Jim Evans, 'Change in the Doctrine of Precedent during the Nineteenth Century', in Laurence Goldstein, ed., *Precedent in Law*, (Oxford, 1987), pp. 35, 64–70.
[40] See the leading article in the *Daily Telegraph* (30 November 1864) quoted in W. T. S. Daniel, *The History and Origin of the Law Reports* (London, n.d.), p. 238. For Bentham on 'judge-made law' see, e.g., 'Inferences of Judge-made Law' in the *Introductionary View* in *Works*, vol. VI, pp. 53–7, 101, 107, 109, 112, 113, 142; *Rationale of Judicial Evidence* in *Works*, vol. VI, p. 391, vol. VII, p. 195n, p. 447n.
[41] Evans, 'Change in the Doctrine of Precedent', 64; C. K. Allen, *Law in the Making*, 7th edn (Oxford, 1964), pp. 219–21.
[42] See, e.g., *R* v. *Phillips* (1848) 3 Cox CC 88.

1870s, when greater institutional reforms took place, the failure to provide a satisfactory system of criminal appeals continued, and it was not until the establishment of the Court of Criminal Appeal in 1907 that the law of criminal evidence reached a stage at which it could become fully developed as a system of rules.

A change in the conception of case law took place all the more readily in civil cases because of the perception that, as W. T. S. Daniel QC put it, '[t]he want of Certainty in the unwritten law of this country is the great defect in our Jurisprudence'.[43] This was reflected in attempts to codify the law. Piecemeal reforms such as the Criminal Law Consolidation Acts of 1861 did manage to simplify some of the sources of law, and attempts were made to simplify evidence law by means of codification.

In autumn 1872 J. F. Stephen was instructed by Sir John Coleridge, the Attorney General, to draw up a code of the law of evidence on the lines of the Indian Evidence Act, which had been largely drafted by Stephen.[44] Coleridge may have been prompted to instruct Stephen by the presentation of a private member's codifying bill earlier in the year.[45] On the other hand, the Attorney General appears to have had a genuine interest in evidence codification. Stephen described how he and Coleridge settled the bill in frequent consultations. According to Stephen, the bill was ready to be introduced early in the session of 1873, and Coleridge made various attempts to bring it forward but was unsuccessful until the last day of the session. In fact, on that day (5 August 1873), Coleridge said that he had never proposed to do more that session than introduce the bill and print it for the consideration of members, adding that, if he had the opportunity, he would endeavour to pass it into law in a future session. On 2 July, however, he had written to his father: 'I have my speech on evidence to make, and, then, my work for the Session is fairly over', which suggests that earlier he might have had more substantial hopes. In the event, the bill was never printed, Stephen described it as 'drawing on the model of the Indian Evidence Act'

[43] Daniel, *History and Origin of the Law Reports*, p. 32.
[44] Leon Radzinowicz, *Sir James Fitzjames Stephen (1829–1894) and his Contribution to the Development of Criminal Law*, Selden Society Lecture (London, 1957), p. 19; K. J. M. Smith, *James Fitzjames Stephen: Portrait of a Victorian Rationalist* (Cambridge, 1988), p. 76.
[45] *House of Commons Parliamentary Papers* 1872 (69) I 685. The bill was read for the first time on 28 February 1872 but was dropped at the second reading.

and as containing 'a complete system of law upon the subject of evidence'. In the latter part of 1873, Coleridge was promoted to the Bench, and Stephen's bill was not proceeded with by his successor as Attorney General.[46]

In both the Indian Evidence Act and the 1872 bill the underlying principle on which Stephen attempted to base the law of evidence was that of relevancy. This principle could have led to the anti-nomianism favoured by Bentham, but Stephen used relevancy as the foundation for an exclusionary, rule-based structure. Unlike Bentham, Stephen had a respect for the way in which the judges had developed evidence law. It possessed

in the highest degree the characteristic merits of English case law. English case law, as it is, is to what it ought to be, and might be if it were properly arranged, what the ordinary conversation of a very clever man on all sorts of subjects written down as he uttered it, and as passing circumstances furnished him with a text, would be to the matured and systematic statement of his deliberate opinions. It is full of the most vigorous sense, and is the result of great sagacity applied to vast and varied experience.[47]

Although Stephen stipulated a few circumstances in which, under strict conditions, hearsay evidence might be admitted, he defended the general rule of exclusion on the ground that hearsay evidence was *irrelevant*. It was, he said, a matter of common experience that conversational statements were made so lightly and were so liable to be misunderstood or misrepresented that they could not generally be depended on for any important purposes. He allowed that there was some degree of truth in the criticism that this was an objection to weight and not to relevancy, but justified the rule on the grounds that to allow reliance on hearsay would 'present a great temptation to indolent judges to be satisfied with second-hand reports' and would 'open a wide door to fraud'.[48]

---

[46] *House of Commons Parliamentary Papers* 1873 II 355; Ernest Hartley Coleridge, *Life & Correspondence of John Duke Lord Coleridge Lord Chief Justice of England* (London, 1904), vol. II, p. 217; James Fitzjames Stephen, *A Digest of the Law of Evidence* (London, 1876), pp. iii–iv; *Parl. Deb.* 3rd series, ccxvii, 1559.

[47] James Fitzjames Stephen, *The Indian Evidence Act with an Introduction on the Principles of Judicial Evidence* (Calcutta, 1872), p. 7. Cf. Stephen's *A Digest of the Law of Evidence*, 2nd edn (London, 1876), p. xviii, where he described Bentham as 'too keen and bitter a critic to recognise the substantial merits of the system which he attacked'.

[48] Stephen, *Indian Evidence Act*, pp. 123–4. A similarly pragmatic approach can be seen in his justification of the exclusion of evidence as to transactions similar to, but not specifically connected with, the facts in issue. Stephen believed that to

It is not possible to tell how much support would have been given to Stephen's bill had it been presented again. What can be said is that even if his proposals for codification had been accepted, evidence law would have retained many of the exclusionary features condemned by Bentham. Nor would there have been anything to prevent the growth of judicial law-making in the interpretation of the code, whereas Bentham had stipulated that decisions in one case should never be cited as a precedent in any other.[49]

TWO CASE STUDIES

The point has already been made that while civil evidence developed significantly during the nineteenth century as an exclusionary, rule-based system, a similar system of criminal evidence was slow to develop for want of an effective appellate structure. This can be illustrated by two case studies. The first concerns an exception to the rule against hearsay in favour of declarations made in the course of business; the second deals with the law relating to the corroboration of accomplices.

Declarations in the course of business

The history of this exception shows an initial difference of judicial opinion. This arose in part because some judges thought that the common law should adapt to new circumstances, while others favoured the virtues of stability and certainty. But another reason was lack of agreement about what sort of evidence was in principle caught by the rule against hearsay. By the 1840s, the approach that favoured stability and certainty was in the ascendant, and this trend continued for the rest of the century. At the same time, the definition of the scope of the rule against hearsay became clearer. The question came to be not whether the principle that held

admit such evidence would lead to an undesirable inquiry into the whole life and character of the parties concerned. 'A very slight acquaintance with French procedure is enough to show the evils of not keeping people close to the point in judicial proceedings.' (Ibid., p. 125.)

[49] See, e.g., *Equity Dispatch Court Proposal* in *Works*, vol. III, p. 389; Postema, *Bentham and the Common Law Tradition*, pp. 418–19.

hearsay in disfavour should be given more or less weight in a
particular case, but whether the facts of that case were covered by
the relevant legal rules. This process of clarification appears in the
development of the exception in favour of declarations in the
course of business. Over several decades, the conditions in which
it was allowed to operate were restricted by requirements that the
declaration should be contemporaneous with the matters referred
to, and that the declarant should have a duty to make the
declaration.

The case which came to be accepted by writers as the foundation
for the exception was a decision of Holt CJ at nisi prius in *Price* v.
The Earl of Torrington (1703).[50] In this case the plaintiff, who was
a brewer, brought an action for the price of beer allegedly sold and
delivered to the defendant. A difficulty arose in proving delivery,
because the drayman who made this particular delivery had since
died. Evidence was given of the plaintiff's usual course of business, in accordance with which his draymen used to come every
night to the clerk of the brewhouse, to whom they would give an
account of the beer that they had delivered. The clerk used to
record this information in a book kept for the purpose and the
draymen would set their hands to their respective entries. Holt CJ
held that the entry in the book to which the deceased drayman had
set his hand was good evidence that the beer in question had been
delivered to the defendant.

The report of the judgment gives no reasons for this decision.
The headnote in 2 Ld Raym reads: 'If a tradesman uniformly
obliges his servants to subscribe in his books an account of the
goods they deliver, proof of the subscription of a servant who is
dead is evidence of the delivery of the goods contained in the
account subscribed.' This emphasises the requirement that the
entry be made in accordance with the servant's duty to his
employer, but otherwise takes the matter little further.

Some time appears to have passed before this decision was
referred to in the reports. In *Calvert* v. *The Archbishop of Canterbury* (1798)[51] the only evidence of a contract was an entry of the
terms made in the plaintiff's book by his deceased servant.
Counsel for the plaintiff argued that this was admissible on the
basis of the decision in *Price* v. *Torrington*.[52] Lord Kenyon CJ

---

[50] 1 Salk 285.   [51] 2 Esp 646.   [52] See n. 50.

took the view that the evidence was inadmissible because the entry was not contrary to the servant's interest. By excluding the evidence on that ground he provided a rationale for the exception.[53]

This rationale, however, was not available in *Pritt* v. *Fairclough* (1812),[54] where the disputed evidence was nevertheless admitted. At the trial of the action before Lord Ellenborough CJ it became necessary to prove the contents of a letter sent by the plaintiff to the defendants. The plaintiff produced an entry that had been made in a letter-book by his deceased clerk. This professed to be a copy of a letter sent on the same date from the plaintiff to the defendants. It was also proved that, according to the plaintiff's course of business, the letters that he wrote were copied by this clerk, then sent by post, and that in other instances copies made by the clerk had been compared with the originals and had always been found to be accurate. Lord Ellenborough CJ held that this evidence was admissible to prove the contents of the letter and observed: 'The rules of evidence must expand according to the exigencies of society.'[55]

Lord Ellenborough CJ displayed a similarly flexible approach in *Doe d Reece* v. *Robson* (1812),[56] where he admitted as evidence entries in the books of a deceased attorney to prove the date of execution of a lease. In the course of his judgment he stated: 'The ground upon which this evidence has been received is, that there is a total absence of interest in the persons making the entries to pervert the fact and at the same time a competency in them to know it.'

In *Barker* v. *Ray* (1826),[57] Lord Eldon expressed doubt about the way in which the law appeared to be developing:

The cases satisfy me that evidence is admissible of declarations made by persons who have a complete knowledge of the subject to which such declarations refer, and where their interest is concerned; and the only doubt I have entertained was as to the position – that you are to receive evidence of declarations, where there is no interest. At a certain period of my professional life, I should have said that that doctrine was quite new

---

[53] Similar reasoning may have been applied in *Rowcroft* v. *Basset* (1802) Peake Add Cas 199.
[54] 3 Camp 305.
[55] 3 Camp 307. Similar evidence was held admissible by the same judge in *Hagedorn* v. *Reid* (1813) 3 Camp 377, and in *Champneys* v. *Peck* (1816) 1 Stark 404.
[56] 15 East 32, 34.   [57] 2 Russ 63.

to me. I do not mean to say more than that I still doubt concerning it. When I have occasion to express my opinion judicially upon it I will do so; but I desire not to be considered as bound by that as a rule of evidence.[58]

Little had been done to clarify the basis of the decision in *Price* v. *Torrington*.[59] There was a suggestion in the argument in *Goss* v. *Watlington* (1822) that such entries were admissible to prove not the truth of the entries themselves, but some other fact with which they were connected. In modern terms, the evidence of the entry was not covered by the rule against hearsay because it was admitted merely to show the fact that it had been made, and not the truth of its contents.[60] This way of looking at the problem emerged clearly in another case frequently cited as an authority in favour of the admissibility of declarations in the course of business. In *Doe d Patteshall* v. *Turford* (1832)[61] the Court of King's Bench had to consider whether to make absolute a rule nisi for a nonsuit in a case where the trial judge had admitted evidence in the following circumstances. It had been the usual course of practice in an attorney's office for the clerks to serve notices to quit on tenants and to indorse on duplicates of such notices the fact and the time of service. One day, the attorney himself prepared a notice to quit for service on a tenant. He took it out with him, together with two others prepared at the same time, and served the various tenants. On returning to his office he indorsed on the duplicate of each notice a memorandum of his having delivered it to the tenant. There was independent proof that he had served two of the notices, but none in relation to the third. The attorney had since died; therefore, the question arose of whether the indorsement was admissible to prove service of the third notice.

The Court found no difficulty in overcoming the fact that the indorsement had been made by the principal and not his servant. The indorsement was treated as tantamount to that of a clerk, on the assumption that the principal would do what he required his clerk to do, and that there was therefore a duty on the principal to make out the indorsement. On those rather dubious assumptions the question then arose of whether the evidence was admissible.

---

[58] 2 Russ 76.   [59] See n. 50.
[60] 2 Brod & B 132, 136. The decision itself throws no light on the problem.
[61] 3 B & Ad 890.

Lord Tenterden CJ was content to rely on the authorities cited in favour of admissibility without any further examination. Littledale J dealt with the duty of the attorney but went no further than Lord Tenterden CJ in considering the basis of admissibility. Taunton J was in favour of admissibility, provided there were other circumstances that corroborated the fact recorded – a reversion to an earlier, more flexible approach to hearsay. Only Parke J gave any real consideration to the grounds of admissibility.

In his view the entry was admissible 'because the fact that such an entry was made at the time of his return from his journey, was one of the chain of facts ... from which the delivery of the notice to quit might lawfully be inferred'. Delivery might be proved either by direct evidence from the person who made the delivery, or by circumstantial evidence.

In this point of view, it is not the matter contained in the written entry simply which is admissible, but the fact that an entry containing such matter was made at the time it purports to bear date, and when in the ordinary course of business such an entry would be made if the principal fact to be proved had really taken place. The learned counsel for the defendant has contended that an entry is to be received in two cases only; first, where it is an admission against the interest of a deceased party who makes it, and, secondly, where it is one of a chain or combination of facts, and the proof of one raises a presumption that another has taken place: but it is contended that the facts here do not fall within the latter branch of the rule, because [the attorney] who served the notice was not shewn to have been in the habit of serving notices. I agree in the rule as laid down, but I think that, in the second case, a necessary and invariable connection of facts is not required; it is enough if one fact is ordinarily and usually connected with the other: and it appears to me that the present case is not, in its circumstances, an exception to that part of the rule.[62]

Parke J thus appears to have taken the view that a statement would not be caught by the rule against hearsay if its probative force did not come solely from the words uttered, but also from the statement itself as a piece of original evidence.[63]

---

[62] 3 B & Ad 896–7. See also *R* v. *Inhabitants of Dukinfield* (1848) 11 QB 678, where Erle J, after referring to *Doe d Patteshall* v. *Turford*, said, on p. 687, 'If the indorsement usually followed the fact in question, it is admissible as evidence of that fact, on the general principle that an antecedent may be inferred from a consequent as soon as the usual sequence of facts is proved.'

[63] For discussion of this distinction see Stephen Guest, 'The Scope of the Hearsay Rule', *Law Quarterly Review* 101 (1985), 385–404. In 1834, Parke was moved from the Court of King's Bench and began twenty-two years of office as a baron of the Exchequer. By 1837, he had so revised his views in favour of a strict

Turford's case was relied on by the Court of Common Pleas in *Poole* v. *Dicas* (1835).[64] In this case it was held that an entry of dishonour of a bill of exchange, made at the time of dishonour in a book by a notary's clerk acting in the usual course of his business, was admissible in an action on the bill. But the decision seems likely to have been the result of pragmatism as much as anything else. Tindal CJ stated: 'The rejection of the evidence which has been received would be a great injury to the commercial classes, by casting an unnecessary difficulty on the holders of bills of exchange.'[65]

These cases show that prior to the 1840s there was no single foundation upon which an exception for declarations in the course of business rested, and that the scope of the exception had yet to be clearly defined. The way in which treatise writers dealt with the subject confirms this state of affairs. In the seventh edition of Phillipps's *Treatise*, published in 1829, the author first referred to the rule against hearsay as having been recognised and approved from the earliest times as a fundamental principle of the law of evidence that was always to be strictly observed. There were, he added, certain exceptions to the general rule, but they were perhaps as ancient as the rule itself and had been allowed either because the usual inconvenience and danger of such evidence was absent, or because greater inconvenience would result from exclusion than from admission.[66] Phillipps described one of these exceptions as follows:

> Entries in the books of a tradesman by his deceased shopman, who therein supplies proof of a charge against himself, have been admitted in evidence, as proof of the delivery of goods, or of other matter there stated within his own knowledge.[67]

The cases to which Phillipps referred as authority for his proposition were later to be cited as authority for the exception in

---

application of the rule against hearsay that he was able in that year to deliver his memorable judgment as a member of the Court of Exchequer Chamber in *Wright* v. *Doe d Tatham* (1837) 7 A & E 313. His judgment in this case was heavily relied on by a majority in the House of Lords when the strict application of the rule against hearsay was reaffirmed in *R* v. *Kearley* [1992] 2 AC 228.

[64] 1 Bing NC 649.   [65] 1 Bing NC 654.

[66] Phillipps, *Treatise* (1829), vol. I, pp. 229–34. Earlier editions had contained shorter statements of the rule, without any reference to antiquity to support either the rule or its exceptions.

[67] Ibid., p. 263.

its fully developed form.[68] What distinguished the exception in this form from its later expressions was chiefly the reference to the shopman's having by his entry supplied 'proof of a charge against himself'.

Phillipps realised that this justification of the exception presented a difficulty. The declaration by a tradesman's servant that he had delivered certain goods was an implied admission that he had received them for that purpose, and such a declaration would have been evidence against the servant in an action brought against him for failure to deliver the goods in accordance with his instructions. But in any other proceedings, such as an action for the price against the person to whom the goods were alleged to have been delivered, the declaration of the servant as to delivery would not be contrary to the interest of the maker. The probability of the truth of the declaration would then be 'neither greater nor less than the probability of [the maker's] being honest or dishonest, which is nothing more than may be said in any case of hearsay'. Phillipps concluded that such declarations by shopmen should be only cautiously admitted in evidence to charge third persons with the receipt of goods, especially as tradesmen could easily be given evidence of delivery by taking a memorandum from the purchaser, or by requiring some other security.[69]

In 1838 Phillipps brought out the eighth edition of his *Treatise* jointly with Andrew Amos. By then the narrow reference in the seventh edition to 'entries in the books of a tradesman by his deceased shopman' had given way to the more general 'declarations and entries made in the course of duty or employment'. More importantly, the exception had by then lost its previous link with declarations against interest. The authors explained the matter in this way:

According to the observations of several Judges on different occasions, it might seem that where there was a competency of knowledge, or at least peculiar means of knowledge in an individual making a declaration, and a total absence of interest to pervert the facts to which he has spoken, his declarations would be admissible evidence after his death, even though the declarations did not operate against his interest.

---

[68] These were *Price* v. *Torrington* (1703) 1 Salk 285, *Pitman* v. *Madox* (1700) 2 Salk 690, *Calvert* v. *Archbishop of Canterbury* (1798) 2 Esp 646, *Hagedorn* v. *Reid* (1813) 3 Camp 377.

[69] Phillipps, *Treatise* (1829), vol. I, pp. 263–4.

Phillipps and Amos made it clear, however, that such judicial observations were too loose, and perhaps contradictory to established principles. What the authors needed to do to rationalise the law was to reject the intellectually embarrassing requirement that such a declaration should be against the interest of the maker. At the same time, it was necessary to tie down the scope of the exception as closely as possible, and to provide reasons for permitting this exception to the general exclusionary rule. This is what Phillipps and Amos proceeded to do.

After recognising the need for some departure from the requirement that the declaration be against the maker's interest, Phillipps and Amos continued:

> There appears, however, more reason for considering that a rule exists, which allows of declarations of deceased persons being received in evidence, even though not made against their interest, provided that in addition to a peculiar knowledge of the facts, and the absence of all interest to pervert them, the declarations appear also to have been made in the ordinary course of official, professional, or other business or duty, and been immediately connected with the transacting or discharging of it, and contemporaneous, or nearly so, with the transaction to which they relate.

Justification was based on reliability and necessity. With regard to the former, there could be no temptation to deceive because the declaration would not be available to the maker during his lifetime. Ordinary error was made less likely by the requirements that the declaration be made in the ordinary course of business and contemporaneously. As business transactions were frequently confined to the knowledge of a few persons, 'there is some reason, on the ground of necessity, arising out of the subject matter of the declarations, which may be thought to warrant, under proper safeguards, some relaxation of the strict rules of evidence'. Even for this there were precedents. Similar reasons of necessity, it was pointed out, were the foundation of the admissibility of hearsay in cases of pedigree and matters of general interest, and also, to some extent, in dying declarations.

There was also a suggestion that such declarations might operate outside the hearsay rule because they could be regarded as the ordinary incidents of the transactions to which they related rather than as narratives of them.[70]

Such clear and reasoned lines of development were not,

[70] Phillipps and Amos, *Treatise* (1838), pp. 332–4, 341.

however, perceived by the other leading treatise writer of the time. Starkie, in the 1833 edition of his *Treatise*, dealt with the exception in favour of declarations against interest. He then stated that there were also 'several instances to be found where the declaration of a party as to a fact, where he possessed peculiar means of knowing the fact, and laboured under no temptation, bias, or influence, to misrepresent it' had been admitted in evidence after his death. But he added that, as the rules by which the reception of this class of evidence did not appear to be very distinctly defined, the decisions on the subject would be detailed at a future opportunity. Those cautious words were merely repeated in the 1842 edition.[71]

In the first edition of Best's *Treatise* in 1849, however, the law was stated on the lines laid down by Phillipps and Amos. The exception was said to cover declarations by deceased persons in the regular course of a business, office, or employment, where the declarant had had personal knowledge of the facts, and no interest in stating an untruth. Such declarations were said to differ from declarations against interest in that they must have been made contemporaneously with the acts to which they related.[72]

During and after the 1830s the judges developed a more restrictive approach to hearsay exceptions generally, and in doing so built up a body of case-law rules that sometimes threatened to become unmanageable. Phillipps and Amos noted this in 1838, when they observed that several of the exceptions had been much narrowed within modern times.[73] They acknowledged that the existence of exceptions might be thought 'to obviate many objections which would exist, if the rule [against hearsay] were unlimited in its operation'. But they recognised that the exceptions had also 'occasioned a substantive mischief in the mass of legal decisions arising out of them, – decisions, which present many subtle distinctions, and not unfrequently conflicting opinions of the Courts'.[74]

Initially, exceptions in favour of declarations in the course of business had rested not on a single foundation, but on an intuition that such declarations were more likely to be reliable than those usually falling within the hearsay category, and on an idea that

[71] Starkie, *Treatise* (1833), vol. I, p. 46; Starkie, *Treatise* (1842), vol. I, p. 45.
[72] Best, *Treatise* (1849), p. 376.
[73] Phillipps and Amos, *Treatise* (1838), p. 219.   [74] Ibid., p. 222.

hearsay was not really involved at all – that all the court was doing was admitting one fact from which others might be inferred. Later reports on declarations in the course of business showed a more regulated approach, which confined the exception by strictly applying the requirements of duty, routine, and contemporaneity.

The cases on duty

These established two important restrictions. The first was that the existence of a duty had to be clearly proved: it would not be inferred. The second was that even where it was clear that the declarant had a duty to make a declaration, it still had to be proved that the declaration in question had been made pursuant to that duty.

The first of these restrictions appears from *Poore* v. *Ambler* (1843).[75] A barrel of stout had been delivered by a brewery at the house where the defendant lived. The delivery was allegedly made upon the credit of the plaintiff, who had paid the brewery. The question arose at trial of whether the stout had in fact been supplied on the plaintiff's credit, and whether it had been supplied to the defendant or to another person living at the same house. The plaintiff tendered in evidence a memorandum in the hand-writing of a deceased clerk of the brewery. This was produced from the custody of the brewery and purported to show both that the stout had been supplied on the plaintiff's credit, and that it was the defendant to whom it had been supplied. The trial judge rejected this evidence and the Court of Queen's Bench upheld his decision on a motion for a new trial. No evidence had been given that it was the duty of the clerk to make the memorandum, and the Court could not infer that it was his duty to do so.

A similar decision was *Bright* v. *Legerton* (No. 1) (1860).[76] In this case the question arose of whether a solicitor had acted for the plaintiff on an occasion some twenty years earlier. The solicitor being dead, Sir John Romilly MR admitted in evidence a letter formerly written by the solicitor in which he had professed to be acting on behalf of the plaintiff in making an offer to settle a claim that the plaintiff then had. In admitting this evidence, Sir John Romilly observed:

I must say it would have been a great surprise to me if I had found, on an

---

[75] 1 LTOS 253.   [76] 29 Beav 60.

examination of the authorities, that such a letter was not receivable in evidence, as it clearly would have been contrary to all commonsense; for if a respectable solicitor comes to a person against whom A.B. has claims, and says, 'I am the solicitor of A.B., and I am authorized to make you this proposition', there are certainly very few persons who would not believe that he was authorized by A.B. to act for him accordingly; and it is every day's practice.[77]

On appeal, however, Lord Campbell LC held that, in order to make the letter admissible, it had to be proved independently that the writer had been duly authorised by the individual for whom he professed to act as solicitor.[78]

It might be clear that a record had been kept in the ordinary course of business by an employee. But it had still to be proved that the keeping of the record was done in accordance with a duty. In *Massey* v. *Allen* (1879)[79] the plaintiff claimed to be indemnified by the defendants in respect of 200 shares transferred into the plaintiff's name as trustee for the defendants. The plaintiff wished to prove that the shares had been bought on the Stock Exchange for one of the defendants through his brokers, Griffiths & Druitt. Griffiths, who had transacted the greater part of the firm's business, was dead. But the plaintiff tendered in evidence an entry in the firm's day-book showing a purchase of 200 shares by Griffiths for one of the defendants. The plaintiff proved that the entry was in the handwriting of Griffiths, and that it had been made by him in the ordinary course of business at the time of purchase as a memorandum of the transaction.

It was argued that the entry was admissible as a declaration in the ordinary course of business. Hall VC decided that it had not been made in the performance of any duty. The plaintiff had not established that it had been the duty of Griffiths as between himself and his client, the defendant, to keep the day-book. The Vice Chancellor distinguished *Doe d Patteshall* v. *Turford* (1832)[80] by saying that in that case the entry had been made in discharge of the clerk's duty.[81]

---

[77] 29 Beav 65–6.   [78] *Bright* v. *Legerton* (1861) 2 De G F & J 606.
[79] 13 Ch D 558.   [80] See n. 61.
[81] But the clerk's duty to serve the notice to quit and make out the indorsement had in that case been to his employer. This point eluded Coleridge J in *R* v. *Inhabitants of Worth* (1843) 4 QB 132. For a similarly restrictive approach see the decision of the Court of Appeal in *Hope* v. *Hope* [1893] WN 20. Cf. the robust approach of Lord Coleridge CJ in *Esch* v. *Nelson* (1885) 1 TLR 610.

The second restriction, which required a duty to make the particular declaration in question, appears to have first appeared in *Chambers* v. *Bernasconi* (1834).[82] This was an action brought by a bankrupt against his assignees in bankruptcy. It became necessary at trial to inquire whether the plaintiff had been arrested in a particular place on 9 November 1825 by a sheriff's officer who had died before trial, but who had left a record of the circumstances of the arrest.

In the Court of Exchequer Chamber counsel for the plaintiff in error relied principally on the broad rule 'that an entry written by a person deceased in the course of his duty, where he had no interest in stating an untruth, is to be received as proof of the fact stated in the entry and of every circumstance therein described, which would naturally accompany the fact itself'. But all the judges were of the opinion that:

whatever effect may be due to an entry made in the course of any office reporting facts necessary to the performance of a duty, the statement of other circumstances, however naturally they may be thought to find a place in the narrative, is no proof of those circumstances. Admitting, then, for the sake of argument, that the entry tendered was evidence of the fact, and even of the day when the arrest was made (both which facts it might be necessary for the officer to make known to his principal), we are all clearly of opinion that it is not admissible to prove in what particular spot within the bailiwick the caption took place, that circumstance being merely collateral to the duty done.[83]

This approach was confirmed in *Smith* v. *Blakey* (1867),[84] an action to recover the balance alleged to be due on an advance made by the plaintiffs to the defendant on a consignment of boots and shoes. The plaintiffs' business in Liverpool had been carried on by a confidential clerk named Barker, whose duty and practice it had been to keep his principals constantly advised of all the business that he transacted for them. Barker had had dealings with the defendant, but had since died.

In order to prove the transaction between the plaintiffs and the defendant, a letter describing it, written by Barker to the plaintiffs, was admitted in evidence. The question subsequently arose of whether it had been rightly admitted. It was argued amongst other things that it was admissible as a declaration by a deceased person

82 1 Cr M & R 347.   83 1 Cr M & R 368.   84 LR 2 QB 326.

in the performance of his duty to his employers in the ordinary course of business.

The Court of Queen's Bench rejected this argument. Blackburn J said:

I think all the cases shew that it is an essential fact to render such an entry admissible, that not only it should have been made in the due discharge of the business about which the person is employed, but the duty must be to do the very thing to which the entry relates, and then to make a report or record of it.[85]

Mellor J showed the feeling of constraint that a strict system of rules could produce when he said that it was with some reluctance that he had come to the conclusion that the letter was not admissible, because there could be no doubt in anybody's mind on reading it that the contract had been as the plaintiffs alleged. But when the judges considered that the law jealously guarded against statements made behind the back of a party being admissible against him, they had to take care how they enlarged the exceptions to the general rule against hearsay evidence.

The present case does not fall within the exception. It was the duty of Barker to communicate all transactions to his principals, and keep them advised of all that he had done; and the letter was written in the performance of that general duty; but it is not a record of having done a particular duty within the cases which have established the exception. If we were to hold this letter admissible, I do not know where the limit is to be put; but all letters and correspondence between principals and their agents might become admissible against third persons.[86]

The requirement of contemporaneity

In the context of declarations made in the course of business, contemporaneity was originally a feature that marked the declaration as part of an action and so outside the scope of the rule against hearsay. Later, when it had become settled that such declarations were in principle caught by the hearsay rule, contemporaneity

---

[85] Ibid., 332–3.

[86] Ibid., 334. Lush J expressed a similar fear that if this letter were admissible, 'it would follow that every commercial traveller, who writes to his principals that he has received orders from different customers, might enable his principals, in the event of his death, to charge every one mentioned in his letters' (ibid., 335). See also *Coleman* v. *Mellersh* (1850) 2 Mac & G 309; *Percival* v. *Nanson* (1851) 7 Exch 1; *Polini* v. *Gray* (1879) 12 Ch D 411, 420–1, 426, 430–1; *Trotter* v. *Maclean* (1879) 13 Ch D 574, 579–80; *Lyell* v. *Kennedy* (1887) 35 WR 725; *Sturla* v. *Frescia* (1880) 5 App Cas 623.

remained a necessary condition of admissibility, but for a different reason. At that stage it was a security against inaccuracy. Two cases, separated from each other by a little under thirty years, illustrate this development.

In *Doe d Kinglake* v. *Beviss* (1849)[87] Maule J stated his opinion that the declaration in question should have been so contemporaneous that the recording of it was part of the action in question. After the cases of *Torrington* and *Turford*[88] had been cited in argument, he said:

In all those cases, the entry was part of the transaction it purported to record. Of the same order is the presumption that a letter has been posted, where the ordinary course of business in an office would be to do so.[89]

By contrast, contemporaneity was relied on as a security against inaccuracy in *The Henry Coxon* (1878).[90] Two vessels, the *Gange* and the *Henry Coxon*, had come into collision on a Saturday. On the following Monday the mate of the *Henry Coxon* made an entry in the ship's log concerning the circumstances of the collision. In a subsequent action for damages between the owners of the two vessels the question arose of whether this log entry was admissible in evidence. Testimony was given that the entry was in the mate's handwriting, that he had signed it, and that he had been lost at sea on a subsequent voyage. One of the reasons given by Sir Robert Phillimore for refusing to admit the entry as evidence was that he was not satisfied as to its contemporaneity, the collision having occurred on Saturday and the entry having been made only on the following Monday.[91]

In summary, it can be said that the law relating to the admissibility of declarations in the course of business began to emerge in the period before the 1840s. At that stage there were differences of judicial opinion as to whether such evidence came within the scope of the rule against hearsay at all, and, if it did, whether and on what basis an exception should be allowed to develop in favour of admissibility. Among the treatise writers, Phillipps and Amos were the most creative, suggesting a future line of development and a rationale. In this they were followed by Best, though ignored by the editors of Starkie. But there was also

---

[87] 7 CB 456.   [88] See nn. 50 and 61.   [89] 7 CB 503.   [90] 3 PD 156.
[91] See also *Ellis* v. *Cowne* (1849) 2 Car & Kir 719, *Re Djambi (Sumatra) Rubber Estates Ltd* (1912) 107 LT 631.

a tendency, which can be seen during and after the 1830s, for judges to adopt a more restrictive approach to the operation of hearsay exceptions generally. This was shown in the case of declarations in the course of business by emphasis on duty and contemporaneity as essential conditions of admissibility.

Corroboration of accomplices

By contrast with the hearsay exception already described, the development of case law on corroboration of accomplices proceeded in a haphazard way throughout the period under consideration. Two major questions had to be decided: the first was whether it was possible to convict on the uncorroborated evidence of an accomplice; the second concerned the nature of corroboration itself. To neither question were the courts able to give a satisfactory answer. On this subject a system of rules was slow to emerge because of the lack of an effective appellate structure.

Was corroboration essential for a conviction?

In the eighteenth century, where clear evidence was lacking and the crime had been committed with others, the Crown's best hope of securing a conviction lay in persuading one of those accused to give evidence against their companions in return for an undertaking that they would not be prosecuted.[92] The disadvantages of evidence obtained in this way are obvious. A popular saying was that such witnesses 'fished for prey, like tame cormorants, with ropes round their necks'.[93] By the 1750s, the dangers inherent in the Crown witness system had led to the development of a rule that required corroboration of an accomplice's testimony before it could be admitted as evidence against the accused. Leach's edition of Hawkins's *Pleas of the Crown*, published in 1787, supported the view that 'the bare, uncorroborated testimony of an accomplice is not thought of sufficient credit to put a prisoner upon his defence'.[94] But by that time it was felt that the rule was too

[92] John H. Langbein, 'Shaping the Eighteenth-Century Criminal Trial: a View from the Ryder Sources', *University of Chicago Law Review* 50 (1983), 1, 1–4.
[93] Lord Macaulay, *The History of England from the Accession of James II* (repr. London, 1880), vol. II, p. 250. Macaulay recalled the expression in the context of the treason trials that followed Monmouth's rebellion.
[94] W. Hawkins, *A Treatise of the Pleas of the Crown*, T. Leach ed., 6th edn (London, 1787), vol. II, p. 609.

favourable to accused persons. In the following year the opinion of
the Twelve Judges in *R* v. *Atwood & Robbins* was that, since it had
long been settled that accomplices were competent to testify, any
objection to uncorroborated accomplice testimony could go only
to weight. Such testimony was therefore to be left to the jury
'under such directions and observations from the Court as the
circumstances of the case may require'.[95]

But might a court still direct a jury to acquit in the absence of
corroboration? In *R* v. *Durham & Crowder* the decision in *Atwood
& Robbins* was referred to in argument, and Perryn B observed,
presumably on the strength of it, that 'the practice of rejecting an
unsupported accomplice, is rather a matter of discretion with the
Court than a rule of law'.[96] There followed a period of uncertainty
about the extent to which a court might intervene to keep
uncorroborated accomplice evidence from a jury.

In *R* v. *Jones* (1809)[97] counsel for the accused apparently felt
able to contend that, as the Crown case rested solely on the
uncorroborated evidence of an accomplice, his client could not be
legally convicted. But Lord Ellenborough said:

No one can seriously doubt that a conviction is legal, though it proceeded
upon the evidence of an accomplice only. Judges in their discretion will
advise a jury not to believe an accomplice, unless he is confirmed, or only
in as far as he is confirmed; but if he is believed, his testimony is
unquestionably sufficient to establish the facts which he deposes. It is
allowed that he is a competent witness; and the consequence is inevitable,
that if credit is given to his evidence, it requires no confirmation from
another witness ... Strange notions upon this subject have lately got
abroad; and I thought it necessary to say so much for the purpose of
correcting them.

Perhaps the writers of treatises had had something to do with this
state of uncertainty. In *R* v. *Hastings & Graves* (1835)[98] Lord
Denman CJ reiterated that a jury might act on the unconfirmed
evidence of an accomplice. The editors of the report of the case

---

[95] (1788) 1 Leach 464.
[96] *Durham & Crowder*, though heard after *Atwood & Robbins*, was reported before
the latter case in (1787) 1 Leach 478. The judges in *Atwood & Robbins* did not
come to a completely novel decision. In *R* v. *Smith & Davis* (1784) at the Old
Bailey, the court stated that there was an established rule of law that the
uncorroborated testimony of an accomplice was legal evidence, but thought it
too dangerous to allow a conviction to take place on such testimony; the accused
was acquitted. See the note to the report of *Durham & Crowder*.
[97] 2 Camp 131.   [98] 7 Car & P 152.

observed in a note: 'In the Text Books it does not clearly appear that it is not necessary to have any confirmation of an accomplice; this case, therefore, seems to us important as a distinct decision to that extent.'

But there was still little uniformity of approach. In *R* v. *Keats* (1843)[99] Coleridge J directed an acquittal where there was no evidence to corroborate an accomplice. A contrary approach was adopted by Erle J two years later in *R* v. *Avery* (1845).[100] After counsel had submitted that there was no case to go to the jury, because the evidence of an accomplice was uncorroborated, Erle J declared that he had no right to withdraw any case from the jury where there was one competent witness for the prosecution, even though that witness was an uncorroborated accomplice. In the same year Coleridge J appeared to have revised his opinion when, in *R* v. *Andrews & Payne*,[101] he said that even the entirely unconfirmed evidence of an accomplice must go to the jury. In another case in the same year Erle J decided that, though he could not withdraw the case from the jury where the only evidence was that of an uncorroborated accomplice, he could tell them that such evidence was very unsatisfactory and advise them not to act on it.[102]

Despite all this, when Dr Lushington attempted to describe the common law practice in 1847, he stated:

[I]t is usual with the Judge, where the evidence of an accomplice stands uncorroborated in material circumstances, to direct an acquittal ... The result, then, is that, though the law in theory is satisfied with the conviction founded upon the evidence of an accomplice alone, in practice the Judge modifies that law.[103]

Yet, in 1848, Maule J said that the directions of judges about corroboration 'are not directions in point of law which juries are bound to adopt, but observations respecting facts which judges are very properly in the habit of making.'[104]

In 1855, the corroboration of accomplices was considered by the Court for Crown Cases Reserved in *R* v. *Stubbs*.[105] Four prisoners had been variously indicted for stealing or receiving a quantity of metal. The sole evidence against Stubbs was that of the accom-

---

[99] 1 LTOS 552.   [100] 1 Cox CC 206.   [101] 1 Cox CC 183.
[102] *R* v. *Skiller* (1845) 9 JP 314.
[103] *Simmons* v. *Simmons* (1847) 1 Rob Ecc 566, 574.
[104] *R* v. *Mullins* (1848) 3 Cox CC 526, 531.   [105] 7 Cox CC 48.

plices. At the conclusion of the prosecution case, counsel for Stubbs asked the chairman of quarter sessions to direct the jury that the evidence of the accomplices in respect of his client was not corroborated, and that it ought to have been corroborated as to each prisoner individually, whereas in fact it was corroborated as to only two of the four prisoners. The chairman directed the jury that it was not necessary that the accomplices should be corroborated as to each individual prisoner, and that their being corroborated as to material facts tending to show that two of the prisoners were connected with the crime was enough. He added, though, that the jury should look with more suspicion at the evidence in Stubbs's case than in the cases of the prisoners against whom the prosecution evidence was corroborated.

As well as considering what constituted corroboration, the Court for Crown Cases Reserved also considered the effect of the lack of corroborative evidence against Stubbs. Jervis CJ said that although they might regret the result that had followed from the chairman's departure from usual practice, they could not interfere because it was not a rule of law that an accomplice must be confirmed. 'In point of law the judge is bound to tell the jury that they may find a verdict of guilty upon unconfirmed testimony of an accomplice; but the usual course is to advise them not to do so.'[106]

In 1861 the Court of Queen's Bench affirmed that although it was 'a rule of general and usual practice to advise juries not to convict on the evidence of an accomplice alone', the application of that rule was a matter for the discretion of the judge by whom the case was tried. It followed that failure to give the warning could not lead to any action by a court of review.[107] This was recognised to be the law as late as 1894; the law was not changed until 1914, in the case of *R* v. *Cohen*, in which Lord Reading CJ justified the decision of the Court of Criminal Appeal by stating that there were 'rules of practice which crystallize into rules of law'.[108]

The existence of a discretion of this kind was a source of some embarrassment to treatise writers. Starkie, after stating that a prisoner could be convicted on the unconfirmed testimony of an accomplice, added that 'as a rule of *discretion* and in practice, it is

---

[106] Ibid., 49.   [107] *R* v. *Boyes* (1861) 1 B & S 311.
[108] *In re Meunier* [1894] 2 QB 415; *R* v. *Cohen* 10 Cr App R 91, 101.

said that he ought not to be convicted unless the testimony of the accomplice receive *material* confirmation'.[109] In an attempt to explain this, he continued:

> Regarding the rule as one of discretion and not of strict law, it can scarcely be understood that it is a rule which the Judge may enforce or disregard at his option, but rather that it belongs to the court to decide, under the circumstances of each particular case, whether they supply a material confirmation of the accomplice's testimony.[110]

But this was to confuse two separate matters. The state of the law was that in a case where the sole evidence against a prisoner was that of an uncorroborated accomplice, a judge *did* have an unreviewable discretion to withdraw the case from the jury, leave it to them with a warning, or leave it to them with no warning at all. Starkie had referred to something quite different: the *judgement* exercised by the judge in deciding whether certain matters given in evidence were capable of amounting to confirmation of the accomplice's testimony.

In another passage, in which Starkie discussed the case of *Durham & Crowder*,[111] he assessed the situation more accurately when he wrote:

> The decision seems to go the full length of wholly dispensing with the necessity for confirmation, even as a discretionary rule, for there was no confirmation whatsoever of the witness as far as appears, not even as to the *corpus delicti*: and though it is reported to have been said in that case, that the practice of rejecting an unsupported accomplice was rather a matter of discretion with the court than a rule of law, yet it is difficult to understand how it can be looked upon as any rule at all, if it may be utterly dispensed with and disregarded.[112]

The truth of the matter was that in this respect at least the judges resolutely refused to establish any rule and persisted in giving carte blanche to the trial judge in his conduct of the proceedings.

The nature of corroboration

This was another problem left unresolved during the nineteenth century. In the first two decades it appeared to be generally accepted that if an accomplice's evidence was confirmed in any respect, that sufficed to establish the credibility of the witness; it

---

[109] Original emphases. [110] Starkie, *Treatise* (1842), vol. II, p. 13, n.(d).
[111] See n. 96. [112] Starkie, *Treatise* (1842), vol. II, p. 15, n.(d) continued.

was not necessary that the confirmatory evidence should implicate the accused.[113]

The first sign of a different approach appeared in *R* v. *Webb* (1834).[114] This was a trial before Williams J and a jury, in which the prisoners were charged with breaking into a warehouse and stealing a large quantity of cheese. An accomplice was called to prove the case. He stated that during the commission of the offence the thieves had taken a ladder from the premises of a Mr Player. To confirm the accomplice, Player's servant was called to prove that his master's ladder had been taken away on the night when the offence had been committed. Greaves, for the prosecution, then said that he proposed to call other witnesses to confirm the accomplice's account of the way in which the offence had been committed. At this, Williams J intervened:

Mr Greaves, you must shew something that goes to bring the matter home to the prisoners. Proving by other witnesses that the robbery [*sic*] was committed in the way described by the accomplice is not such confirmation of him as will entitle his evidence to credit so as to affect other persons. Indeed, I think it is really no confirmation at all, as every one will give credit to a man who avows himself a principal felon for at least knowing how the felony was committed. It has been always my opinion that confirmation of this kind is of no use whatsoever.[115]

Two years later, Alderson B in summing up a case to a jury said: 'The confirmation which I always advise juries to require is a confirmation of the accomplice in some fact which goes to fix the guilt on the particular person charged.'[116] Thereafter, most reported cases in which the problem arose showed support for this view.[117]

In *R* v. *Jordan & Others* (1836)[118] Gurney B held it unnecessary that an accomplice should be confirmed in relation to each particular prisoner. But the same judge in *R* v. *Dyke* (1838)[119] observed that in the majority of cases it had been laid down that confirmation should be as to some matter that connected the

---

[113] *R* v. *Birkett & Brady* (1813) Russ & Ry 251, *R* v. *Dawber & Others* (1821) 3 Stark 34, *R* v. *Barnard* (1823) 1 Car & P 87. All were decisions by trial judges.
[114] 6 Car & P 595.   [115] 6 Car & P 595–6.
[116] *R* v. *Wilkes & Edwards* (1836) 7 Car & P 272.
[117] *R* v. *Moores & Spindlo* (1836) 7 Car & P 270, *R* v. *Farler* (1837) 8 Car & P 106, *R* v. *Kelsey* (1838) 2 Lewin 45, *R* v. *Fletcher & Others* (1838) 2 Lewin 45n, *R* v. *Birkett* (1839) 8 Car & P 732, *R* v. *Keats* (1843) 1 LTOS 552 *R* v. *Jenkins & Another* (1845) 1 Cox CC 177, *R* v. *Mullins* (1848) 3 Cox CC 526.
[118] 7 Car & P 432.   [119] 8 Car & P 261.

prisoner with the commission of the offence. He added that he thought it would be 'highly dangerous' to convict any person of such a crime as that charged – stealing a lamb – on the evidence of an accomplice that was unconfirmed with respect to the party accused. The only exception to this approach appears to have been taken in *R* v. *Andrews & Payne* (1845),[120] where Coleridge J said that he did not think it necessary that there should be confirmation as to each of the two prisoners indicted; confirmation as to one would be sufficient.

All these were decisions of trial judges. It appears that the only case in which the Court for Crown Cases Reserved considered the matter was *R* v. *Stubbs* (1855).[121] Of the judges who dealt with this point, Parke B and Cresswell J required confirmation of the accused's involvement in the offence. A third judge, Wightman J, contented himself with the observation that there had 'certainly been some diversity of practice upon this subject'.[122]

As with the question of whether any warning should be given at all, there seems throughout this period to have been no willingness either to say that a rule existed, or to create one. The subject remained one that was the subject of customary practice, but no more. Thus in *R* v. *Gallagher & Others* (1883), in a trial at the Central Criminal Court before Lord Coleridge CJ, the Master of the Rolls, and Grove J, Lord Coleridge's summing-up to the jury contained a reference to the practice of requiring corroboration of an accomplice, but made no reference to any requirement that it should implicate the accused, saying only that 'there must be a certain amount of corroboration sufficient to satisfy the jury'.[123] The rule that common law corroboration must implicate the accused was not finally settled until 1916 by the decision of the Court of Criminal Appeal, sitting with five members, in *R* v. *Baskerville*.[124]

[120] 1 Cox CC 183.   [121] 7 Cox CC 48.
[122] Ibid., 50–1.   [123] 15 Cox CC 291, 318.
[124] [1916] 2 KB 658. It was accepted that where corroboration was required by *statute*, it had to implicate the accused. Lord Reading went to considerable lengths to conceal the fact that at common law two inconsistent lines of authority had existed: Julius Stone and W. A. N. Wells, *Evidence: its History and Policies* (Sydney, 1991), pp. 717–18.

3

INCOMPETENCY FROM DEFECT OF RELIGIOUS PRINCIPLE

Statutes in the nineteenth century did much to extend the range of admissible evidence. At the beginning of this period two great classes of witnesses were excluded: those who, as Phillipps put it, were incompetent 'from defect of religious principle',[1] and those who were incompetent by reason of an interest in the outcome of the proceedings. In addition, there were some cases where witnesses were excluded on account of their criminal convictions. This chapter deals with the reforms, completed by 1869, which affected the first of these classes. A short account of the common law as it stood at the beginning of the century in relation to incompetence on religious grounds is followed by an outline of the arguments used by Bentham in favour of reform. There follows a summary of the legislative reforms, and a discussion of the influences that helped to bring them about.

THE COMMON LAW

The common law required that all witnesses should take an oath, which was believed to operate as 'a solemn invocation of the vengeance of the Deity upon the witness, if he do not declare the whole truth, so far as he knows it'.[2] As late as 1852, Phillipps justified this requirement by stating that without belief in the existence of God, by whom truth was enjoined and falsehood punished, one sanction was wanting: the fear of Divine punishment invoked by the witness upon himself. It was not enough that the witness should believe himself bound to speak the truth from a

---

[1] Phillipps, *Treatise*, 10th edn (1852), vol. I, p. 12.
[2] Starkie, *Treatise*, 2nd edn (1833), vol. I, p. 22.

regard to his own good character, or to the common interests of society, or through fear of punishment for perjury. 'Such motives have indeed their influence, but they are not considered as affording a sufficient safeguard for the strict observance of truth.'[3] It therefore followed that atheists were not competent to give evidence.[4] Coke had held that infidels could not be witnesses.[5] But, while Hawkins had thought it a sufficient objection to the competency of a witness that they believed neither the Old nor the New Testament,[6] Hale had pointed out the unreasonableness of excluding indiscriminately all heathens, as well as the inconsistency of compelling them to swear in a form that they might not consider binding.[7]

These differences were resolved by the decision in *Omychund* v. *Barker*,[8] which held that the depositions of witnesses professing the Gentoo religion,[9] who had been sworn according to the ceremonies of their religion under a commission out of Chancery, ought to be admitted in evidence. It was afterwards regarded as an established rule 'that not only Jews, but infidels of any country, believing in a God who enjoins truth and punishes falsehood, ought to be received as witnesses'.[10] *Omychund* v. *Barker* also established that, although the substance of the oath must be the same in all cases, it was obviously necessary to allow persons to swear according to the particular ceremonies of their religion in such a manner as they considered binding on their conscience.[11]

Prospective witnesses could be examined before taking the oath for the purpose of determining their competency in relation to

---

[3] Phillipps, *Treatise*, 10th edn (1852), vol. I, pp. 15–16.
[4] *Omychund* v. *Barker* (1744) 1 Atk 21, 40, *per* Parker LCB.
[5] Sir Edward Coke, *The First Part of the Institutes of the Laws of England; or, a Commentary upon Littleton*, ed. Francis Hargrave and Charles Butler, 19th edn (London, 1832), vol. I, sec. 6b. According to Willes LCJ, he had included Jews as well as heathens under this head. See *Omychund* v. *Barker* (1744) 1 Atk 21, 44.
[6] William Hawkins, *A Treatise of the Pleas of the Crown*, ed. Thomas Leach, 7th edn (London, 1795), vol. IV, pp. 443–4.
[7] Sir Matthew Hale, *The History of the Pleas of the Crown*, ed. George Wilson (London, 1778), vol. II, p. 279.
[8] See n. 4. The case was heard before the Court of Chancery, where it was determined by Lord Hardwicke in consultation with the common law Chief Justices Willes and Lee, and Parker LCB.
[9] A contemporary term for the Hindu religion.
[10] Phillipps, *Treatise*, 8th edn (1838), vol. I, p. 12.
[11] 1 Atk 21, 42, 48–9.

religious principle. However, the proper mode of such examination was not to question the witness as to their particular opinions, but to ask whether they believed in a God, in the obligation of an oath, and in a future state of rewards and punishments.[12] Although Quakers had been permitted to make a solemn affirmation in civil proceedings, an oath was still required of them in criminal trials, and they could be punished for contempt of court if they refused to comply.[13]

BENTHAM'S CRITIQUE

In Bentham's view, the true sanction for securing the truthfulness of testimony was not the sanction of religion, but that of public opinion. 'The same formulary, which undertakes to draw down upon a man the resentment of the Deity in case of contravention, does actually, in the same event, draw down upon him (as experience proves) the resentment and contempt of mankind.' An oath could have a powerful effect, but only where it invoked the force of public opinion. Unorthodox religion, and even atheism, were therefore improper grounds for the exclusion of testimony. The religious opinions of a witness should lead to the exclusion of their evidence only, perhaps, if their religion enforced lying in court.[14] Bentham directed a number of arguments, chiefly in *Swear Not At All* (1817) and the *Rationale of Judicial Evidence* (1827),[15] against the use of oaths. For example, he argued that false testimony could be punished without having been given on oath, and that the existing law led to absurdities such as the exclusion of those with honest scruples and the admission of anyone willing to lie about their beliefs.[16] He also argued that oaths led to a double standard of veracity, because the effect of requiring an oath to support some assertions, such as those

---

[12] *R* v. *Taylor* (1790) Peake 14.
[13] 16 Charles II c 4; 7 & 8 William III c 34; 13 William III c 4; 1 George I Stat 2 c 6.
[14] *Works*, vol. VI, pp. 311–12; vol. VII, pp. 420–1, 423.
[15] *Swear Not at All* was printed in 1813 but not published until 1817. The title page indicated that the pamphlet was 'Pre-detached from an Introduction to the "Rationale of Evidence"' (A. D. E. Lewis, 'The Background to Bentham on Evidence', *Utilitas* 2 (1990), 195, 210–11).
[16] *Works*, vol. VII, pp. 421, 424.

contained in testimony given in court, was to provide a 'menda-city-licence' in other contexts, such as pleadings, where an oath was not required to support assertions.[17]

One of Bentham's fundamental objections was that the exclusion of testimony which resulted from insisting that witnesses be sworn weakened the efficiency of the law. For example, he pointed out that the existing law in effect granted a licence 'to all such crimes as from time to time it shall happen to any man to feel himself disposed to commit (other persons out of the question) upon the bodies, or in the presence, of any number of quakers'.[18] Another objection was that oaths were supported by bad theology because they involved the unwarranted assumption not only that God would invariably punish an oathbreaker, but that such divine intervention could be compelled as the result of a human cere-mony.[19] In any case, he argued, such ceremonies were prohibited according to the precept 'Swear not at all', ascribed to Jesus in St Matthew's gospel.[20] Even according to the Articles of 'that modification of the religion of Jesus which is established in England', the use of oaths, though allowable, was not in any case enjoined.[21]

One of Bentham's arguments was that oaths were inadequate as security for the trustworthiness of testimony because the threat-ened divine punishment was of such an uncertain nature that the mere utterance of an oath could not be relied upon to indicate the honesty of the person taking it.[22] That oaths were accorded little weight was shown by the regular violation of jurors' oaths when verdicts were reached that mercifully, but knowingly, under-estimated the value of stolen property so as to avoid a sentence of death.

And this under the eyes and direction of a never-opposing, frequently applauding, or even advising judge: so that here we have in perpetual activity as many schools of perjury as there are courts of justice, having cognizance of these the most frequently committed sorts of crimes; schools in which the judge is master, the jurymen scholars, and the by-standers applauders and encouragers.[23]

---

[17] *Works*, vol. VI, p. 316.   [18] *Works*, vol. V, p. 201.
[19] Ibid., p. 192.   [20] Matt. 5:34.
[21] *Works*, vol. VI, pp. 28–9. See 'Articles of Religion', *Book of Common Prayer* (1662).
[22] *Works*, vol. V, p. 192.   [23] *Works*, vol. VI, p. 308.

Bentham's opposition to oaths cannot be fully understood without seeing it in the context of his opposition to the sinister interests of the legal profession and to those of the established church. According to him, the existing system of procedural law, an important feature of which was the requirement that testimony should be on oath, had been framed 'not in pursuit of the ends of justice, but in pursuit of private sinister ends – in direct hostility to the public ends'. The sinister interests of 'Judge & Co.' had encouraged the growth of the 'technical' or 'fee-gathering' system.[24] The first object of this system was to render the number of claims and defences, whether or not bona fide, as great as possible in order to increase the number of occasions for the payment of fees. But, provided there was no loss of opportunity to earn fees, it was in the interest of judges to keep hearings short. On one pretence or another, witnesses were therefore excluded. Among the benefits to the judge of excluding parties Bentham identified:

Making ease (without prejudice to profit) by exempting himself from the plague and indignity of having to do with low people, with the mob, the rabble, the populace, – *i.e.* the great majority of the people; wretches, who, being ignorant of things in general, and of jurisprudential science in particular, are in proportion to their ignorance, apt to be troublesome.[25]

To hear too many witnesses would be 'a work of trouble', and deciding a case after hearing too many would be even more troublesome.

To free himself from this trouble, [the judge] lays hold of the difficulty and converts the magnitude of it into a pretence for shrinking from it. To untie the knot would be too much trouble. In this pretence he finds a sword, with which he cuts it.[26]

One obvious such sword was the law that excluded witnesses who would not give testimony on oath.

Another reason for Bentham's opposition to the administration of oaths may well have been that he regarded the legal requirement as upholding the sinister interests of the established Church. Bentham's destructive criticisms of religious doctrine make it probable that he was an atheist, though too cautious to acknow-

---

[24] See generally *Works*, vol. VII, pp. 197–214, 598.
[25] *Works*, vol. VII, p. 232.   [26] UCL 58:136.

ledge this openly.[27] In Bentham's writings on procedure and evidence, however, jurisprudence and religion are on several occasions linked in critical comments. For example:

In jurisprudence as in religion, swallowing absurdities is an exercise of faith, and faith is fortified by exercise.[28]

Religion excepted, jurisprudence is the only science – pretended science, in which the use of reason continues to be openly discountenanced, in which the adherence to unkind barbarism has been commended as a duty: in which the privilege of thinking for one's self has been made the object of monopoly in the hands of those that are no more.[29]

Priests and lawyers were criticised equally for self-interest:

Priests, if bound by any tie political or moral to maintain for true propositions relative to religion whatever may be their opinions concerning the truth of them, are the natural and implacable enemies of whatever is true in matter of religion. Lawyers whose emoluments in all shapes arise out of and are proportioned to the imperfections of the law are the natural enemies of whatever is good in matters of law.[30]

If in the instance of such a multitude of religions, theology according to a universal and universally reciprocal observation ... had no other end in view than the power exaltation and enrichment of the contrivers of them the priests, why should jurisprudence have any other view than the exaltation and enrichment of the lawyers?[31]

The accumulated force of all these arguments suggests that Bentham would have preferred to see oaths abolished altogether. This was certainly the wish of the writer of an article in 1826, whose express purpose was to extend knowledge of Bentham's writings to those who would not read them in their original form, and who concluded with the hope that the 'fruitless and pernicious ceremony' of the oath might be 'forever abolished'.[32] Bentham did believe, however, that if the oath ceremony was to continue it should be reformed, so as to emphasise the force of political and moral sanctions as well as those of religion. In support of the religious sanction, he suggested that in every court of justice there should be a painting or engraving of the death of Ananias and Sapphira, and that the oath should be administered by a minister of the established religion, or of the witness's own religion if it

---

[27] James E. Crimmins, *Secular Utilitarianism: Social Science and the Critique of Religion in the Thought of Jeremy Bentham* (Oxford, 1990), p. 282.
[28] UCL 58:140.   [29] UCL 58:227.   [30] UCL 47:63.   [31] UCL 58:152.
[32] *Westminster Review* 5 (1826), 23, 58.

were different.[33] To emphasise the political sanction, tables stating the punishment for perjury should be set up in courts. While the witness was pronouncing the oath, an officer of the court should point with a wand to the appropriate provision. On special occasions, where the temptation to lie was thought to be particularly great and where the cause was an important one, a curtain should be drawn up to reveal 'a graphical exhibition, representing a convict suffering the characteristic punishment for perjury'. The moral sanction was to be emphasised by changing the wording of the oath, so as to make reference to the contempt or abhorrence of all good men in cases of mendacity.[34]

THE LEGISLATIVE REFORMS

The reforms took place in two stages. During the first, attention was directed towards the relief of persons, such as Quakers, who had religious scruples against taking an oath. After some piecemeal reforms, complete success was achieved so far as civil actions were concerned with the passing of the Common Law Procedure Act 1854. The reform contained in that Act was extended to criminal trials in 1861. Attention then turned to the relief of those who refused to take an oath because they subscribed to no religious belief whatsoever. These attempts succeeded with the passing of the Evidence Further Amendment Act 1869.

1828–1861

In 1828, the Marquis of Lansdowne introduced in the House of Lords a bill that extended to Quakers and Moravians[35] the right to

---

[33] For the fate of Ananias and Sapphira see Acts 5: 1–10. A writer in the *Edinburgh Review* thought that Bentham's recommendation for court ornamentation was 'passing strange', considering that perjurers 'instead of dropping down dead in court walk out as lively as their truth-telling neighbours' (*Edinburgh Review* 59 (1834), 465).

[34] *Works*, vol. VI, pp. 319–20.

[35] Members of the Moravian Church, also known as the Renewed Church of the Brethren, or Unitas Fratrum. It originated as an evangelical Christian communion in Bohemia among followers of John Huss (*c.* 1372–1415). Persecution reduced its members, but a renewal took place during the eighteenth century in Saxony. Moravian congregations were later founded in other countries, including Holland, England, the West Indies, and North America.

affirm in criminal cases, which they already possessed in civil proceedings. The bill rapidly passed both Houses, and received the royal assent on 27 June 1828.[36] In 1833 the statutory benefits which had been given to Quakers and Moravians were extended to Separatists,[37] but there was as yet no general permission for evidence to be given on affirmation, even by those whose unwillingness to take an oath stemmed from religious, as opposed to deistic or atheistic, beliefs. Nevertheless, a cautious parliamentary movement for reform developed, which was led by Lord Denman in the Lords and by Benjamin Hawes, member for Lambeth, in the Commons.

In the parliamentary session of 1838, Denman brought before the Lords a proposal that an affirmation should be substituted for an oath wherever a witness had conscientious scruples against being sworn. This was the effect of the second clause of a bill that he introduced, the first being a far less controversial provision that all witnesses taking an oath should be sworn according to the form that they regarded as binding on their consciences. Before putting the bill forward, Denman had communicated with all members of the House of Lords who filled, or had filled, judicial situations. With but one exception, he had discovered them to be in favour of the measure.[38] He lacked, however, the general support of the common law judges.[39] Opinion in the Lords was opposed to the second clause. Denman, seeing the strength of his opponents, was content to split the bill, having the first clause passed and the second made the subject of a separate bill. This latter bill was defeated in the Lords on 19 July. The more acceptable of the two

---

[36] 9 George IV c 32. See further *Parl. Deb.*, New Series, xviii, 1357–8 (28 March 1828); xix, 350–1 (5 May 1828). In the debate on 5 May in the Commons, the member for Norwich, William Smith, emphasised that the exception in favour of Quakers and Moravians had 'become expedient for the sake of the interests of the public' (*The Times*, 6 May 1828). For the reluctance of Quakers themselves to press for reform, see a letter from a former Quaker in *The Times*, 14 April 1828.

[37] 3 & 4 William IV c 82. Separatism, later known as Congregationalism, was a form of protestant church organisation in which each local group, or congregation, had control over its own affairs. The movement began in the sixteenth and seventeenth centuries in England as a revolt against the established Church.

[38] *Parl. Deb.*, 3rd series, xliv, 148 (12 July 1838).

[39] Joseph Arnould, *Memoir of Thomas, First Lord Denman* (London, 1873), vol. II, p. 92; *Parl. Deb.*, 3rd series, xliv, 318–19.

bills passed both Lords and Commons, and received the royal assent on 14 August 1838.[40]

In 1839, a bill to provide a general right to affirm for those opposed on religious grounds to taking an oath was proposed in the commons by Benjamin Hawes. It was defeated by 125 votes to 93. Hawes made a second attempt with a similar bill in 1840. To meet the earlier objections that a witness might make a pretence of religious scruples on the spur of the moment to avoid taking the oath, Hawes proposed elaborate safeguards. To obtain the benefit of the legislation applicants must previously have obtained a certificate from a bench of two or more justices of the peace sitting in the area where they resided. Afterwards, they must have produced the certificate, have signed a register kept for the purpose, and have made a solemn affirmation and declaration to the effect that they believed the taking of any oath to be forbidden by their duty to God. This bill was passed in the Commons by a majority of thirty-two, but failed subsequently in the Lords.[41]

On 10 March 1842, Lord Denman presented a bill in the House of Lords for rendering Baptists' affirmations equivalent to an oath in courts of justice. The bill was read for a first time, but on 2 May Denman announced that he had since found that strong objections were entertained against making the measure applicable to Baptists alone. He therefore begged leave to withdraw the bill and said that he would return to the general question in a day or two.[42] On 6 June 1842, Denman moved the first reading of a bill 'to provide a general Form of Affirmation for all Persons who believe the taking of any Oath to be forbidden by their Duty towards God'. The form of declaration provided for such persons included a declaration of belief 'that the taking of any Oath is contrary to the Law of God'. This was not, therefore, legislation from which an honest atheist could benefit. In the debate on the second reading the Lord Chancellor suggested that a committee should be directed to inquire into the general subject of the

---

[40] 1 & 2 Vict c 105.
[41] *Parl. Deb.*, 3rd series, liv, 681–2 (28 May 1840); lv, 869–80 (22 July 1840), 1246–51 (4 August 1840).
[42] *Parl. Deb.*, 3rd series, lxi, 418, 1357–8.

administration of oaths in courts of justice and elsewhere, and Lord Denman consented to withdraw the bill.[43]

When Denman next turned to the matter in Parliament, in 1849, it was to speak in support of a bill which had already passed the Commons. The object of this bill also was to relieve those who had a religious objection to taking an oath, and it contained provisions similar to those of the 1840 bill to ensure that objection to the administration of an oath could not be made on the spur of the moment. This bill, like its predecessor, was defeated in the Lords.[44]

The question of examination on oath was considered in the Second Report of the Common Law Commissioners, published in the 1852–3 parliamentary session.[45] The Commissioners recited the arguments that they had heard for and against a general practice of insisting on sworn evidence and said that they were unable to agree on any recommendation. They remarked, though, that sometimes an individual, not being a Quaker, Moravian, or Separatist, refused to be sworn from conscientious religious motives. In such a case, that witness's evidence was lost, and sometimes the individual was punished for contempt of court. They continued: 'In principle, there does not appear to be any reason why the same regard which is had to the scruples of a body of persons should not be extended to those of an individual.'[46] On 12 August 1854, the Solicitor General stated in the House of Commons that the Government would introduce a bill in the next session that would be founded on the Report of the Commissioners and would make proper provision for witnesses who had a religious objection to taking an oath.

The bill, which in due course became the Common Law Procedure Act 1854, provided in clause 21 that if any person called as a witness should refuse from alleged conscientious motives to be sworn, it should be lawful for the court or judge or other presiding officer, upon being satisfied of the sincerity of the objection, to permit the witness instead to make a solemn

---

[43] *House of Lords Sessional Papers*, 1842 II. 7 (122); *Parl. Deb.*, 3rd series, lxiv, 617–35; Arnould, *Lord Denman*, vol. II, pp. 135–6, 415–25.

[44] *Parl. Deb.*, 3rd series, civ, 441–51 (18 April 1849); cvi, 714–29 (22 June 1849).

[45] *Second Report of H. M. Commissioners for Inquiring into the Process, Practice, and System of Pleading in the Superior Courts of Common Law*, PP 1852–3 [1626] XL.

[46] Ibid., 14–15.

affirmation or declaration. Thus far there was nothing to prevent
an atheist from taking advantage of the legislation, but this was
precluded by the form of the affirmation or declaration, which
required the witness to declare that the taking of any oath was,
according to their religious belief, unlawful. In the Lords there
was a division on a motion by Lord St Leonards to omit the
clause, as a result of which the clause was retained by a majority of
ten. In the Commons the bill was passed with no significant
debate on the new power to affirm.[47]

The result of this legislation was that different rules applied to
the admissibility of evidence on affirmation in civil and criminal
cases. The removal of this anomaly was proposed by a Criminal
Proceedings Oath Relief Bill, which was introduced with the
approval of the Law Officers of the Crown by John Locke QC,
member for Southwark, on 2 May 1861. The bill was passed in
the Commons on 22 July. It was later passed in the Lords, where
it had the support of Lord Denman and the Lord Chancellor, and
received the royal assent on 1 August 1861.[48]

1861–1869

During the 1860s, attempts were made, unsuccessfully until 1869,
to legislate in order to permit those without religious beliefs to
give evidence on affirmation.

On 21 February 1861, Sir John Trelawny, member for Tavi-
stock Borough, obtained leave to bring in a bill that provided that
persons should be allowed to affirm if they stated that an oath
would not in their judgement add to their obligation to speak the
truth. By a majority of seventy it was resolved that the bill be put
off for six months, thereby ensuring that it would be lost through
the expiration of time.[49] In the following year, Trelawny brought
in a similar bill, but for lack of time it did not proceed beyond a
first reading. He failed in a similar attempt in 1863.[50]

[47] *Parl. Deb.*, 3rd series, cxxxiii, 797 (23 May 1854), 145–56 (30 May 1854).
[48] *Parl. Deb.*, clxii, 1372 (2 May 1861); clxiii, 601–4 (5 June 1861), 977–8 (13 June
1861); clxiv, 1032–4 (17 July 1861), 1284 (22 July 1861), 1340 (23 July 1861),
1479–80 (25 July 1861), 1779 (30 July 1861), 1816 (1 August 1861).
[49] *Parl. Deb.*, 3rd series, clxi, 697 (21 February 1861), 1936–40 (13 March 1861);
clxiii, 953–73 (12 June 1861).
[50] *Parl. Deb.*, 3rd series, clxvii, 1024–6 (24 June 1862); clxix, 223 (10 February
1863), 1285–1302 (11 March 1863). See also *The Parliamentary Diaries of Sir*

The next move to achieve this reform was not made until 26 February 1869, when George Denman[51] brought in a bill for further amendment of the law of evidence. One of its main provisions was, as he described it in moving for leave, that parties should not be deprived of the evidence of witnesses through some defect in the witnesses' religious belief. On this occasion the proposal for reform had the support of the Attorney General, Sir Robert Collier. The bill was read a second time without a division. No argument at all appears to have been directed against the proposed amendment of the law concerning the right to affirm. The bill experienced a similarly smooth passage in the Lords, where it had the support of the Lord Chancellor, Lord Hatherley. As originally drafted, the bill had allowed witnesses to avoid the oath where they simply objected to taking it. This was amended in committee to require witnesses to satisfy the judge that taking an oath would have no binding effect on their conscience.[52] In this form, the legislation received the royal assent on 9 August 1869.

INFLUENCES ON THE REFORMS

Why had religious considerations ceased to be a ground of incompetency by 1869? I argue that this came about as a result of the convergence of two lines of development: one of religious scepticism; the other of social stability. Until the 1860s, it was difficult for Members of Parliament to support legislation that might seem to weaken the connection between the state and

John Trelawny, 1858–1865, ed. T. A. Jenkins, Camden Fourth Series, vol. XXXX (London, 1990), pp. 151–263, passim.
[51] 1819–96. 4th son of Lord Denman and member for Tiverton Borough. Barrister, 1846; QC 1861; Justice of the Court of Common Pleas, 1872; Justice of the Common Pleas Division of the High Court of Justice, 1875; Justice of the High Court of Justice, Queen's Bench Division, 1881–92.
[52] The bill brought in by George Denman appears in *House of Commons Sessional Papers* 1868–9 II.411 [Bill 25]. The form in which it reached the Lords is in *House of Lords Sessional Papers* 1868–9 IV.583 (110). For the bill as amended in committee and finally on report see *House of Lords Sessional Papers* 1868–9 IV.587 (239); 589 (260). Trelawny commented: 'Such is progress! Why, in 1861, the Tories I believe thought me inspired by the Devil, whereas today, the Bill was read a 2d time without a division' (*The Parliamentary Diaries of Sir John Trelawny, 1868–1873*, ed. T. A. Jenkins, *Camden Miscellany* XXXII, Camden Fifth Series, vol. III (London, 1994), pp. 359–60).

Christianity. In the earlier decades of the century, it had even been difficult to support measures that might seem to weaken the position of the form of Christianity represented by the established Church. The reason for this was that, until at least the 1850s, there were substantial fears among the propertied classes for the stability of society. Christianity, particularly in its established form, was seen as a social cement, and any attempts at reform that might diminish its influence were opposed. The sanction of oaths, which were administered not only in courts of law but as a condition of entry to many positions of responsibility, was seen as an essential part of the public aspect of Christianity. By the late 1860s, however, a change in outlook had developed. The state of society seemed far more stable; the need for established religion, even any religion at all, as a social cement appeared to have diminished. Oaths had become less important, and so the reforms could be made. Probably as a result of this change in the way society was viewed, some convinced Christians developed a distaste for the compulsion of consciences involved in the administration of oaths under the unreformed law.

The period 1828–61 saw four changes in the relevant law: the 1828 grant to Quakers and Moravians of the right to affirm in criminal cases; the 1833 extension to Separatists of the rights already granted to Quakers and Moravians; the general grant in 1854 of the right to affirm in civil cases to persons with religious scruples against taking an oath; and, in 1861, the extension of that right to criminal cases.

The 1833 extension, while perhaps of interest to historians of English nonconformity, appears to have no special significance for the development of the law of evidence. Furthermore, whilst an extension of competency from civil to criminal proceedings aroused great controversy in the period that preceded the Criminal Evidence Act 1898, no controversy was aroused over the very much more limited proposals enacted in 1861.

By contrast, the 1828 legislation is potentially of some interest, occurring as it did in the year of Brougham's famous reform speech and against a background that featured the publication in the previous year of Bentham's *Rationale of Judicial Evidence*. But the 1828 Act stands in isolation from the later reforms of 1854 and 1869. The legislation of 1854 was quite different in kind from that of 1828. Unlike the earlier Act, its object was to grant a general right to affirm, albeit confined to those who wished to do so on religious grounds, and it generated a substantial controversy. The 1869 Act, which extended the general right to atheists and those who would later be called agnostics, was similarly controversial. Despite the difference in scope between the legislation of 1854 and that of 1869, the arguments employed differed very little, and I therefore consider the influences on these reforms as part of the development of a general right to affirm.

It will be convenient to consider first the influences on the 1828 legislation, and then those on the development of a general right to affirm.

The 1828 legislation

In the early decades of the century, irreligion could excite great hostility, whether it amounted to atheism or took some less extreme form. This was at least partly due to its connection with the radical movement, originating with Thomas Paine and Robert Owen, which had developed in Britain in response to the French Revolution.[53]

Two incidents show the kind of emotions that could be excited. The first occurred in 1826, when Joseph Hume, member for the Montrose district, wished to present to the House of Commons, a petition that he believed to be that of Robert Taylor, a clergyman of the established Church. This document declared that the petitioner, after a most mature consideration, found himself unable any longer to give credence to the doctrines of Christianity, and that he had in consequence resigned his cure and now declared himself to be a deist. The document then stated that in various instances deists had been deprived of legal protection because they could not take an oath according to the prescribed forms. The petition concluded by reciting that 'your petitioner considers the law, as it now stands, is injurious to the fair and equal administration of justice, and is at variance with the interests of the State, inasmuch as it allows persons guilty of atrocious crimes to escape with impunity, and deprives your petitioner and others of justice'.

In presenting the petition, Hume said that the rights of a British

---

[53] Edward Royle, *Victorian Infidels: the Origins of the British Secularist Movement 1791–1866* (Manchester, 1974), p. 25.

subject and the cause of civil and religious liberty were deeply
concerned. He argued that it was inconsistent to refuse the oath of
a person who disbelieved in Christianity, but at the same time to
receive the oaths of those who were Hindus, sworn according to
the form of their faith. The profession of a belief in God was
surely sufficient for the purpose of taking an oath in a court of
justice. Every man, he asserted, should be allowed to enjoy liberty
of conscience uncontrolled by civil disability.

In the debate that followed, Mr Serjeant Onslow said that
Hume's speech had been 'such as should never have been
addressed to a British House of Commons', and he asked what
form of oath could bind someone who openly professed no creed.
Onslow's opinion was shared by at least one of the younger
members, as the remarks of the member for Beverley, Charles
Batley, show. He intervened to say that a person who did not
believe in our Saviour ought not to be tolerated in a British House
of Commons, and that it was astonishing that Hume had not been
interrupted in giving his speech and no objection taken to his
arguments before they had been suffered to proceed. Sir Edmund
Carrington expressed his horror that any gentleman, educated in a
Christian country, could be found to entertain the doctrine stated
in the petition. The member for Norwich, William Smith, to
some extent redressed the balance by saying that the interests of
justice were much more likely to suffer from the oath of a man
who swore on the gospels, though unbelieving, than from that of a
man who, though denying the gospels, acknowledged the existence
of a God. Yet when Hume later moved that the petition be printed
so that members should be acquainted with its objects he was met
by a general cry of 'No, no', which forced him to withdraw the
motion.[54]

The second incident took place at the Old Bailey in November
1833. On that occasion a man called Henry Berthold was on trial
for theft. He called as a defence witness a man who, when handed
the Bible to be sworn, declared that he had no belief in its contents
and that he was an atheist. This observation evoked 'strong marks
of disapprobation and disgust from all parts of the court'. Having

---

[54] *Parl. Deb.*, New Series, xvi, 171–8 (29 November 1826). The affair had a
strange sequel: on 12 April 1827 Hume informed the House that the petition he
had presented had been discovered to be a forgery (*Parl. Deb.*, New Series, xvii,
389–90).

established that he was unable to take the oath, the witness retired 'amidst the strongest manifestations of disgust and execrations from all present'. Another defence witness presented the same problem. According to the report: 'It was some minutes before silence was produced, so general were the expressions of execration at the declaration and demeanour of the witness, who left the court amid hisses and loud cries of "Turn him out" in which several of the jury joined.'[55]

The violence of opinion illustrated by these two incidents might have been expected to create some difficulties for Lansdowne's bill of 1828. In fact, the bill encountered no opposition. There were several reasons for this. In the first place, it was a government bill. By contrast, the member who had tried to present the petition and who had spoken in support of deists in 1826 had been notorious for his radical views and may himself, as Batley's remarks suggest, have been regarded as a deist, if not worse. Further, the extent of reform proposed in 1828 was very limited. It applied only to Quakers and Moravians – persons who were undoubtedly Christians – and merely increased the extent of a reform that had already been conceded to them in civil cases.

Another reason may have been the realisation that public safety would benefit from this reform. In his speech in support of the bill, Peel emphasised that it was not intended as a boon to Quakers and Moravians – they had not wanted that – but 'as a means of rendering them competent witnesses for the purpose of benefiting thereby the community'. Lansdowne had made the same point at the committee stage of the bill in the Lords.[56] During the period 1821–7 crime had substantially increased,[57] and contemporary commentators were aware of this. In February 1828, *The Times* summarised a pamphlet, recently published by Sir Eardley Wilmot, on what the newspaper described as 'the awful subject of the increase of crime in England'. In April of that year, the same newspaper noted a return printed by order of the House of Commons, which showed that in the period 1821–7 there had

---

[55] *Annual Register* (1833), 159–61 (23 November).   [56] See n. 36.

[57] Commitments in England and Wales (excluding London and Middlesex) showed an increase of 86% over the period 1811–17; convictions in this period increased by 105%. The increase in London and Middlesex was not as great, but was still considerable: commitments increased by 48% and convictions by 55% (Sir Leon Radzinowicz, *History of English Criminal Law*, vol. I, pp. 588–9).

been an increase in convictions outside London and Middlesex of between a half and one-third, while within those areas convictions had increased by over a half.[58]

Finally, the bill may have been viewed as a tactical device to further Catholic emancipation. By 1828, the success of this cause appeared to be only a matter of time, but the perception remained that anti-Catholics were too strong to be immediately overthrown by direct assault, and that success was more likely to be achieved by indirect methods. One of the tactics adopted by supporters of Catholic emancipation was to press for repeal of the Test and Corporation Acts to the extent that they affected Protestant dissenters, for it had become a familiar argument of opponents of emancipation that Catholics should not be put in a better position than Protestant dissenters. In accordance with this policy, Lord John Russell, backed by a powerful Nonconformist pressure group known as the United Committee, introduced a bill in February 1828 for the repeal of the Test and Corporation Acts to the extent that they excluded Protestant dissenters from office. At first, Wellington and Peel opposed it; then they tried to compromise, and the bill was eventually passed with very minor amendments later that year.[59] Lansdowne himself was much engaged at this time in the cause of Catholic emancipation,[60] and his evidence bill may have been intended as part of the project of Protestant emancipation designed to precede that of the Catholics.

Lansdowne's bill may therefore have been initiated, and could certainly have been supported, for several reasons. Might the influence of Bentham have been one more? The *Rationale of Judicial Evidence* had been published in 1827, and Lansdowne could have been no stranger to Bentham's ideas. His father, the second Earl of Shelburne and first Marquis of Lansdowne, had been a friend of Bentham, and it was probably on the latter's advice that he had chosen Edinburgh rather than Oxford for his son's further education. After Edinburgh the young man had

---

[58] *The Times*, 9 February 1828, 2 April 1828. See also William Draper Best, *The Substance of a Charge Delivered to the Grand Jury of Wiltshire at the Summer Assizes 1827, by the Lord Chief Justice Best* (London, 1827), pp. 6, 9.

[59] E. Halévy, *A History of the English People in the Nineteenth Century*, trans E. E. Watkin, 2nd edn (1949), vol. II, pp. 263–4; Asa Briggs, *The Age of Improvement: 1783–1867*, rev. edn (London, 1979), p. 230.

[60] *Dictionary of National Biography*, s.v. 'Petty-Fitzmaurice, Henry, third Marquis of Lansdowne'.

proceeded to Cambridge, whence, in 1802, he had set out on the grand tour in the company of Etienne Dumont, Bentham's translator and redactor.[61] The real difficulty with the suggestion that the 1828 legislation might have been influenced by Bentham's ideas is the minimalist nature of the reform. With such good reasons already available to account for the introduction of the bill and for the support that it gained, it seems superfluous to look beyond those reasons to the much wider scope of Bentham's vision, or to that of Brougham, who, in his speech on law reform on 7 February 1828, had urged that any person who believed in the existence of a God and a future state of rewards and punishments should be able to give evidence in civil and criminal proceedings.[62]

The development of a general right to affirm

Thomas Gisborne,[63] writing at the end of the eighteenth century, thought that religious scepticism had made significant progress in the higher and middle classes of society. He attributed this to several causes. Some, such as travellers or historians, had compared different societies and had concluded that all religions were alike. In their view, the Supreme Being had enabled mankind to discover by the power of reason the plain precepts of morality; the object of all religions, albeit encumbered with fanatical rites and doctrines, was to inculcate those precepts. Others thought that religion of every kind was superstition, and that, though certain modes of conduct ought to be followed from principles of honour and for the good of society, it was absurd to judge that people were bound to act thus by reference to the supposed will of a deity. Some had become unbelievers through the study of philosophy. Others had persuaded themselves of their unbelief through a desire to pursue a way of life that was incompatible with

---

[61] Ibid.

[62] Henry Brougham, *A Speech on the Present State of the Law of the Country; delivered in the House of Commons, on Thursday, February 7, 1828*, 2nd edn (London, 1828), p. 41.

[63] Religion and social control were subjects considered in the mid-1790s by a number of Christian thinkers, from the utilitarian William Paley to his Evangelical critic Thomas Gisborne. In his *Enquiry into the Duties of Men* (1795), Gisborne examined the Christian basis of duty (Robert Hole, *Pulpits, Politics and Public Order in England 1760–1832* (Cambridge, 1989), pp. 81, 136).

Christian beliefs. Others had reached a stage of disbelief through immersion in political, commercial, or professional business, or through 'a continued succession of dissipated amusements'.[64]

By 1845, a writer in the *British Quarterly Review*[65] felt able to state that a large number of educated men had come to reject Christianity, considered as a divine revelation, and that only a small minority of the educated and upper classes, including perhaps one-fifth of the House of Commons, were earnest and convinced adherents of Christianity. The 1830s, 1840s, and 1850s saw the development of what John Morley called 'dissolvent literature',[66] and rational Christian writers such as Paley may also have helped to spread an attitude that was essentially secular and pragmatic.[67] The lives of individual men and women show the doubts that were being felt. For example, in 1863, James Fitzjames Stephen indicated in private correspondence that he was supported by the belief that God ordered all things; but by 1879, his correspondence showed that he had reached an agnostic position: 'The whole theory about the relations (if any) between God (whatever he may be) and man is so hopelessly obscure that one is simply reduced to silence.' But he worried about the implications of this: 'However it may go with individuals I feel much alarmed at the spread of my own opinions. I do not doubt their truth but I greatly doubt the capacity of people in general to bear them.'[68]

Tractarianism, before losing its original impetus in the late 1840s, had strengthened the defences against scepticism.[69] By the 1860s, however, a change in intellectual spirit could be seen. In 1868, Carlyle wrote in his journal: 'An immense development of *Atheism* is clearly proceeding, and at a rapid pace, and in joyful

---

[64] Thomas Gisborne, *An Enquiry into the Duties of Men in the Higher and Middle Classes of Society in Great Britain*, 2nd edn (London, 1795), vol. II, pp. 472–7.

[65] Quoted in W. L. Burn, *The Age of Equipoise: a Study of the Mid-Victorian Generation* (London, 1968), p. 274.

[66] John Morley (Viscount Morley), *Critical Miscellanies* (London, 1886), vol. III, p. 242. See also Burn, *Age of Equipoise*, p. 274.

[67] William Paley, *The Principles of Moral and Political Philosophy* (London, 1785 and subsequent edns); Hole, *Pulpits, Politics and Public Order*, pp. 83–4.

[68] See the letter to his wife, 22 October 1863, and letters to Lord Lytton, 2 April and 1 October 1979. *Stephen MSS*, Cambridge University Library, quoted in Burn, *Age of Equipoise*, pp. 274–5.

[69] Burn, *Age of Equipoise*, pp. 275.

exultant humour, both here and in France.' A year later he made
the same observation:

The quantities of potential and even consciously increasing Atheism,
sprouting out everywhere in these days, is enormous. In every scientific or
quasi-scientific periodical one meets it ... Not only all Christian churches
but all Christian religion are nodding towards speedy downfall in this
Europe that now is ... France is amazingly advanced in that career.
England, America, are making still more passionate speed to come up
with her, to pass her, and be the vanguard of progress.

A similar entry appeared in 1870.[70]

The campaign to extend the right to affirm to those without a
religious belief found organised support outside Parliament.
When Trelawny was preparing to introduce the first of his bills in
1861, George Jacob Holyoake[71] set up an 'Evidence Committee'
to gather arguments against the existing law. He announced a
policy, based on Bentham's ideas, of carrying bad law into operation until all the mischief it could produce had an effect on the
legislature. He even went so far as to institute a collusive action
that was designed to fail because of the law requiring testimony on
oath. However, this scheme was forestalled by reality in the case of
Madan v. *Catanach*, a case decided in November 1861, which was
given considerable publicity and became the subject of a leading
article in *The Times*.[72]

The case was heard by the Court of Exchequer, sitting in banc
on appeal from a decision of the Rochdale County Court. The
plaintiff had issued a plaint in detinue for a pianoforte that had
belonged to his wife before her marriage to him. In the County
Court Mrs Madan had gone into the witness box to give evidence
in support of the claim. She had been about to take the oath when
she had been stopped by the advocate for the defendant, who had
then asked her about her religious beliefs. It had become clear that
she believed neither in a deity, nor in a future state of rewards and
punishments. The judge had thereupon ruled that she was not
competent to give evidence. In the Court of Exchequer it was

[70] James Anthony Froude, *Thomas Carlyle: a History of his Life in London,
1834–1881*, new impression (London, 1919), vol. II, pp. 399, 414–15.
[71] 1817–1906. English social reformer and follower of Robert Owen; established a
free-thought movement that campaigned for a secular, pluralist society. His
movement formed the basis for the National Secular Society set up by
Bradlaugh (1866). See Royle, *Victorian Infidels*, pp. 2–4.
[72] *The Times*, 12 November 1861, p. 9; 16 November 1861.

argued that the decision of the judge had been wrong, and that such a circumstance ought not to have deprived her of the right to give evidence, but should have affected only her credibility. The Court of Exchequer dismissed the appeal without calling on counsel for the respondent. However, the extent of organised support for secularism is shown by the fact that Mrs Madan obtained support from two secular societies: the Rochdale Secular Society, which funded her appeal, and the Manchester Secular Society, which raised a subscription for a new piano.[73]

The advance of secularism was both illustrated and encouraged by the publication from the end of the 1850s of more books encouraging a secular, or at least critical, outlook. Mill's essay *On Liberty* was published in 1859, a year that also saw the publication of Charles Darwin's *On the Origin of Species*. In 1860, a collection of broad church essays entitled *Essays and Reviews* was published. This was followed in 1861 by J. W. Colenso's commentary on *St Paul's Epistle to the Romans*, in which everlasting punishment and other orthodoxies were denied. William Lecky's *History of the Rise and Influence of Rationalism in Europe* was published in 1865.[74] Owen Chadwick summed up the intellectual changes of the 1860s in this way:

The forties was the time of doubts, in the plural and with a small d; turmoils of Arthur Hugh Clough or John Sterling or young James Anthony Froude. In the sixties Britain and France and Germany entered the age of Doubt, in the singular and with a capital D.[75]

Until the 1860s, people who were sceptical of the claims of revealed religion had tended to conceal their opinions. To be open might have exposed them to prosecution under the criminal law.[76] But pressure might also be indirect, for example, the careers of

---

[73] Royle, *Victorian Infidels*, pp. 270–2. The case attracted the attention of Sir John Trelawny, who asked a question in Parliament about it: *Trelawny Diaries 1858–1865*, pp. 149–50.

[74] Royle, *Victorian Infidels*, p. 291; Owen Chadwick, *The Secularization of the European Mind in the Nineteenth Century*, Canto edn (Cambridge, 1990), p. 202.

[75] Chadwick, *Secularization of the European Mind*, p. 184.

[76] The Blasphemy Act 1697 barred from office all those, educated as Christians, who denied the doctrine of the Trinity, the truth of Christianity, or the divine authority of the Bible. A second offence might incur penalties of inability to hold land, to bring an action at law, or to receive a legacy, and imprisonment for up to three years. A prosecution might also be brought for the common law offence of blasphemous libel. The Blasphemy Act was not repealed until 1813, and the common law offence remained unaffected by the repeal. Its abolition

Mark Pattison and Benjamin Jowett were probably hindered by their reputation for unorthodox opinions.[77] As late as 1863, Edward Bowen referred to the 'notoriety and odium' that opposition to religious dogmatism, especially the dogma of biblical infallibility, incurred.[78]

Another reason for reticence could have been that a person who was sceptical of religious beliefs might have feared the results of a widespread loss of faith. J. S. Mill described the 1850s as a period 'in which real belief in any religious doctrine is feeble and precarious, but the opinion of its necessity for moral and social purposes almost universal'.[79] A similar view was taken by J. F. Stephen as late as 1879,[80] and in 1881 Henry Sidgwick wrote to J. R. Mozley:

While I cannot myself discover adequate rational basis for the Christian hope of happy immortality, it seems to me that the general loss of such a hope, from the minds of average human beings as now constituted, would be an evil of which I cannot pretend to measure the extent. I am not prepared to say that the dissolution of the existing social order would follow, but I think the danger of such dissolution would be seriously increased, and that the evil would certainly be very great.[81]

By the beginning of the nineteenth century a close connection between religion and civil government had been a commonplace of political thought in England for at least three hundred years. In the sixteenth century, Hooker had recognised what he called the 'politic use of religion':

Men fearing God are thereby a great deal more effectually than by positive laws restrained from doing evil; inasmuch as these laws have no farther power than over our outward actions only, whereas unto men's inward

---

was recommended by the Law Commission in 1985 (J. C. D. Clark, *English Society 1688–1832* (Cambridge, 1985), pp. 283–9, 379–82; Law Com. No 145).

[77] V. H. H. Green, *Oxford Common Room: a Study of Lincoln College and Mark Pattison* (London, 1957), pp. 154–7; Peter Hinchcliff, *Benjamin Jowett and the Christian Religion* (Oxford, 1987), pp. 40–1, 93–4, 107–8.

[78] Edward Bowen, 'Bishop Colenso on the Pentateuch', *The National Review* 31 (January and April 1863), 25.

[79] J. S. Mill, *Autobiography*, in *Collected Works of John Stuart Mill*, ed. John M. Robson and Jack Stillinger (Toronto, 1963–91), vol. I, p. 73.

[80] See n. 68.

[81] A. and E. M. Sidgwick, *Henry Sidgwick: a Memoir* (London, 1906), p. 357. Cf. J. W. Cross, *George Eliot's Life as Related in her Letters and Journals* (Edinburgh and London, 1885), vol. II, p. 343.

cogitations, unto privy intents and motions of their hearts, religion serveth for a bridle.[82]

In particular, the use of oaths to ensure order and stability had long been recognised. For example, in 1637, the Earl of Manchester declared in the Star Chamber:

Now, my lords, your lordships well know, that every man's state, every man's credit, his possessions and livelihood, much depends upon oaths; for if not upon the jurors, yet the witnesses in any case of evidence, be it for matter of title, or matter of fact ... if they be caused to swear against their consciences, and that tye be taken away whereby they stand obliged before God and men to give right to the truth, no man is sure of any thing that he enjoys, nor can expect to get any thing that is unjustly detained and withheld from him in the proceedings of any court whatsoever.[83]

In the judgement of Hale CJ, Christianity was 'parcel of the laws of England', and to say that religion was a cheat was to dissolve all those obligations whereby civil societies were preserved.[84] Lord Raymond CJ believed that 'whatever strikes at the very root of Christianity, tends manifestly to the dissolution of the civil government'.[85]

During the eighteenth century, Christian political thought had concentrated less on the social function of religion and more on themes made significant by the Revolution Settlement of 1688–9, such as the origin of political authority and obligation, the importance of representation and consent, and the nature of political, civil, and religious rights. But this emphasis was changed as a result of the fears for political stability aroused at the end of the century by events in France. These encouraged a reversion to the old theme of the social function of religion in preserving order. So, for example, on the eve of the French Revolution, Bishop Tomline argued that civil government in general was ordained by God, and that a man sinned who, by word or action, weakened the particular form duly established and justly administered in his community.

It is allowed even by atheists, that society derives the greatest advantages from the influence of religion ... And of all religions the Christian is

---

[82] Richard Hooker, *Of the Laws of Ecclesiastical Polity*, bk V [2], Everyman's Library edn (London, 1907), vol. II, p.19.

[83] *Cobbett's Complete Collection of State Trials and Proceedings for High Treason and other Crimes and Misdemeanours from the Earliest Period to the Present Time* (London, 1809), ed. T. B. Howell, vol. III, pp. 789–90.

[84] *Taylor's Case* (1676) 1 Vent 293.   [85] *R* v. *Woolston* (1729) Fitzg 64.

indisputably the best adapted to restrain the turbulent passions, and control the unruly appetites, of mankind. Duty to God, and just submission to our earthly Governors, are in their own nature, and by the doctrines and tenor of the Gospel, as closely joined together, that they cannot, without the utmost violence and most heinous guilt, be put asunder.[86]

A theory developed that the revolution in France was the result of a conspiracy between freethinkers and others to destroy religion and government. This theory and the war with France, bringing invasion scares and food crises, ensured that the social function of religion remained uppermost in the years after 1789. This situation was unchanged during the first three decades of the nineteenth century because of general poverty and unrest. Vivid examples of the function of Christianity as a stabilising force can be found in the writings of Hannah More. For example, in her *Christian Morals*, first published in 1812, she emphasised that it was

no less our interest, than our duty, to keep the mind in an habitual posture of submission ... If the barbarian ambassador came expressly to the Romans to negotiate from his country for permission to be their servants, declaring, that a voluntary submission, even to a foreign power, was preferable to a wild and disorderly freedom, well may the Christian triumph in the peace and security to be attained by a complete subjugation to Him who is emphatically called *the God of order*. [Original emphasis.]

More regretted the decline in the practice of family prayers, remarking that this institution could be a bond of political, as well as moral, union. It was the only occasion on which rich and poor

[86] George Pretyman, afterwards Tomline, *A Sermon Preached before the Lords Spiritual and Temporal in the Abbey Church of Westminster, on Friday, January 30, 1789* (London, 1789), p. 16. Cf. Lord Chedworth's charge to the Grand Jury in 1793: 'A very little Attention will enable any one to see that it is manifestly the Intention of the Supreme Ruler of the Universe that there should be Inequality in this World, the Comforts of which are not distributed according to Merit; if they were, this World would not be what it is evidently intended for, a State of Probation and Trial. This unequal Distribution of Things affords the strongest Argument of which Natural Religion is in Possession for a future State, to which we must look for the Rectification of these Irregularities. ... The Extinction of Religion, considered merely in a temporal View, would be a most deplorable Calamity. As little Religion as there seems to be in the World, it has nevertheless a very great Influence in promoting the general Tranquility, and restraining Men from the Commission of Crimes' (Georges Lamoine, ed., *Charges to the Grand Jury 1689–1803*, Camden Fourth Series (London, 1992), vol. XXXXIII, pp. 489–90).

in a household met together and, '[i]n acknowledging their
common dependence on their common Master, this equality of
half an hour would be likely to promote subordination through
the rest of the day'. The interests of the superiors would be
promoted by periodically reminding dependants of the latter's
duty to God, which necessarily involved every human obligation.[87]

Fear of revolution remained a factor in political and religious
thought until after the collapse of the Chartist movement in 1848.
For example, in 1844, the Bishop of Ripon said of a Chartist
demonstration that it was mainly prompted not 'by the urgency of
temporal want', but by 'principles of discontent and insubordina-
tion', which had been 'too readily imbibed by hearts undisciplined
by religious restraints'. By contrast, 'it was equally evident that
just in proportion as the sound doctrine and discipline of the
Church was inculcated did respect for the law and a patient and
exemplary submission to privations generally prevail'.[88]

The French Revolution had produced among the propertied
classes in England a continuing fear of mob violence. Sir Samuel
Romilly observed the result:

If any person be desirous of having an adequate idea of the mischievous
effects which have been produced in this country by the French Revolution and all its attendant horrors, he should attempt some reforms on
humane and liberal principles. He will then find not only what a stupid
spirit of conservation, but what a savage spirit, it has infused into the
minds of his countrymen.[89]

Although this attitude did not prevail in extreme form for much
more than a decade after 1815, instability continued for different
reasons.

The fall of Charles X of France in 1830 caused considerable

---

[87] Hannah More, *Christian Morals* (1812), in *The Works of Hannah More*
(London, 1853), vol. IX, pp. 55, 87–8. See, generally, Hole, *Pulpits, Politics and
Public Order*, to which I am indebted for a number of references on this topic.
Best LCJ believed that 'the hopes and terrors of religion may and ought to be
employed to produce order and good conduct in life, as well as consolation in
death'. His order of priorities is revealing (*The Substance of a Charge ... by the
Lord Chief Justice Best*, p. 31).
[88] Charles Thomas Longley, *A Charge Addressed to the Clergy of Ripon at the
Triennial Visitation in September 1844* (1844), p. 9.
[89] Quoted in Walter Bagehot, *Biographical Studies*, ed. R. H. Hutton, new edn
(London, 1907), pp. 315–16. Bagehot gives no reference, and I have been unable
to trace his source.

excitement in England, and brought about a revival of interest in parliamentary reform. During autumn 1830 troubles broke out in the agricultural districts of southern England, and many towns in the north were disturbed by strikes. In January 1831, a writer in the *Quarterly Review* thought that the 'appellations of Whig and Tory' should be dropped; the struggle was no longer 'between two political parties for the ministry, but between the mob and the government, between the conservative and subversive principles, between anarchy and order'.[90] In the debate on the first reform bill, Macaulay appealed to the Commons to '[s]ave the multitude, endangered by their own ungovernable passions'. He thought the danger terrible, and the time short.[91] When the Lords rejected the bill in October 1831, riots broke out in Derby and Nottingham, and there were lesser disturbances in Leicester, Tiverton, Yeovil, Blandford, Sherborne, Exeter, and Worcester. The greatest disorder broke out in Bristol almost three weeks after the rejection of the bill. A mob sacked the Bristol Mansion House, broke into prisons, and burned a number of buildings, including the bishop's palace. Troops had to be used to restore order.[92] Despite the eventual passing of the Reform Act in 1832, social stability remained elusive. By 1838, ideas of violent revolution were gaining ground in the Chartist movement, and the threat to stability from this source was a cause of anxiety to the government and propertied classes for the next ten years.[93]

Behind the unrest during these decades was a pattern of economic crises, which peaked in 1837 and 1842, leading contemporary observers to deplore a divided society, where a cash nexus had taken the place of older patterns of social relationships. 'Distress after 1815 had quickened the pace of English politics; in the late 1830s and early 1840s it dominated the whole mood of the nation.'[94] The period 1843–50 was one of revival, despite a further financial crisis in 1847. The middle of the 1840s saw an economic boom, based largely on the rapid expansion of railways. This

[90] *Quarterly Review* 44 (1831), 315.
[91] *Parl. Deb.*, 3rd series, ii, 1204–5 (2 March 1831).
[92] John Stevenson, *Popular Disturbances in England 1700–1870* (London, 1979), pp. 220–1.
[93] Sir Llewellyn Woodward, *The Age of Reform 1815–1870*, 2nd edn (Oxford, 1962), pp. 19–20, 77–83, 137–45.
[94] Briggs, *Age of Improvement*, pp. 294–7, 404–5.

expansion stimulated demand for the products of other industries such as coal, iron and engineering; it also permitted the cheaper movement of goods, and so widened local markets.[95] A sense of greater tranquillity emerged between 1848 and 1851. *The Times*, for example, commenting on the size of the crowds at the Great Exhibition, observed that only a few years before such numbers would have been regarded as most dangerous to the safety of the state, yet there had been no disorder and very little crime.[96] Mill's comment in the 1850s on the need for religion[97] shows that the new prosperity and stability were greeted with caution. But by the 1840s, even some Christians had criticised the use of their religion as a social cement. Charles Kingsley complained that it reduced the Bible to a 'mere special constable's hand-book, an opium dose for keeping beasts of burden patient while they were being over-loaded'.[98] In the event, the need for the restraining influence of religion diminished, for in almost every respect the 1860s 'seemed either to confirm assumptions of prosperity based on the boom of the fifties or to promise expectations of increased prosperity for the future'.[99]

Parliamentary debates on the proposed reforms showed an over-whelming concern on both sides for the stability and security of society. This concern was at the root of the arguments of those supporting reform, who maintained that the community would benefit from having more evidence available and that the exclusion of evidence weakened the efficiency of the law.

There are many examples of arguments based on the benefit to the community that would result from making testimony more freely available. In a Commons debate in 1839, Daniel O'Connell, member for Dublin, recalled a case in which he had been counsel

---

[95] Ibid., pp. 296–8; P. S. Atiyah, *The Rise and Fall of Freedom of Contract* (Oxford, 1979), pp. 225, 227.
[96] *The Times*, 13 October 1851; reproduced in C. R. Fay, *Palace of Industry, 1851: A Study of the Great Exhibition and its Fruits* (Cambridge, 1951), p. 131.
[97] See n. 79.
[98] Parson Lot, 'Letters to the Chartists, No. II', in *Politics for the People* (London, 1848), pp. 58–9.
[99] Richard Shannon, *The Crisis of Imperialism 1865–1915*, Paladin edn (London, 1976), p. 29. But popular disturbances continued on some issues. There were anti-Catholic and anti-Irish disturbances, disturbances at election times, and during labour disputes, and as part of political demonstrations in London, especially in connection with the passing of the second Reform Bill in 1867 (Stevenson, *Popular Disturbances*, pp. 275–6).

for a man accused of 'a horrible crime imputed to him by a female'. Only the evidence of a Quaker who had been prepared to violate his conscience had enabled the accused to establish an alibi and secure an acquittal.[100] In 1840, Henry Warburton, member for Bridport, said in a Commons debate that in ninety-nine cases out of a hundred, the testimony in question was for the benefit of other parties; the House was not legislating for individuals but for the public generally.[101]

In 1842, Lord Denman, moving the second reading of his bill, stated that his grievance was 'the exclusion of Truth – an inevitable consequence of the rejection of such witnesses as are convinced that they are forbidden by the word of God to take an oath'. He then pointed to the consequences of excluding evidence: the most just of debts might be lost to a creditor, property might be unjustly taken away and, above all, crime was encouraged because criminals escaped justice – and this at a time when crime was increasing.[102] In a letter written to Denman on the subject of the bill, Sidney Smith commented:

Your great difficulty is akin to that of proving that two and two are equivalent to four. All that the Legislature ought to enquire is, *whether this scruple has now become so common as to cause the frequent interruption of justice.* This admitted, the remedy ought to follow as a matter of course. We are to get the best evidence for discovering truth – not the best we can imagine, but the best we can procure – and if you can't get oaths you must put up with affirmations as far better than no evidence at all; but one is ashamed to descant on such obvious truths.[103]

In the debate in May 1854 on the bill that in due course became the Common Law Procedure Act, Lord Cranworth, the Lord Chancellor, said that to ask why persons were to be relieved from the obligation of taking oaths was to put the question upon a most absurd foundation. The person to be considered was the party who required the testimony of the witness. It was entirely unimportant to the witness whether their testimony was received or not; but it was a serious misfortune to a tradesman suing a debtor if the only person who could prove the debt was a very honest person, who neither was nor had been a Quaker, a Moravian, or a

---

[100] *Parl. Deb.*, 3rd series, xlv, 826–7 (22 February 1839).
[101] *Parl. Deb.*, 3rd series, lv, 877 (22 July 1840).
[102] *Parl. Deb.*, 3rd series, lxiv, 617–27 (27 June 1842).
[103] Quoted in Arnould, *Lord Denman*, vol. II, p. 137. (My emphasis.)

Separatist, who might be a member of the Church of England, a Baptist, or connected with some other persuasion, but who entertained conscientious scruples against taking an oath, and whose evidence, therefore, could not be received. Ought the plaintiff to be punished because a court of law refused to take the witness's evidence, except on oath?[104]

In these and similar arguments there appears one major concern: the security of property. This was threatened by a law that enabled just debts to be avoided or property wrongly taken away, and which assisted criminals to avoid conviction. It is therefore not surprising to find this concern reflected in the debates. As opportunities for trade increased from the middle of the 1840s onwards, so did opportunities to default on debts, and those engaged in commerce can have had little patience with laws that deprived them of the means to establish their just claims. At the same time, published statistics appeared to show an ever-increasing rise in crime. This has been noted earlier in the century, but concern is particularly evident in the 1840s and 1850s, possibly because, as a result of the railway boom during the 1840s and the more general expansion of the 1850s, greater prosperity had increased the number of potential victims.[105]

Other arguments were directed towards establishing that security would not be diminished by the absence of an oath. For example, in a Commons debate in 1839 Dr Lushington expressed the belief that the mainstay with respect to the lower class of witnesses was not so much the oath that they took as the fear of the consequences if they were proved guilty of perjury.[106] A further

---

[104] *Parl. Deb.*, 3rd series, cxxxiii, 797 (23 May 1854). See also the speech of Lord Campbell, who thought that to commit a man for refusing to take the oath was cruel not only towards the witness, but also towards the parties who were deprived of his testimony. The argument was not a new one. See, e.g., a speech of Lord Ashburton in 1838: *Parl. Deb.*, 3rd series, xliv, 315–17 (19 July). Similar arguments were adopted after 1854 in support of an extension of the right to affirm to those without religious beliefs. See, e.g., the speeches of Sir John Trelawny and Lewis Dillwyn in 1861: *Parl. Deb.*, 3rd series, clxi, 1936–40 (13 March 1861); clxiii, 953–73 (12 June 1861). See also the speeches of George Denman and Sir Robert Collier AG in 1869: *Parl. Deb.*, 3rd series, cxcv, 1798–1814 (28 April 1869).

[105] Martin J. Wiener, *Reconstructing the Criminal: Culture, Law, and Policy in England, 1830–1914* (Cambridge, 1990), pp. 14–16.

[106] *Parl. Deb.*, 3rd series, xlv, 833 (22 February 1839). Stephen Lushington DCL was member for Tower Hamlets Borough. He had been a practitioner in civil law, and in the year of this debate he was appointed a judge of the High Court

argument was that the existing law did little to support credibility. Thus Sir John Trelawny argued that if an honest unbeliever stated that he was such, he was credible, but the law disbelieved him. Yet if another unbeliever said that he was a Christian, he told a lie, but his evidence was received.[107]

Opponents of reform laid equal emphasis on the stability and security of society. Of the arguments marshalled against proposals in the period before 1854, the ones most frequently used were that an extension of the right to affirm would weaken the weight of evidence, and that society would also be weakened. Thus Henry Goulburn, member for Cambridge University, argued in 1839 that an unwilling witness would be able to reduce the weight of their testimony by electing to affirm instead of taking the oath. The witness might thereby seriously affect the rights, character, and property of individuals.[108] In the same debate, Sir Robert Peel's speech showed a fear that the value of evidence would be reduced, and the administration of justice impeded, if the bill were to be passed.[109]

Similar fears were expressed by Brougham in 1849. Contrary to the views expressed in 1828, he argued, when opposing a bill to extend the right to affirm, that affirmations did not encourage truth to the same extent as oaths.[110] Brougham said that he had had experience of persons who would tell an untruth without a scruple but who would refuse to swear to it. He had seen a man staggered when it had been put to him, after some careless assertion: 'Upon your oath will you say so – upon your oath?' In the case of those allowed to affirm, however, such a form of examination was never used. 'Upon your affirmation will you say

---

of Admiralty. As was then permitted, he remained in Parliament after submitting himself for re-election. See, generally, S. M. Waddams, *Law, Politics and the Church of England: the Career of Stephen Lushington 1782–1873* (Cambridge, 1992).

[107] *Parl. Deb.*, 3rd series, clxi, 697 (21 February 1861). See also Lewis Dillwyn, *Parl. Deb.*, 3rd series, clxiii, 953–5 (12 June 1861), and George Denman, *Parl. Deb.*, 3rd series, cxcv, 1798 (28 April 1869).

[108] *Parl. Deb.*, 3rd series, xlv, 817–19 (22 February 1839).

[109] Ibid. 834–7.

[110] *Parl. Deb.*, 3rd series, cvi, 720–2 (22 June 1849). Cf. Brougham, *Speech on the Present State of the Law*, p. 41. But Brougham may have been engaged only in tactics. At the time he was conducting a campaign that he had begun in 1845 to make the parties to civil actions competent witnesses; he may have wanted to do nothing to alienate conservative opinion more than necessary. See ch. 4.

so?' did not have the same effect, and was never used in pressing a witness. Admittedly, Quakers, Moravians, and Separatists had already been exempted. But, Brougham said, there was a great difference between a man who merely declined to take an oath and a man who was bound to declare as well that he belonged to one of these sects. The bill tended to take away one at least of their securities against false testimony.

Brougham also argued that to extend the power of affirmation would involve the evasion of all law. If a lawgiver were to listen to all the objections of private individuals, however respected they might be, there would be no end to the evasion of law. Another man would say that it was against his conscience to pay his debts, because by doing so he would rob his children, who must then either starve or go to a workhouse. Another would refuse to give evidence at all, either on oath or affirmation, because it would injure his neighbour, whom he was commanded to love.

This part of Brougham's argument reflected the fears of the staunchest opponents of a general right to affirm: that it would, in some way, lead to the weakening of society. For example, Lord Ashburton, arguing in 1838 against a bill proposed by Lord Denman, said that the lives and property of the people would be less secure under 'so loose a mode of admitting evidence'.[111] In a debate in the Commons, Sir Robert Inglis, member for Oxford University, thought that, if a bill granting a general right to affirm were to be passed, within a year there would be an attempt to get rid of oaths altogether. No civilised society, he declared, had ever been kept together without these solemn appeals to God; in fact, belief in God had in some less civilised countries been kept alive by them.[112] There may have been many Members of Parliament who believed, as did Lord Abinger, that oaths were in all countries part of the system for administering justice, or who feared, like the Bishop of London, that a general extension of the right to affirm would lead to the abolition of oaths in courts of justice, and so to the removal of a natural security against misdecision and injustice.[113]

---

[111] *Parl. Deb.*, 3rd series, xliv, 315–19 (19 July 1838).
[112] *Parl. Deb.*, 3rd series, xlv, 824–5 (22 February 1839). See also his speech in 1840: *Parl. Deb.*, 3rd series, lv, 873–4 (22 July).
[113] *Parl. Deb.*, 3rd series, lxiv, 627–8, 630–1 (27 June 1842). Lord Abinger was wrong. In a few legal systems there has been either a weak oath tradition or

In 1854, Lord St Leonards defended the existing law, which favoured Quakers, Moravians, and Separatists on the basis that their testimony was more likely to be truthful because members of those sects had at least some ties with the community. There was security, he argued, in that 'the witness allowed to affirm was a man who, in the face of the world, and to the particular knowledge of everybody around him, had joined a particular sect, and they knew that he was influenced, or affected to be influenced, by religious motives in objecting to an oath'. But the bill then under consideration would enable any person, upon their own mere unsupported assertion that they had a religious scruple, to avoid taking an oath.[114]

When the wider question of extending the right to affirm to atheists was being debated, similar considerations were taken into account. Opponents of reform argued that the absence of the oath would allow unacceptably weak evidence to affect the outcome of the case, or, worse still, that the removal of oaths would loosen the bonds of society. In 1842, for example, *The Times* realised that the limited reforms proposed by Lord Denman might be the beginning of a process that would end with the extension of competency to atheists. A leading article on 15 June presented a careful argument confined to the effect that such a change would have on the weight to be given to testimony.

The writer began by acknowledging that 'we are far from wishing to exclude from our court the evidence of Jew, Mahometan, or Hindoo'. What should be excluded was the least credible evidence. The atheist stood on quite a different footing from those of non-Christian faiths, and 'we cordially assent to the caution which refuses any judicial weight to his statement'. An oath was plainly necessary to ensure that the mass of professing Christians gave evidence that was true, 'a fact which is not less true because it is humiliating'. How could it be safe to remove that sanction in

none at all. The oath never became the focal point of Russian procedure in the way that it did in Germanic procedure. In several Swiss cantons the oath had disappeared by the eighteenth century. The Chinese never had an oath tradition. It has been suggested that the last example can be attributed to the influence of Confucian teachings, the basic tenets of which were that mankind is by nature good, and that government by the influence of ethical standards is preferable to government by law (Helen Silving, 'The Oath: I', *Yale Law Journal* 68 (1959), 1329, 1375–81).

[114] *Parl. Deb.*, 3rd series, cxxxiii, 1151 (30 May 1854).

the case of others who had torn themselves free from the authority of those motives that sway the mass of men to follow truth and honesty?

They are incapable of fulfilling those conditions which the law exacts as a security for truth; and they proclaim themselves uninfluenced by those great motives, the admission of which, almost alone, makes other men credible. We have not the same reasons for trusting even to their word which we have in the case of other men, and they are incapacitated from giving us any more powerful voucher. Call it weakness, ignorance, super-stition – call it what names you will – it is absolutely certain that the mass of men, even of notorious liars, if you choose to take such, do shrink from perjury, and that, not from a fear of fine or imprisonment, but from a consciousness, more or less distinctly brought out, that they are invoking ONE who knows all truth and falsehood, and who will reward and punish even the fantastic resources by which bad and uneducated men strain to elude the obligation of an oath – their kissing of thumbs – their taking the Testament in the wrong hand – their evasions and equivocations still show, wretched and senseless as they are, a sense of the supernatural power which they are provoking – an awe of that which they so miserably understand – a basis of fear, if not of goodness, on which society draws much, and might draw more, protection against falsehood.

Arguments on these lines were being used in Parliament twenty years later. Thus, in 1861, the Solicitor General, in opposing a bill introduced by Sir John Trelawny, said that the interests of society required that persons without religious conscience and belief should not be accepted as witnesses in courts of justice.[115] In the same debate Sir William Heathcote, member for Oxford University, allowed that many would give their evidence as truly unsworn as sworn. But equally, he said, it was true that the administration of an oath made most people more careful and accurate in their statements than without it. There were also many who believed that their obligation to tell the truth depended solely on the complete and formal administration of the oath. He observed that as recently as 1858 an Act had been passed to enable the House of Commons to swear witnesses before committees, it having been felt that committees of the Lords secured more accuracy from their witnesses because they were always sworn.[116]

One of the most vigorous exponents of the 'bonds of society' argument was Lord Robert Montagu. In the 1861 debate he drew

---

[115] *Parl. Deb.*, 3rd series, clxiii, 972–3 (12 June 1861).
[116] Ibid., 967–8.

a picture of atheists as persons who had deliberately rejected Christianity. For him, such people had been presented with a choice that could equally well have been exercised in favour of religion. There is even a suggestion that atheists were insincere in their disavowal of religious belief. Trelawny, referring to the fact that non-believers in India were allowed to affirm, had argued that the right should be extended to English subjects.[117] Montagu replied:

There, no doubt, the Natives were permitted to affirm instead of being sworn; but the affirmation of a black man was taken at what it was worth, and would not be weighed against a white man's oath ... It was one thing to allow these persons, who clung most tenaciously to the scraps and shreds of belief handed down to them by their forefathers, to make affirmations in courts of justice, and quite another to allow those persons who had been taught the Christian religion and knew all its doctrines, and had learnt from childhood about God, but who had deliberately discarded and rejected them and professed to disbelieve in God to do the same.

For Montagu, the religious sanction was fundamental to the worth of any testimony because religion was fundamental to morality:

What is honour? What is honesty without belief in God? I challenge any honourable Member to define these terms. He cannot do so without assuming the presence of a God who orders all the events and arranges all the details in the world. Honour and honesty, apart from religion, were nothing but pride and self-interest.

Amongst other things, religion was a social cement without which society would fall apart. 'A consistent Atheist must be a bad citizen and capable of every Machiavellian scheme and false-hood.'[118]

John Walter, owner of *The Times* and member for Berks County, supported Montagu's arguments for the most part, but had a different opinion of atheists. In Walter's view they were mad rather than bad. How, he asked, could a man believe in the distinction between right and wrong if he did not believe in the moral government of the world? He objected to the bill because it would destroy the principle of conduct, which was the main distinction between man and the beasts. It might be a hard case not to receive the evidence of an atheist, but the same hardship

[117] Trelawny observed that by 6 & 7 Vict c 22 'barbarians and uncivilized people', destitute of the knowledge of God and of any religious belief, were allowed to make affirmations in lieu of oaths.
[118] *Parl. Deb.*, 3rd series, clxiii, 957–9 (12 June 1861).

would occur in the case of a lunatic. In Walter's opinion, they ought to treat the wretched persons whose minds were so constituted that they were unable to see what everyone else saw, and to believe in the existence of an Almighty Power, as not in their right minds.[119]

Such views took a long time to die out completely. For example, three years after the law had been changed in 1869, John Pitt Taylor commented:

The policy of thus relaxing in favour of Atheists one of the fundamental safeguards of truth, and of encouraging the public avowal, if not the collusive assumption, of infidelity and irreligion, may admit of a serious doubt; and the more so, as the cases, in which any inconvenience could arise from the old law, are unquestionably of very rare occurrence.[120]

But, by the 1860s, such views had become a rarity. In a debate on Sir John Trelawny's bill in 1863, Sir Francis Goldsmid QC, member for Reading Borough, showed how far religious scepticism and social stability had developed. He argued that, although those who were strongly attached to revealed religion might rationally maintain that, had there been no revelation, the leading principles of morality would not have been as clearly recognised as they were, those principles had come so completely to form part of public opinion that they were admitted by all, whether believing or not in the source from which they might originally have proceeded. In the same debate William Coningham, member for Brighton Borough, said that he for one did not regard speculative or abstract religious opinions as the true measure of a man's veracity – though it might be of his intelligence. What was required was that a man should be restrained by moral convictions, which appeared to Coningham to be altogether independent of speculative ideas on sacred matters.[121]

J. F. Stephen, writing in the same year, saw the rule that rendered atheists incompetent to give evidence as the residue of an obsolete political theory.

The real reason why the rule is maintained is a vague impression that it is a legal protest against atheism, and sets a stigma on that way of thinking, and that its removal would indicate something like a relenting on the part of the nation at large towards atheists. This reason is perfectly intelligible,

---

[119] Ibid., 964–5.
[120] Taylor, *Treatise*, 6th edn (1872), vol. II, para. 1248.
[121] *Parl. Deb.*, 3rd series, clxix, 1297–8, 1301 (11 March 1863).

but hardly any one would explicitly avow it. It has passed into a common-place that it is no part of the duty of the state to stigmatize opinions, and that the principal effect of the attempt to do so is to prejudice generous minds in their favour.[122]

Throughout the period when the granting of a general right to affirm, either to a limited or to a full extent, was being debated, other subsidiary arguments did appear; but their proportion in relation to the major arguments based on stability and security was small. Some of these subsidiary arguments remind the reader of parts of Bentham's critique. For example, it was quite often argued that the existing law gave rise to contradictions, absurd-ities, or embarrassments. As early as 1838, the Attorney General, Sir John Campbell, had acknowledged that a general measure to allow affirmation on religious grounds must come soon, and that in many cases justice had been defeated as a result of the existing law.[123] Lord Denman referred in 1842 to the invidious position of the judge when an oath was refused, adding that the exceptions for Quakers and Separatists highlighted the injustice done in other cases.[124] In the debate on Sir John Trelawny's bill in 1861, Lewis Dillwyn, member for Swansea Borough, pointed out that if a man was willing, from his regard for truth, to submit to the obloquy of avoiding his doubts and being rejected as a witness, he was likely to be a person who would give truthful evidence.[125]

Another criticism was that the use of oaths established a double standard of veracity. It recognised a principle that it was possible by some human contrivance to increase the obligation to tell the truth. The natural consequence of this was to discredit the simple assertion of an individual, and to encourage the notion that what a person said was immaterial so long as they were not put on their

---

[122] James Fitzjames Stephen, *A General View of the Criminal Law of England* (London, 1863), pp. 293, 289–90.

[123] *Parl. Deb.*, 3rd series, xliv, 999 (3 August 1838). His opinion was echoed in the *Law Magazine*, where a commentator thought that objectors who relied on the superior sanctity of an oath mistook 'the nature of the check by which offenders against public justice are restrained ... Perjury will be as much restrained by any species of solemn affirmation as by an oath, so long as the same punishment is denounced against false testimony' (*Law Magazine* 20 (1838), 233–4).

[124] *Parl. Deb.*, 3rd series, lxiv, 617 (27 June 1842); Arnould, *Lord Denman*, vol. II, p. 420.

[125] *Parl. Deb.*, 3rd series, clxiii, 955 (12 June 1861). Cf. the speech of George Denman in 1869: cxcv 1803, 28 April.

oath.[126] On this basis Philip Harwood, writing in the *Westminster Review* in 1843, criticised Denman's proposals for reform, because they would have allowed sworn and unsworn testimony to exist side by side. If the law once allowed that a solemn affirmation was trustworthy, why complicate the matter 'by showing this morbid anxiety to get, if possible, something more and better'?[127]

An argument used mainly by writers was that false testimony could perfectly well be punished even in the absence of an oath. For example, the writer of an article in the *Law Magazine* in 1834 thought it probably right that in the large majority of cases the fear of being punished by a criminal court for perjury was the only operative sanction. Because the existing law of perjury could be adapted to cover those who wilfully gave false evidence, the oath was superfluous.[128] Best observed in his *Treatise* that there were four sanctions of truth; atheism merely meant that one of these, the religious sanction, did not operate on the mind of the witness, while the other three remained. These latter sanctions were the natural sanction, which resulted from the fact that it was easier to tell the truth; the moral sanction, by which infamy was attached to liars by public opinion; and the political or legal sanction, by which the state punished false testimony.[129] The same point was made by a speaker at the congress of the Social Science Association in 1868.[130]

The argument that an oath was not a necessary prerequisite for the punishment of false testimony seems to have played no part in the parliamentary debates, perhaps because it could have been used to support the total abolition of oaths in legal proceedings. This, for example, had been the argument of the writer in the *Law Magazine* in 1838.[131] Ironically, the force of such contentions was acknowledged by the Lord Chancellor, Lord Hatherley, in the final stages of the 1869 legislation, when he declared that he had long been of the opinion that it was undesirable to draw a

[126] *Law Magazine* 12 (1834), 269–87.
[127] *Westminster Review* 39 (1843), 80–104. Cf. the speech of the Earl of Wicklow: *Parl. Deb.*, 3rd series, lxiv, 627 (27 June 1842).
[128] *Law Magazine* 12 (1834), 279–81, 283. See also *Law Magazine* 20 (1838), 233–4 and *Westminster Review* 39 (1843), 80–104.
[129] Best, *Treatise*, 4th edn (London, 1866), pp. 15–16, 62, 231–3. This was a point made by Bentham: see n. 16 and text.
[130] *Law Magazine and Law Review* 24 (1868), 157–8, 265–78.
[131] See n. 128.

distinction between the duty of telling the truth at all times and the duty of telling it in a court of law. All that was necessary in giving evidence was that, instead of taking an oath, a witness should know that they had a solemn duty to perform, for any breach of which they would be liable to a legal penalty.[132]

It is likely that a belief in the efficacy of prosecutions for perjury was not confined to writers of critical jurisprudence. In an article published in the *Jurist* in 1827, a year after the incident involving Joseph Hume and six years before the trial of Berthold,[133] the writer described an apparently recent case in which a Mr Taylor had appeared before the Lord Mayor to answer a charge brought against him by a Mr Collins. Collins was sworn, whereupon Taylor asked him if he believed the book on which he was sworn. The witness said that he did, but the Lord Mayor interjected, saying that he did not know what this had to do with the question. Taylor said that he wished to know what security he had that the witness would speak the truth. The Lord Mayor replied that the law attached penalties to those who were guilty of perjury, and that these penalties were the security that the prisoner had on the one hand, and the public justice on the other, that nothing but the truth would be spoken. The writer in the *Jurist* thought that this was 'the language of common sense', but noted that common sense and the law were 'not unfrequently at variance'.[134]

As well as the arguments that Bentham had used, there can be found arguments that suggest a different critique based on individual rights. For example, Joseph Hume referred to the rights of a British subject and the cause of civil and religious liberty when he attempted to present a petition in 1826.[135] In 1839, Benjamin Hawes reminded the House of Commons that the effect of the existing law was to exclude 'from civil rights', including the right to membership of a profession, all those who had conscientious objections but were not covered by existing legislation in favour of members of particular sects.[136] In 1849, in support of a bill to

---

[132] *Parl. Deb.*, 3rd series, cxcviii, 678 (26 July 1869). Cf. the comment in the *Law Times* after the Act was passed: 'The value of an oath is very questionable. The only punishment a false witness fears is prosecution for perjury.' (*Law Times* 46 (1868–69), 422.)

[133] See nn. 54 and 55 and text.

[134] 'Law of Evidence', *Jurist, or Quarterly Journal of Jurisprudence and Legislation* 1 (1827), 91, 93–4.

[135] See n. 55 and text.   [136] *Parl. Deb.*, 3rd series, xlv, 823 (22 February 1839).

relieve individuals who had a religious objection to taking an oath, Lord Denman argued that such a bill was the necessary result of accepting the principle of religious toleration. In the same debate, the Duke of Argyll declared that in supporting the measure he would take 'the highest and broadest and firmest ground at once'. The bill should be passed, because 'it was needed to give effect to the rights of individual conscience; for until that great principle was conceded to the greatest possible extent, he held that the Government could not be said to have paid due respect to the rights of the individuals over whom it ruled'.[137]

It has already been seen that the 1828 legislation can be explained without reference to Bentham. However, it remains to be considered whether his thinking had any influence on the extension of a general right to affirm. Bentham undoubtedly had a place in the intellectual background to the reforms. But such a position can be occupied without an inevitable influence on later developments, and it is improbable that there was any Benthamite influence on these particular reforms.

Bentham's opinions received their most extensive publicity in the 1820s, which decade saw the publication of *Traité des preuves judiciaires*, in 1823, followed by an English translation in serial form in 1824 and as a complete work in 1825. The *Rationale of Judicial Evidence* followed in 1827.[138] It was also a period when several articles were published that set out his ideas in more accessible form. For example, in March 1824 Denman reviewed Dumont's *Traité* in an article that drew attention to defects in the law of evidence, while showing that Denman was not an uncritical supporter of Bentham's ideas.[139] In 1826, Bentham's arguments in *Swear Not At All* (1813) were set before a wider audience in an article, probably by Peregrine Bingham, in the *Westminster Review*.[140] In 1828, an article by J. A. Roebuck in the *Westminster Review* summarised a number of the arguments contained in the *Rationale of Judicial Evidence*.[141] In the same year, William

---

[137] *Parl. Deb.*, 3rd series, cvi, 717, 724 (22 June 1849).
[138] See the bibliography by C. W. Everett in Halévy, *Growth of Philosophic Radicalism*; Lewis, 'Bentham's View of the Right to Silence', in *Current Legal Problems 1990*, pp. 138–9.
[139] *Edinburgh Review* 40 (1824), 169–207.
[140] *Westminster Review* 5 (1826), 23–58.
[141] *Westminster Review* 9 (1828), 198, 245.

Empson published a lengthy review of the *Rationale of Judicial Evidence* in the *Edinburgh Review*.[142]

Thus what was probably the most extensive publicity to be given to Bentham's writings on evidence appeared nearly two decades before the first stage of the extension of a general right to affirm in 1854, and over forty years before the right was finally granted to those without any religious belief. Had there existed the opportunities for irradiation, suscitation, and permeation that Finer saw at work in the administrative reforms of the nineteenth century,[143] these lapses of time might not have been significant. But the methods described by Finer of bringing influence to bear on administrative developments depended on the effective organisation of Bentham's followers. This could not be achieved in the field of legislation because of the numbers that had to be won over before a private bill could be successful. While a group of Benthamites might sway other members of an administrative committee, the House of Commons and House of Lords were too unwieldy for such attempts. There were also time constraints, which tended to block any reform lacking government support. If a measure did not succeed within a session it was therefore lost, and the whole process of getting up support had to start again.[144]

Despite the passing of time, Bentham's position as an advocate of evidence law reform was occasionally acknowledged, but not always with approval. For example, in 1861, a leading article in *The Times*, commenting on the decision in *Madan* v. *Catanach*,[145] observed that, so long as it was supported by public opinion, the effect of the oath was not to be measured by the faith or scepticism of the witness taking it:

He knows that, however he may pretend to laugh at it, the mass of spectators regard it with unaffected reverence, and that one perjury will sink him far deeper in the estimation of his neighbours than a lifetime of falsehood. These considerations must fairly be set off against those which might dispose us to accept BENTHAM'S guidance in this difficult question.[146]

---

[142] *Edinburgh Review* 48 (1828), 457–520. See Twining, *Theories of Evidence*, pp. 106–7.
[143] See n. 28 to ch. 1 and text.
[144] See, e.g., the bills introduced by Sir John Trelawny in 1861, 1862, and 1863: nn. 49 and 50 and text.
[145] See n. 72 and text.　　[146] *The Times*, 16 November 1861.

In 1863, Sir John Trelawny quoted from Bentham and Mill in a speech in support of his bill to extend the right to affirm to atheists.[147] A leading article in the *Solicitors' Journal and Reporter* noted Sir John's attempts, but expressed the opinion that, notwithstanding that his principle had been advocated by writers such as Bentham and W. M. Best, his attempts were likely to remain unsuccessful.[148]

A difficulty in detecting a specific Benthamite influence on the reform of the law requiring testimony to be on oath is that supporters of reform from time to time adopted arguments that Bentham had used, but could well have done so independently. For example, it has already been shown that at least one of Bentham's arguments against the use of oaths pre-dated him by over two hundred years.[149] A similar point was made by a contemporary critic, who remarked on Bentham's lack of originality when, in a review of the *Rationale of Judicial Evidence*, he complained of 'the parade with which there is so often trumpeted to the world the laying of an egg, whose chickens have long been selling in the public market'.[150]

The need for caution in detecting Benthamite influences is shown by an article on oaths published in 1834 in the *Law Magazine*.[151] Although the writer and Bentham shared some views on this subject, Bentham was mentioned only in connection with a criticism of his idea of the nature of an oath. This is unlikely to have been a mere diplomatic distancing from Bentham on the part of the writer; the tone of the *Law Magazine* at about this time does not seem to have been in favour of radical reform. A few years later, for example, the writer of an article referred to 'Mr Bentham and his disciples, who, by their utter ignorance of the

---

[147] *Parl. Deb.*, 3rd series, clxix, 1288–90 (11 March 1863).
[148] *Solicitors' Journal and Reporter* 7 (1862–3), 902–4.
[149] See n. 30 to ch. 1 and text.
[150] *Edinburgh Review* 48 (1828), 457, 461. In the *Rationale of Judicial Evidence* Bentham himself disclaimed originality for his views, but he did so on the assumption that to find models for his proposed improved system it was necessary only to look at systems that had been adopted locally in former times. 'By doing away the work of five or six hundred years, and throwing back the system of procedure, as to the most fundamental parts, into the state in which it was at the time of Edward I and much earlier, a mountain of abuse might be removed, and even a near approach to perfection made' (*Works*, vol. VII, p. 599).
[151] *Law Magazine* 12 (1834), 269–87.

real character of the evil, and the ludicrous extravagance of their amending schemes, have probably done more to retard the progress of rational measures than ever was or ever could be effected by Lord Eldon and the now rapidly decreasing supporters of his principles'.[152]

Because Parliament was almost exclusively the arena in which this reform was discussed and developed, one way of trying to resolve the question of Bentham's influence might be to construct a sort of intellectual family tree for those taking a leading part in the legislative process. In such a structure Lord Denman and his son George would have the closest connection to Bentham. Although Lord Denman was by no means an uncritical follower of Bentham, he pursued a limited reform of the law requiring testimony to be on oath, and his connections with Lansdowne and Brougham, as well as his interest in Dumont's work, suggest that he may have been influenced by Bentham's ideas. George Denman was influential in extending competency to those without religious beliefs, a reform of which Bentham would certainly have approved. Denman's speech in the Commons debate on 28 April 1869 referred to an argument in favour of this reform used by Mill.[153] It is likely that he came into contact with Bentham's ideas either through his father or through the writings of Mill, whose task it had been to edit the *Rationale of Judicial Evidence*.

Brougham, though closer to Bentham than either Lord Denman or his son, played little part in promoting this reform; in 1849, he actually opposed one of Denman's bills in the Lords.[154] Hawes, Trelawny, Dillwyn, and others who supported legislation in the Commons may have been influenced by Bentham's writings at either first or second hand.

The intellectual family tree is suggestive but little more. What cannot be ignored is the fact that the part of Bentham's critique that was typically Benthamite – its radical nature – hardly appeared at all. Very occasionally, a writer, though never a politician, can be found who seems to have taken up the full Benthamite critique. But the rarity with which this is encountered emphasises the lack of support given to Bentham's critique as a whole. One example is an article in the *Jurist* commenting on

[152] *Law Magazine* 23 (1840), 357.
[153] See n. 125.   [154] See n. 110 and text.

Brougham's law reform speech of 1828. The writer favoured competency not only for those then rendered incompetent because of interest, but also for those who were incompetent because of criminal conviction, or for failure to believe in God or a future state. All these matters, he insisted, affected weight only. This was a perception that lay at the root of Bentham's critique, but it was not often expressed by those who supported reform.[155]

A similarly radical critique was adopted in 1843 by Philip Harwood,[156] who argued in the *Westminster Review* that the proposed reforms of Denman and Hawes did not go far enough. Harwood's recommendation was that all oaths whatsoever should be forthwith abolished.

We object, first and chiefly, to the present law of oaths, that it contains provisions for excluding evidence from the ear of justice; giving, to the extent of such exclusion, impunity and inducement to wrong, and inflicting right with helplessness and impotence. We put this objection first, because it seems to us to stand first in importance; and also because, on looking through the debates on the subject during the last few years, we find it much less insisted on than it deserves.

He excepted Denman's speech from this criticism, but pointed out that the argument had previously been centred on the indulgence of individual consciences, which was not the point:

The point is the admission of truth into courts of justice. The relief really needed is not merely, nor chiefly, relief of a comparatively small number of estimable persons from legal obligations that offend their particular consciences, important and desirable as such relief always is. It is the relief of that very much larger class – potentially co-extensive with the whole community – of individuals who have suffered, or may suffer, or may know or fancy themselves liable to suffer, in property, person, reputation, or civil rights, in consequence of the legal silencing and suppression of facts.

The present state of the law tended 'to exclude evidence, to silence truth, to paralyse justice, and to license crime'. Yet if you dissociated the oath sanction from the other, natural, sanctions associated with telling the truth – such as self-respect, love of truth, and fear of prosecution for perjury – the power of the oath

---

[155] *Jurist* 2 (1828), 26–7.
[156] 1809–87. Harwood was a unitarian pastor who, at various stages of his life, also worked on a number of periodicals, including the *Examiner*, the *Spectator*, and the *Morning Chronicle*. From 1854, he worked on the *Saturday Review*, becoming its editor in 1868. See *Dictionary of National Biography*.

to ensure veracity was 'expressible only by *zero*'. He concluded
that on every ground, the universal abolition of oaths was greatly
preferable to a 'mere legalising ... of the nonjuring scruples of
individuals'.[157]

While it is likely that Bentham would have preferred to see the
oath ceremony abolished altogether,[158] that was never the aim of
the parliamentary reformers. Nor does one find in the parliamentary debates any echoes of Bentham's criticism of oaths as an
instrument of sinister interest. It has already been shown that
those who favoured and those who opposed reform were in the
main concerned to preserve the stability and security of society
and differed only in the way in which they thought this objective
should be achieved. Ultimately, Bentham's own position was
based on an acknowledgement that security was 'the principal
object of law *in general* and in every branch'.[159] But in his view
security required the destruction of Judge & Co and of their
sinister interest. This was the characteristically Benthamite critique; unsurprisingly, it found no reflection in the parliamentary
debates.

In those debates some speakers used less radical arguments that
Bentham had also used, such as arguments based on the contradictions and absurdities of the existing law, or the 'double
standard of veracity' argument. But it was not necessary to have
read Bentham, or a summary of Bentham, to use such arguments
and, in any case, these played a minor part in the debate by
comparison with arguments based on concern for the stability and
security of society. Change came about primarily because of a
perception that stability and security had sufficiently increased to
make it safe to allow public acknowledgement of increasing
religious scepticism. The probability is that Bentham played little
or no part in the story of the reforms considered in this chapter,
and that he was mistakenly thought to have done so because of his

---

[157] *Westminster Review* 39 (1843), 80, 89–90, 95–7, 98–104 (original emphasis).
[158] See n. 27 and text.
[159] *Constitutional Code* in *Works*, vol. IX, pp. 11–13; *Principles of the Civil Code* in
Works, Vol. I, p. 307, and generally pp. 322–6; *Pannomial Fragments* in *Works*,
vol. III, pp. 211–13; and *Leading Principles of a Constitutional Code for any
State*, in *Works*, vol. II, pp. 269–70. See also Ross Harrison, *Bentham*,
pp. 248–59; Gerald J. Postema, *Bentham and the Common Law Tradition*,
pp. 168–83.

strenuous opposition to the compulsory administration of oaths. Insufficient weight has been given to the fact that the law was changed in limited ways, and for reasons that had nothing to do with Bentham's radical critique.

4

INCOMPETENCY FROM INFAMY AND INTEREST

The nineteenth century also saw the removal of witness disqualifications based on criminal convictions and on interest in the outcome of proceedings. This took place in three stages. The first was reached in 1843; in that year Lord Denman's Act abolished the rule whereby persons convicted of certain criminal offences had, in principle, been disqualified from giving evidence. The Act also made a substantial inroad into the rule excluding witnesses with an interest in the outcome of the action in which they were called to testify. The second stage was reached in 1851, when the Evidence Amendment Act, also known as Lord Brougham's Act, made the parties to civil proceedings competent in most cases. The third stage was reached only in 1898, when the Criminal Evidence Act accepted as a general principle the competency of the accused in all criminal cases. The first two stages are dealt with in this chapter, and the third stage in chapter 5.

THE COMMON LAW

Incompetency from infamy

Persons who had been convicted of an 'infamous' crime and who had had judgment recorded against them were in principle disqualified from giving evidence because it was thought that no sufficient weight could attach to any testimony that they might give. Starkie explained the rule in this way:

Where a man is convicted of an offence which is inconsistent with the common principles of honesty and humanity, the law considers his oath to be of no weight, and excludes his testimony as of too doubtful and suspicious a nature to be admitted in a court of justice to affect the property or liberty of others.[1]

It was originally the infamy of the punishment, not the nature of the crime itself, that was the test of incompetency.[2] However, well before the beginning of the nineteenth century it came to be the crime that rendered the offender unworthy of belief.[3] The rule gave rise to many anomalies.

> Witnesses of the most infamous and depraved character, though not credible, may yet be competent; and it frequently happens that a witness is suffered to give evidence, because not absolutely disqualified by the rules of law, though at the same time he may be far lower in point of credit and real character, than another, who is at once excluded as incompetent.[4]

Probably because of this, the rule was restricted in a number of ways by both statute and common law, yet in many cases the restrictions served only to emphasise the anomalies.[5]

Incompetency from interest

The general rule was that all witnesses with an interest in the outcome of a cause were to be excluded from giving evidence in that cause. According to Phillipps, the ground of this exclusion was a presumed lack of integrity or impartiality rather than a desire to save the proposed witness from the temptation to commit perjury. Had the latter been the true principle, he argued, there would have been some inconsistency in excluding witnesses even if they had an interest that was minute, while admitting others who might be subject to the more powerful influence of relationship or friendship.[6] Starkie provided a similar justification but recognised the need to limit the operation of the rule for the sake of certainty in the law and to prevent an excessive exclusion of evidence.[7] Although Phillipps and Starkie may have accurately reflected the justification for the rule current at the time when they

---

[1] Starkie, *Treatise*, 2nd edn (1833), vol. I, p. 94.
[2] *R* v. *Crosby* (1694) 5 Mod 15, *per* Holt CJ.
[3] *Pendock* v. *Mackender* (1755) 2 Wils KB 18.
[4] Phillipps, *Treatise*, 7th edn (1829), vol. I, p. 27.
[5] A summary of the law can be found in Starkie, *Treatise*, 3rd edn (1842), vol. I, pp. 97–100.
[6] Phillipps, *Treatise*, 7th edn (1829), vol. I, p. 45.
[7] Starkie, *Treatise*, 3rd edn (1842), vol. I, p. 17.

were writing, it may be that the original purpose of the rule had been to save witnesses from perjury. Stephen Shapin has shown the importance of truthfulness as a characteristic of gentility in the seventeenth century;[8] it may be that the exclusion of interested witnesses in the superior courts of common law was not dictated by the need to protect the court from being misled, but by the need to protect members of the gentry from being put in a position where they might be found to be liars. Such a finding might have damaged not only the integrity of the witnesses, but the social class to which they belonged. It is true that this problem might have arisen where there was a suggestion that evidence was affected by friendship or kinship; but a general rule of exclusion on these grounds would have been unworkable. The question of kinship, in particular, could too readily have given rise to collateral issues, which would have been difficult or impossible to resolve.

Whatever the origin of the rule may have been, it is clear that a disqualifying interest had to be a present, certain, vested interest in the outcome of the suit and not one that was uncertain or contingent.[9] This could give rise to anomalies. For example, the heir apparent to an estate was competent to give evidence in support of the claim of his ancestor because he had as yet no vested interest. But a remainderman, who did have such an interest, was incompetent.[10] Brougham highlighted this inconsistency in a speech in 1828 on the state of the law:

If I have the most distant interest, even the interest of a shilling in reversion, on an estate of 50,000 *l.* a year, I am incompetent to give evidence on any point that affects that estate; but supposing that I have a father, ninety years of age, lunatic, bed-ridden, and quite incapable of doing any legal act for himself, and that he is in possession of an estate in fee simple, and not in fee tail, and that I expect to be his heir, and that nothing can prevent me from becoming so, I may be a witness on any point which affect his estate.[11]

As Brougham observed, the size of the interest was immaterial.[12] This was justified on the ground that a plain and simple rule was

---

[8] Steven Shapin, *A Social History of Truth: Civility and Science in Seventeenth-Century England* (Chicago, Ill., 1994), see especially pp. 3–125. Cf. Brougham on the connection between honour and high station: *Parl. Deb.*, 3rd series, cxvi, 20.

[9] *Goss* v. *Tracy* (1715), 1 P Wms 287.

[10] Starkie, *Treatise*, 3rd edn (1842), vol. I, p. 19.

[11] Brougham, *A Speech on the Present State of the Law*, pp. 39–40.

[12] *Burton* v. *Hinde* (1793) 5 TR 174.

absolutely necessary; if a small degree of interest did not disqualify a witness it would be impossible to draw a practicable line of distinction.[13]

A party on the record was not a competent witness, and neither was the husband or wife of a party.[14] It was held by Tindal CJ in *Worrall* v. *Jones* (1831)[15] that the basis for this exclusion was the interest that a party usually had in the outcome of the proceedings, rather than the mere fact of being a party. No other relation of the party was excluded. The reason for excluding the husband or wife of a party to an action from giving evidence either for or against that party was founded partly on their identity of interest, and partly on a principle of public policy, which deemed it 'necessary to guard the security and confidence of private life, even at the risk of an occasional failure of justice'.[16]

BENTHAM'S CRITIQUE

Bentham believed that justice had two ends. The first, to give effect to substantive law, was the special task of adjective law, of which the law of evidence was a part. The other was the reduction of injustice caused by concomitant vexation, expense, and delay. At times a utilitarian calculation would have to be made. If the price in vexation, expense, or delay of obtaining the benefit of the substantive law exceeded the value of that benefit, it ought not to be paid. 'Even evidence, even justice itself, like gold, may be bought too dear. It always is bought too dear, if bought at the expense of a preponderant injustice.' He was optimistic about the ease with which such a calculation could be made.

Here and there a case may present itself, in which it may be matter of doubt on which side the balance lies, but in general there will be no difficulty: all doubt will be removed by clear and indisputable principles.[17]

Other reasons justifying the exclusion of evidence were that it was irrelevant; that it was superfluous because there was enough evidence without it, either from a different source or of a better

---

[13]   Starkie, *Treatise*, 3rd edn (1842), vol. I, p. 117.
[14]   *Mant* v. *Mainwaring* (1818) 8 Taunt 139.   [15]   7 Bing 395.
[16]   Phillipps, *Treatise*, 7th edn (1829), vol. I, p. 77.
[17]   *Rationale of Judicial Evidence* in *Works*, vol. VII, pp. 335–6, 362–3.

kind from the same source; and that it was useless 'because sure to be refuted or outweighed by other evidence'.

Bentham emphasised that in every case where exclusion in accordance with his principles was being considered, the question to be decided was one of fact and not law. There was, therefore, no need to refer to any rules of law in the decision process and, in order to ensure that an unwanted body of judge-made law did not develop, Bentham recommended that a judge who decided for admission or exclusion in a particular case should be forbidden to make any reference to what might have been done in an earlier case by himself or any other judge. In arriving at such a decision,

the looking to precedent for a rule would be exactly as incongruous and mischievous as if, on an account between A and B, the balance were to be deduced, not from a comparison of the sum of the items on one side with the sum of the items on the other, but by copying the balance of a former account, in which the items, as well as the persons, were all different: an account between C and D.[18]

Bentham's general view of exclusionary rules of evidence was that they were 'manifestly an extreme and a most disastrous remedy' because of the misdecision to which exclusion might give rise.[19] There was but one mode of searching out truth: 'see everything that is to be seen; hear everybody who is likely to know anything about the matter: hear everybody, but most attentively of all, and first of all, those who are likely to know most about it – the parties'.[20]

As already stated, Bentham thought that the basis of exclusionary rules was not merely fear of deception but sinister interest: 'The more unforeseen exclusions there are, and the more unforeseen exceptions to exclusions, the more arguments; and the more arguments, the more fees.'[21] The real mischief, against which exclusion was unable to provide security, was not deception but misdecision. If you excluded necessary evidence, you were bound to produce misdecision. However, if you admitted evidence that was false, the falsity would not inevitably go undetected.

Against danger of misdecision, resulting from the admission of a lying witness, or rather of a witness disposed to lie, there are abundant remedies. There is the natural sagacity of the jury – there is the cultivated sagacity of the judge – there is the perhaps equally cultivated, and still

---

[18] Ibid., pp. 344–5.   [19] Ibid., p. 368.   [20] Ibid., p. 599.
[21] Ibid., p. 427. See also ch. 3, n. 24 and text.

more keenly sharpened, sagacity of the counsel for the defendant – there is, in penal cases (especially in cases of the most highly penal nature) the candour of the counsel for the prosecution.[22]

Bentham was particularly critical of exclusion on the ground of infamy. In the first place, he condemned the law for its uncertainty. In his *Principles of Penal Law*, he wrote: 'I would wish to give the reader a precise list of the offences to which this punishment [of exclusion from testifying] is annexed, but this I find to be impossible. Every principle delivered on this subject teems with contradiction.'[23] Secondly, he held a witness's past improbity, even including perjury, to be a ground for regarding their evidence with suspicion, but not for excluding it. Often a witness would have been guilty of only a single transgression and, in any case, an exclusionary rule could not take into account degrees of improbity. 'To all these different levels the eye of judicial suspicion has the power of adjusting itself. Exclusion knows no gradations; blind and brainless, it has but one alternative; – shut or open, like a valve; up or down, like a steam-engine.'[24] Besides, the natural instinct of every individual was to speak what they believed to be the truth.

To relate incidents as they have really happened, is the work of the memory: to relate them otherwise than as they have really happened, is the work of the invention. But, generally speaking, comparing the work of the memory with that of the invention, the latter will be found by much the harder work.[25]

In the absence of any interest in giving a false account, 'the most abandoned criminal that ever was upon the earth' might be trusted to testify 'as safely as the man of the most consummate virtue'.[26]

THE LEGISLATIVE REFORMS

In 1842 Lord Denman introduced a bill with a preamble that acknowledged that,

---

[22] *Works*, vol. VII, pp. 386–7.   [23] *Works*, vol. I, p. 486.
[24] *Rationale of Judicial Evidence* in *Works*, vol. VII, pp. 406–7.
[25] *Rationale of Judicial Evidence* in *Works*, vol. VI, p. 262.
[26] *Principles of Penal Law* in *Works*, vol. I, p. 486. See also *Rationale of Judicial Evidence* in *Works*, vol. VI, p. 401.

the Inquiry after Truth in Courts of Justice is often obstructed by Incapacities created by the present Law, and it is desirable that full Information as to the Facts in issue, both in Criminal and in Civil Cases should be laid before the Persons who are appointed to decide upon them, and that such Persons should exercise their Judgment on the Credit of the Witnesses adduced, and on the Truth of their Testimony ...

The bill went on to provide 'that no Person offered as a Witness shall hereafter be excluded by reason of Incapacity from Crime or Interest from giving Evidence'. The major exception to this broad rule and to the spirit of the preamble was that the parties to a suit remained incompetent as witnesses. The bill achieved a second and third reading and was sent to the Commons, but there it was an unintended casualty of a procedural device directed against another piece of legislation.[27] In 1843, Lord Denman presented an identical bill; it passed the Lords without difficulty, and was debated in the Commons on 17 August. The Attorney General, Sir Frederick Pollock, spoke in support. The bill passed the Commons without a division and in due course received the royal assent.[28]

Competency of parties was urged by Lord Brougham when, on 19 May 1845, he made a long speech in the House of Lords reviewing the progress made in law reform since his speech on that subject in 1828. Turning to the law of evidence, he asked why parties to suits should not be examined. It was done in Chancery; why not, under due restrictions, in courts of Common Law? At the conclusion of his speech he presented a number of bills for first reading, among which was 'a Bill to enable Parties to be examined on the Trial of Civil Actions'.[29] But the occasion was in sorry contrast with the situation in 1828. With the solitary exception of Lord Campbell, every peer on the opposition benches had left the House by the end of his speech, and on the government side only the President of the Council remained. Her

---

[27] *Parl. Deb.*, 3rd series, lxiii, 1142 (3 June 1842); lxvi, 196–7 (6 February 1843); *The Times*, 7 February 1843. There appears to have been some confusion on the part of reporters between Denman's bill to deal with incompetency for interest and for criminal convictions and his other bill to extend the right to affirm.

[28] 6 & 7 Vict c 85; otherwise known as the Law of Evidence Act 1843, or Lord Denman's Act.

[29] *House of Lords Sessional Papers* (165) 1845. The bill provided that, in limited cases and after giving notice, one party should have the right to call the other as a witness. In return, the party exercising the right could be cross-examined by the opposing party.

Majesty's Ministers, Campbell supposed, were considering the affairs of the nation, or perhaps refreshing themselves after their labours, and he added that 'the noble and learned Lord on the Woolsack and the noble President of the Council appeared eager to join them'.[30]

The bill to make parties competent made little, if any, progress.[31] Although Brougham's attempt to reform the procedure of the Common Law courts was unsuccessful, the principle of parties' competency was accepted when the new county courts were set up by Parliament in 1846. This itself was a development that Brougham had done much to bring about. For a number of years, he had been attempting to establish a new system of local courts in which parties would to some extent be competent to give evidence. Brougham had not always aimed to make them witnesses at the trial of the action just like any others; his original local courts bill had limited their right to the examination of each other in the presence of the judge before trial – a provision presumably aimed at clarification of the issues between the parties.[32] However, section 83 of the statute setting up the county courts system[33] provided that on the hearing or trial of any action or on any other proceeding under the Act, the parties, their spouses, and all other persons might be examined on behalf of the plaintiff or the defendant on oath, or, where permitted, on affirmation.

In 1851, a bill to allow parties to give evidence in the superior courts of Common Law was prepared by J. Pitt Taylor and submitted to Denman for his approval.[34] Denman approved it, but because of ill health was unable to take charge of it in the Lords. The passage of the bill was therefore entrusted to

---

[30] *Parl. Deb.*, 3rd series, lxxx, 509–15.

[31] Ibid., lxxxviii, 705–6 (14 August 1846).

[32] Sir John E. Eardley Wilmot, *Lord Brougham's Acts and Bills, from 1811 to the Present Time, now first Collected and Arranged, with an Analytical Review Shewing their Results upon the Amendment of the Law* (London, 1857), pp. 574–604.

[33] 9 & 10 Vict c 95.

[34] Taylor had drawn up the report of the Common Law Committee of the Law Amendment Society which had recommended the reform (*Law Review* 14 (1851), 137). He had also drawn up a bill, introduced in 1849 by Brougham, to enable parties and their husbands or wives to give evidence in civil cases (Arnould, *Lord Denman*, vol. II, p. 318; *Parl. Deb.*, 3rd series, cxvi, 1). The 1849 bill is printed in *House of Lords Sessional Papers* (89) 1849.

Brougham. The House of Lords gave the bill a second reading on 11 April 1851; after consideration in Committee it received a third reading on 27 June.[35] In the Commons the bill received a formal first and second reading but was more fully considered in Committee, where there was some debate concerning clause 3, which prevented the examination of a wife on behalf of a husband and vice versa. The Attorney General, Sir Alexander Cockburn, admitted that he could not defend this and knew of no good reason for it, but said that he understood there to be a strong opinion in the House of Lords in its favour. The Commons later agreed an amendment that had the effect of enabling husbands or wives to be examined in civil, but not in criminal, cases, either for or against their partners.[36]

The Commons amendments were considered by the Lords on 5 August 1851. Objection was made to some of them, including the amendment to clause 3. The report of the Parliamentary proceedings indicates that, subsequently, the Commons did not insist on their amendment to this clause and that the bill received the royal assent on 7 August 1851.[37] However, when the Act was printed, section 3 appeared in the amended form approved by the Commons: it provided that nothing in the Act should make competent or compellable any person charged with a criminal offence, or render any person compellable to answer any question tending to criminate himself, or render in any *criminal* proceedings any husband competent or compellable to give evidence for or against his wife, or any wife competent or compellable to give evidence for or against her husband.[38] The Act came into force on 1 November 1851.

One substantial criticism of the legislation was that it left husbands and wives of parties incompetent to give evidence, and it

---

[35] *Parl. Deb.*, 3rd series, cxvii, 444–6, 1312.
[36] Ibid., cxviii, 838–49 (16 June 1851).   [37] Ibid., 1893–5, 1927.
[38] Compare the text of clause 3 as it left the Lords: 'But nothing herein contained shall render any Person, who in any Criminal Proceeding is charged with the commission of any indictable Offence, or any Offence punishable on summary Conviction, competent or compellable to give Evidence for or against himself or herself, or shall in any Proceeding, *civil or criminal*, render any Husband competent or compellable to give Evidence for or against his Wife, or any Wife competent or compellable to give Evidence for or against her Husband' (*House of Lords Sessional Papers* (179) 1851). (Emphasis mine here and in accompanying text.)

was thought that in many cases this worked great injustice. The *Law Times* made the point in this way:

Among the middle classes matters of business are often conducted by [the wife] for her husband. Yet in such cases we have the practical absurdity that the husband, who knows *nothing* about it, *may* be called, while the wife, who knows *all* about it, *may not*. The object of the Lords in excluding her was to prevent the violation of domestic confidence; they forgot that at the same time they prevented the proof of all that had come to her knowledge apart from her husband, and in which there was no confidence to violate.[39]

The Evidence Amendment Act 1853 was passed to meet this criticism. Section 1 provided that on the trial of any matter, husbands and wives of the parties were to be both competent and compellable as witnesses. Section 2 provided that nothing in the Act should apply to any criminal proceeding or proceeding instituted in consequence of adultery.[40] By section 3, no husband was to be compellable to disclose any communication made to him by his wife during the marriage, and wives were similarly protected in relation to communications made to them by their husbands.

INFLUENCES ON THE REFORMS

Lord Denman's Act

As the name given to the 1843 legislation indicates, the man chiefly responsible for the reforms that it enacted was Lord Denman, and some history of his opinions must be given in an attempt to determine the extent to which he was guided by Bentham's critique in his support for reform.

In 1824 Denman, then aged 45, had shown support for some of Bentham's ideas on evidence reform in an article in which he reviewed the recently published *Traité des preuves judiciaires*.[41] In particular, Denman recommended that the rule excluding the evidence of an interested witness should be abolished. His principal argument in favour of this reform was based on the inconsistency of the law, which excluded some evidence where the

---

[39] *Law Times* 18 (1851–2), 122.
[40] The Evidence Further Amendment Act 1869 removed the exception in relation to proceedings instituted in consequence of adultery.
[41] *Edinburgh Review* 40 (1824), 169–207.

witness's interest was only slight but included other evidence where the witness had a more potent interest, although one not recognised by the law.

Denman stated that he was 'nearly prepared' to go further than this and recommend that the parties in civil actions should be able to give evidence. He was deterred only by his 'inexperience as to the practice'.[42] He did not, however, fully accept the inclusionary principle that had been at the root of Bentham's recommended abolition of the rule excluding evidence on grounds of interest. If the danger of deception was sufficiently great, Denman was prepared to exclude evidence. This appears from his recommendation that married persons should be disqualified as witnesses either for or against each other. The reason was not wholly the 'dread entertained by the English law, of conjugal feuds', though he thought that these were 'frequently of the most deadly character'. His main reason was that,

the passions must be too much alive, where the husband and wife contend in a Court of Justice, to give any chance of fair play to the truth. It must be expected, as an unavoidable consequence of the connexion by which they are bound, that their feelings, either of affection or hatred, must be strong enough to bear down the abstract regard for veracity, even in judicial depositions.[43]

In a pamphlet published in 1828, Denman repeated his call for the abolition of the rule excluding evidence on account of interest. But by then his opinion seemed to have hardened against the competency of parties in civil cases.

The opinion professed by many enlightened men, that the contending parties ought themselves to be examined in open court, seems much more open to objection, since the very character of a *party* is inconsistent with the knowledge of any important fact adverse to his interest in the cause. His deposition in his own favour would not be thought to carry his assertion farther than his commencing or defending the action: while an acknowledgment to his prejudice could hardly be expected from human virtue. For, in most cases, he would be placed in the dilemma of either committing perjury, or of publicly confessing an attempt to commit injustice; and the necessity for this torturing probation would be done away by such appeals as are already supposed to have been made to his conscience and personal knowledge, in the stages anterior to the trial.[44]

[42] Ibid., 177.   [43] Ibid., 179.
[44] [Thomas Denman] *Considerations Respectfully Submitted to the Commissioners now Sitting to Inquire into the Proceedings in Actions at Law*, quoted in *The Times*, 8 October 1828, pp. 3–4. See also Arnould, *Lord Denman*, vol. I, pp. 256–7.

However, it was not until 1842 that Denman took steps to achieve even the limited reform that he had recommended. There were probably several reasons for the delay. One was that, although between 1819 and 1826 Denman had been a member of the House of Commons and had supported the proposals of other members for law reform, he made, according to Holdsworth, 'no very great figure in the House' and put his work at the Bar first.[45] When he entered Parliament again in 1830, and on the formation of Grey's ministry in November of that year was appointed Attorney General and later a member of the House of Lords, Denman supported a number of proposals for law reform, of which the reform of evidence law was only a part and may not have seemed to him the most pressing. Among other proposals, for example, he supported legislation to abolish the death penalty for forgery and other offences, to allow the courts to sit in banc outside legal terms, and to allow mothers separated from their husbands to have access to their children.[46] In addition, Denman may have wished to keep his proposals back until he was sure of support from the legal profession, in particular from the judiciary. This is suggested by the fact that in the debate on 8 March 1842 he made a point of stating that his proposal had the direct sanction of several of his brethren on the bench, and that he had received no objection to it from any of them. Confirmation of this lack of opposition was later provided by the Lord Chancellor, Lord Lyndhurst, who said that so far as he had been able to obtain the opinion of Westminster Hall, it corresponded to a considerable extent to that of Lord Denman. Lyndhurst said that he himself had conversed with some of the judges of the highest rank, and they had entirely concurred on the principle of Denman's bill.[47]

In arguing the case for reform, Denman relied on the anomalies of the existing law. For example, he pointed out that persons convicted of certain crimes had their lips closed in a court of justice to the end of their days if their evidence was objected to in formal manner by producing the record of conviction. But the mere commission of crime did not exclude the criminal from the witness box. Often, where accomplices gave evidence against their former partner, it was the sole reason for placing them there. Denman

[45] *History of English Law*, vol. XV, pp. 396–7.   [46] Ibid., pp. 398–9.
[47] *Parl. Deb.*, 3rd series, lxi, 209, 211–14 (8 March 1842).

described the law as 'whimsical' in this matter. If convicts obtained a pardon, which might be done without much difficulty, the effect of the conviction was removed and they again became admissible witnesses. Whether the evidence of a person formerly convicted was to be received or not therefore depended on chance, or probably on the pecuniary means of those who had an interest in the admission or rejection of their testimony. Only in one case could exclusion be plausibly defended: where there had been a previous conviction for perjury. But here the law was equally anomalous, for unless the record of the conviction could be proved in court, the evidence could not be rejected.

Denman expected to receive more opposition to his proposals concerning convictions than to those concerning interest.[48] But there was a widespread feeling that the law concerning convictions could not be supported. The same line of argument was adopted in the following year by the Attorney General, Sir Frederick Pollock.[49] And Starkie, in the third edition of his *Treatise*, published in 1842, commented on the unsatisfactory state of the law, arguing that a confession of turpitude on the part of a witness might just as reasonably excite doubts about their veracity as a recorded conviction, which itself might have been based only on the witness's confession. On the other hand, in the same edition he argued in justification of the existing law concerning interest.[50]

Denman argued that the best judges had always realised the evils of exclusion on the ground of interest. He pointed out that Lord Mansfield and many other judges since his time had felt the inconvenience of the law which prevented the admission of witnesses on the ground of interest. Their opinion had been that all persons, whether interested or not, should be allowed to give their evidence and that it should be left to the jury to estimate its value. From a sense of the evil of exclusion, the judges had been led to evade the operation of the existing law; doubts had thereby been raised, and difficulties created, which had increased litigation to an incredible extent. There was hardly a book of reports that did not contain cases of this kind, in which the expenses of the suitors must have been enormous, quite apart from the delay.[51]

---

[48] Ibid., 209.   [49] *Parl. Deb.*, 3rd series, lxxi, 909–10 (17 August 1843).
[50] Starkie, *Treatise* 3rd edn (1842), vol. I, p. 95, n. (h).
[51] *Parl. Deb.*, 3rd series, lxi, 208 (8 March 1842).

During its passage, Denman's bill was the subject of a critical pamphlet by John Lowndes, a barrister of the Inner Temple.[52] Lowndes's pamphlet is interesting because it is an early example of an argument heard with increasing frequency as many of the barriers raised against competency were broken down. He argued that persons with an interest in the outcome of the proceedings ought not to be allowed to give evidence, as this would lead to an increase in perjury. Lowndes admitted that the existing law gave rise to inconsistencies in admitting many witnesses whose testimony was likely to be biased for various reasons. However, 'the necessity of some general and defined limit to the exclusion of witnesses fully justifies the apparent inconsistency; and if the rule of exclusion is good in the case of *direct* interest in the event of the suit, it cannot fairly be attributed as a defect to it, that it does not embrace every possible case of interest whatever'.[53]

Lowndes pointed out that the reason for the general rule was that if the law were to allow such evidence to be given it would tacitly invite a witness to distort and disguise the truth. He described the reformers' case as starting with the proposition that in everyday situations where a question of fact arose, the evidence of interested persons was not excluded; it would be heard, but with a due allowance for bias. Arguments for reform had then developed in three ways. First, it was said that there was an analogy between the trial of a matter by a jury and investigations made in everyday life. Secondly, it was argued that a hardship was inflicted on the parties who stood to benefit by the rejected evidence. Thirdly, it was urged that an injustice was done to mankind by the supposition of such an extremely low standard of moral integrity. Lowndes rejected the second argument at once. If the rule in question tended to further the elucidation of truth, 'there can be no hardship on the parties, except in individual cases, which must ever submit to general rules for the public welfare'.

As to the first argument, Lowndes argued that the analogy was inappropriate. A private person rarely decided any matter without personal knowledge of the parties between whom he was to

---

[52] John J. Lowndes, *A Few Brief Remarks on Lord Denman's Bill for Improving the Law of Evidence* (London, 1843).

[53] Ibid., p. 7.

adjudicate. If he had to pronounce in a matter where the only witness was one previously unknown to him and also deeply interested in the matter, he would no doubt decline any interference, unless he could make some private inquiry into the character of the man. But a jury almost invariably decided between parties with whom its members were unacquainted. Cross-examination could not satisfactorily show 'what degree of pounds-sterling-pressure a man's conscience can bear without being strained'.

If a witness was competent he could in most cases be compelled to give evidence. But would it be right to compel an interested witness to give evidence, where, if he gave it truly, he would lose a large sum of money? It was not in the best interests of society that a man should be forced into a position where he would be so exposed to temptation. It was said that to argue in this way assumed a false estimate of the standard of public morality. But the frailty of human nature had to be regarded; the struggle between moral principle and self-interest should be carefully avoided, and these antagonistic powers not awakened to strife by the active interposition of the law.

Lowndes recognised that the aim stated in the preamble of the bill would be frustrated until the parties to a suit were allowed to give evidence. He added: 'If such a chimera should ever assume tangible form in the shape of a Legislative project, it will be then time enough to show its utter folly and inexpediency.'[54] But Lowndes's protest appears to have been a solitary one. The ease with which the 1843 legislation was passed shows that the legal profession and members of Parliament alike discounted the danger of increased perjury when the benefits of extending competency were considered.

It is clear that by the early 1840s professional and parliamentary opinion favoured the position on interest that Bentham had earlier adopted. Further, the 1843 legislation was passed as a result of the direct efforts of Lord Denman, whose thinking on law reform had clearly been influenced, as his earlier review article showed, by what he had read of Bentham's work. However, before too much significance is attached to the part played by Bentham's critique, it should be remembered that at this stage Denman was proposing a

[54] Ibid., pp. 13–14.

much diluted version of Bentham's proposals. In particular, he had not yet himself been converted to the idea that competency should be extended to the parties to litigation.[55] In addition, the easy passage of the legislation owed much to the concurrence of the judges, and it is hardly likely that they had suddenly come to see the force of Bentham's arguments. A few years later, many lawyers and nearly all the common law judges were united in opposition to proposals to extend competency to parties.

How, then, are we to account for the attitude of the profession in 1842–3? There seems little doubt that the restriction was felt to be an inconvenience: the speeches of Denman and the Attorney General show this. At the same time, it was a restriction that could be remedied without too great a reversal of existing practice. In this respect, of course, it was unlike the later proposal to make parties competent. Perhaps these factors and a pragmatic approach, which had sometimes favoured exceptions in cases likely to create inconvenience for commerce,[56] created the professional opinion favourable to Denman's proposals.

The Law of Evidence Amendment Act, 1851

If the influence of Bentham on evidence law is to be found anywhere among the legislative reforms of the nineteenth century, it is in relation to the 1851 Act, not least because of the contributions of Denman, Brougham, and the Law Amendment Society.

Although Denman was unable, through ill health, to take charge of the bill prepared by J. Pitt Taylor in 1851, he expressed his approval of it in a letter published in the *Law Review*, thereby departing from the opinion that he had expressed in 1828 against extension of competency to parties.[57] Denman now stated that he had come to 'a clear and decided opinion that that change will be beneficial, or rather, that it is necessary for the discovery of truth, and the promotion of justice, and will greatly tend to prevent the crime of perjury, and ultimately to extinguish unjust litigation'.[58]

Later, in a private letter to Brougham, Denman again showed

---

[55] See n. 44 and text.
[56] See, e.g., *Green* v. *The New River Company* (1792) 4 TR 589; *Pritt* v. *Fairclough* (1812) 3 Camp 305; *Poole* v. *Dicas* (1835) 1 Bing NC 649.
[57] See n. 44 and text.
[58] *Law Review* 14 (1851), 206, 207.

the firmness of his conversion to the cause of reform when he wrote:

Only conceive a legislature *creating* a Court, with special proviso that those who know the facts shall *never* be heard, or, never unless the *adversary makes him a witness*.

And this is to be the Law for those of our Courts which ought to assume pre-eminence, while others of inferior pretensions are coming at the Truth by simple means & a natural process.[59]

A month later, Denman wrote again to Brougham:

In truth our bill is not reform in the ordinary sense, it is the introduction into our practice of a great principle plainly necessary for discovering truth though long unaccountably excluded from English judicature. It has been unexpectedly [? been] at once brought to light & *tested* by [the] County Courts. The arguments a priori & a posteriori are both complete. What would be thought of a legislator who, framing [a] code for a new state, should begin his chapter of justice 'Article 1. The parties to a suit shall never be examined as to what they know'? Is it wiser to say in an old State 'In our superior Courts parties are never [heard], these Courts are deserted for some inferior Courts lately erected in which parties may be examined, a practice undeniably giving to those Courts however inferior in other respects, an advantage in the attainment of truth. It is proposed to give the Superior Courts the same advantage. They seem unwilling to accept it. Why?

Exceptional cases are imagined, in which the disparity of parties in talents & dexterity may possibly work injustice.

But this may be said with equal truth of all conceivable systems, & not only the present . . .[60]

From 1828, Brougham appears to have been in favour of a wider competency for witnesses. In his speech in that year on the state of the law he expressed the opinion that all persons should be admitted to give evidence, leaving it to the jury to determine what weight ought to be placed on their testimony.[61] In the debate on the bill introduced by Lord Denman in 1842, Brougham objected only to the exception that it contained, saying that in all cases the

---

[59] Brougham MSS No 39382, 12 June 1851. Brougham's 1845 bill had a provision for one party to call the other as a witness (*House of Lords Sessional Papers* (165) 1845). In a leading article in *The Times* on 18 July 1851, the writer recommended that either party to a suit should be able to obtain leave, without the delay and expense of a bill of discovery, to examine their adversary viva voce before a judge or any proper officer of the court on the matters in dispute between them.

[60] Brougham MSS No 39383, 13 July 1851. Abbreviations in the original have been expanded in this transcription and in that from No. 39382.

[61] Brougham, *Speech on the Present State of the Law*, pp. 39–40.

parties to a suit should be permitted to be examined.[62] He had himself introduced a bill to achieve this reform in 1845, and he had been the guiding force behind the setting-up of the new county court system in 1846, which had provided the opportunity for widespread testing of this reform. It is true that in an earlier local courts bill he had limited the rights of the parties to examination of each other in the presence of the judge before trial, but it is likely that this was put forward as a compromise in an attempt to draw the sting out of any opposition.[63]

Brougham delivered the principal speech in the debate on the second reading of the Law of Evidence Amendment Bill on 11 April 1851.[64] He reminded the House that, although there may have been a time when parties had been excluded from giving evidence simply because they were parties, the current justification was that it was their interest alone that made them incompetent to testify.[65] But, since Lord Denman's Act had enabled interested persons to give evidence, it followed that the prohibition of evidence should now be removed. The existing law, he argued, was inconsistent in other ways. In cases decided by judges rather than juries, evidence was given on affidavit. Many affidavits were sworn by parties to the suit, but,

these depositions are given without any check whatever upon the parties, any guard whatever against falsehood, except what is afforded by their own consciences. The affidavit is prepared in secret; it is sworn in private. It is prepared by professional skill, and carefully framed to prove the case of him who is to swear it.

In these circumstances,

Ordinary men, parties of an average candour, with advisers of a medium honesty, will just tell such parts of the story as may suit their purpose ... They will not tell the whole truth, even should they tell nothing but the truth, while not a few will defy the dread of perjury, and yield to the motive for falsely swearing, because there is neither the watchful eye of the Judge and jury, and public upon them; nor the risk of detection by being cross-examined.

Brougham also pointed to the fact that in criminal cases the person who had suffered injury was allowed to give evidence; they were, in effect, a party to the proceedings, although the Crown was the nominal party.

---

[62] *Parl. Deb.*, 3rd series, lxi, 214 (8 March 1842).   [63] See n. 29 and text.
[64] *Parl. Deb.*, 3rd series, cxvi, 1–20.   [65] *Worrall* v. *Jones* (1831) 7 Bing 395.

Several harmful consequences of shutting out the testimony of parties were relied on by Brougham. First, it excluded the evidence of those who knew most about the matters in dispute, which must often lead to failure of justice. Secondly, it put some parties at a disadvantage, because their opponents were likely to have witnesses while they themselves had none. Thus tradesmen, with people in their service, would be more likely than their customers to have witnesses to support them. A defendant's potential witnesses could be silenced by making them co-defendants. Lastly, the rule encouraged unmeritorious litigation: there were thousands of cases that would have been settled out of court had the parties been able to give evidence.

Brougham dealt briefly with the objection that examination of parties would give advantage to the able over the dull and to the self-possessed over the nervous, pointing out that the same objection applied to witnesses currently allowed to give evidence. The judge, he asserted, would always be able to redress the balance.

The major part of Brougham's speech, however, was devoted to what he perceived to be the principal objection to the extension of competency to parties – the risk of increased perjury. The arguments that he deployed to deal with this were entirely pragmatic. He did not attempt to tackle the paternalistic point, made by Lowndes and later to be made more frequently by opponents of the extension of competency to accused persons, that it was against the interests of society to force someone into a position where they would be so exposed to temptation. He argued instead that perjury was more likely under the existing law. Opponents of the reform, he said, had failed to take into account the possibility of the subornation of perjury – an offence more likely to occur than perjury by a party giving evidence, because 'men will set on others to swear falsely who may shrink from perjuring themselves'. The exclusion of the parties made it necessary to examine a number of other persons, and the chances of perjury were increased with the number of such witnesses. Moreover, persons who would not swear falsely for their own benefit might colour their evidence to help a friend or employer, and the falsity of their evidence would be less easily detected than in a case of clear perjury. Public opinion was completely against witnesses who gave false evidence for their own benefit, but it was more lenient where a witness swore falsely for the benefit of someone else.

Brougham also argued that the false tale of a party was easier to detect than that of an ordinary witness because the party had to tell the whole story and to particularise fully, so increasing the scope for contradiction by another witness or for the detection of falsity in cross-examination. Other witnesses, however, swore to only a part of the story, and the opportunity to contradict them or detect falsity in cross-examination was correspondingly reduced. He relied on the experience of the county courts as proof that the reform would be beneficial, and thought that perjury would be even less frequently committed in the higher courts than in the county courts. In the former, the parties were 'likely to be of a higher station, and more under the influence of honourable feelings'. Besides, the presence of the judges in the superior courts was 'more awful'. At the conclusion of the debate Brougham showed his own debt to Bentham by declaring that the only feeling to damp his gratification was 'that the most illustrious teacher of jurisprudence who ever lived, either in ancient or modern times, Mr Bentham, had not lived to see this day – there being no one of his doctrines on which he set a higher value, or insisted more strenuously, than this of admitting the testimony of parties'.[66]

Bentham's writing may also have been reflected in a leading article that appeared in *The Times* shortly after the Act had come into force. Reporters observing cases under the new law had produced mainly favourable conclusions but thought that a good deal of perjury had resulted. The writer of the *Times* article asserted, however, that it was no part of the court's duty to avoid leading people into temptation. He then produced an argument that Bentham had often used: the prevalence of perjury could be attributed to the fact that a party could file a pleading that might be utterly false without suffering any punishment or disgrace, and by virtue of which they might even succeed in the action if an opponent made a mistake in pleading. 'It is hardly to be expected that Courts which tolerate pleadings utterly false should be able all at once to obtain from the parties to whom this scandalous licence of mendacity has been granted evidence entirely true.'[67]

[66] *Parl. Deb.*, 3rd series, cxvi, 20.
[67] *The Times*, 17 November 1851. Cf. Bentham's observations on the pleading known as the declaration: *Principles of Judicial Procedure* in *Works*, vol. II, p. 170.

The change in the position of parties in civil actions was assisted by the efforts of the Law Amendment Society. This society, founded by Brougham in 1844, produced a quarterly journal called the *Law Review* and stimulated a number of mid-century reforms in the law. Shortly after the new county court system had been set up, the Society turned its attention to removing the bar on testimony from parties in the superior courts. In a report published in 1848, the Common Law Committee of the Society concluded in favour of the reform, stating that the dangers of an increase in perjury had been greatly over-rated. Yet even if perjury were to be increased, the Committee was not prepared to resist a change in the law on that ground alone.

The folding of sheep by night on lands at a distance from the homestead, no doubt affords facilities for sheep-stealing; the exposure of goods in front of shops leads to larceny; nocturnal travelling may tempt to the commission of highway robbery; but no one thinks of prohibiting these innocent acts on the ground that they hold out temptations to crime. Why is this? Because the inconveniences that would result from such a prohibition would be felt far more by the public than those engendered by a partial increase in the number of offences.

In this case, the advantages of examining persons best conversant with the facts 'would far more than counterbalance any evils which the cause of morality would be likely to sustain, from the crime of perjury becoming somewhat more frequent.'[68]

In a further attempt to encourage the case for reform, the Law Amendment Society conducted an opinion poll of all the county court judges and invited their answers to the question: 'In your judgment has the law which enables parties to be examined as witnesses in the County Courts worked well or ill?' The survey showed that the great majority of judges were in favour of

---

[68] *Law Review* 8 (1848), 353–8. It is likely that this closely argued presentation of the case for reform was influential not only in England but also in the state of New York. The legislature of that state had appointed a commission to revise the system of practice and pleading in its courts. The commissioners had reported in 1848 and had published with their report that of the Common Law Committee. A proposed code of civil procedure for the State of New York followed in 1850. The code comprised rules of evidence that were for the most part those followed in England. But two important alterations were proposed. The first involved a wide extension of the admissibility of evidence; in particular, it was proposed to allow parties and others with an interest in the outcome of litigation to give evidence. The second was designed to enable any witness who desired to give evidence on affirmation instead of on oath to do so (*Law Review* 12 (1850), 366–7; 13 (1850–1), 395–418).

admitting such evidence, the benefits of which in their opinion outweighed any increase that there might have been in perjury. The following examples give the flavour of the replies.

George Wilkinson thought that in a large proportion of contested cases there would be failure of justice but for this practice. The additional temptation to perjury and the occasional commission of it were greatly outweighed by the increased facility for doing justice. Henry Stapylton said that at first there had been much perjury, but that this had afterwards decreased. Some judges thought that there had been no increase in perjury. This was William Walker's conclusion, though the picture he painted had its traces of gloom:

That the amount of perjury in the County Courts is very great cannot, I fear, be doubted, though it should be observed that the misstatements made arise more frequently from the extremely careless, hasty, and inconsiderate habits of answering of the lower orders, and from their lowness in understanding questions put to them, than from a deliberate intention to deceive.

But he noted that the children, servants, and other connections of the party were just as ready to swear falsely as the party themself and doubted whether, in proportion to the number of witnesses sworn, there was a greater amount of wilful perjury committed in county courts than in those where the testimony of parties was excluded. On the other hand, J. M. Herbert thought that suborned perjury was much rarer in the county court than in superior courts.

T. J. Birch had no doubt that 'a frightful amount of perjury' was committed in the courts over which he presided, 'but quite as much by witnesses who are not parties as by parties'. Nevertheless, he thought that if the judge took pains he need very seldom be misled. J. D. Burnaby took the same view of the danger that perjury would lead to misdecision: 'I certainly observe many very fearful cases of perjury which are occasioned by the examination of parties, but they are generally easy of detection.' John Wing took a more favourable view of those appearing as witnesses in his court, and thought that 'contradictions in evidence proceed more often from the witnesses representing their suppositions and imperfect recollections as *certainties*, than from a wilful and corrupt determination, on the one side or on the other, to state absolute falsehoods'. Arthur Palmer, the sole judge to disapprove completely of allowing parties to give evidence, was less optimistic. 'I beg to state', he wrote, 'not merely as a matter of opinion, but as a fact, that there is scarcely a week in which the law does not produce, in the Bristol County Court, the *most gross perjury*.' He believed that if the parties were not allowed to give evidence, the commission of crime would be prevented and there would not often be a failure of justice.[69]

There is no doubt that the proposal to make parties competent divided the legal profession. Before the bill became law it was noted that the superior common law judges were unenthusiastic at its prospect. Denman referred to what he perceived as a general judicial characteristic in the letter, which he published in the *Law Review* in support of the bill introduced in 1851.

Besides the constant occupation of their minds in

> their important functions, and the necessity for the undisturbed enjoyment of their hard-earned leisure, there are feelings in the Judges which must ever strengthen the reluctance to assent to alteration. They have administered the law as they found it, with implicit confidence, and even veneration, which unite in them with all the obvious and instinctive motives for abhorring change. It is painful to condemn the past and present. Even if they concur in the projected improvement, they had rather that others should be the persons to counsel it.

According to Denman, some judges believed the fallacy that the system of justice that they had to administer had been established 'on full deliberation by the wisdom of former ages'. Hence, they imputed to all innovators the arrogance of reversing an earlier decision.[70]

Lord Campbell's diary confirms the existence of judicial opposition. Before the bill became law, he wrote:

> The great controversy now is upon the Evidence Bill, allowing the parties to be examined against and for themselves. The Bill is opposed, as might be expected, by the Lord Chancellor. If it passes it will create a new era in

---

[69] *Law Review* 13 (1850–1), 402, 405, 406–7, 408, 415.

[70] *Law Review* 14 (1851), 210, 211. Cf. Bentham's 'Chinese Argument' in *The Book of Fallacies* (*Works*, vol. II, pp. 398–401). See also a leading article in *The Times*, 7 May 1851. The writer believed that the judges, having reached the pinnacle of their professional ambition, had everything to fear and nothing to gain from a change of system. English law protected them from much labour and responsibility, and raised questions for their decision in so abstract a form as to shield them almost entirely from criticism. This was achieved by a highly technical system of pleadings, strict and unbending rules of practice and evidence, and a careful separation of law and fact.

the administration of justice in this country. I support it, and I think it will be carried, although the Common Law judges, with one exception, are hostile to it.[71]

The writer of a leading article that appeared a few months later in *The Times* claimed that there was no doubt that the most numerous and efficient body of persons opposing law reform was to be found in the legal profession. 'A lawyer having acquired, by labour, at a wonderful expense of mental exertion and down-right money outlay, a knowledge of a curiously intricate science so called, on a sudden finds that this mystery, to him so costly, is about to be rendered utterly valueless.' It might be a benefit to the community, but to him it was an unmixed evil – 'it puts an end to his craft, his power, and his profit'. A judge had risen to legal eminence by a craft:

His mind is engrossed by what BENTHAM called an interest-begotten prejudice. He looks back with complacency to the triumphs of his forensic career, and dwells with lingering fondness upon the many points successfully raised by his ingenuity and peculiar knowledge. To abolish at one fell stroke all that gave importance to his past career is to him a most distasteful proceeding.[72]

The writer of a leading article in the *Law Times* supported the bill but acknowledged that many lawyers, if not a majority of them, were hostile to the proposed reform. The *Law Times* encouraged its readers to petition the House of Lords in support of the bill, and provided a precedent that could be used for that purpose. Its great fear was the opposition of the Lord Chancellor, Lord Truro. It may also have felt that something needed to be done to counter the influence of the Incorporated Law Society, which had petitioned against the bill.[73] But a significant part of the profession regarded the reform as a great benefit to litigants. The *Law Times* noticed an 'extraordinary diminution of civil business' on the circuits in the period before the bill became law because impending trials were being delayed to await its passage.[74]

---

[71] Quoted in a debate on the Evidence in Criminal Cases Bill by Lord James of Hereford on 1 August 1898 (*Parl. Deb.*, 4th series, lxiii, 663). Lord James also observed that in 1856 Campbell had added a note to this entry: 'The Act has been made to work most admirably. All mankind praise it.'

[72] *The Times*, 1 September 1851.

[73] *Law Times* 17 (1851), 38, 98, 106, 121.

[74] Ibid., 157–8. A clause was later introduced providing that the new legislation should not apply to pending actions. The *Law Times* thereupon 'lost no time in

In October 1851, a writer in *The Times* took the view that: 'Amid the general impatience of almost all classes in this country for a speedy and sweeping reform of the law, the judges alone regard its progress with dislike and distrust.' In particular, they seemed to look upon a new Act of Parliament reforming the law 'as a challenge rather than a mandate, and address themselves to its interpretation with the view of neutralizing rather than carrying out its provisions'.[75] The complaint was repeated in a leading article on 18 October 1851:

Judicial vanity is easily excited; a judge and a bishop's wife being about equally sensitive on the score of their dignity. We may indeed smile at the anger and the folly of the helpmates of the episcopal bench, but the anilities of Westminster-hall are to the public serious calamities.

On 20 November 1851, and subsequently on 10, 12, and 20 December 1851, letters appeared in *The Times*, signed only with the Greek letter delta. These implied that the judges of the superior courts disliked the 1851 Act and, in deciding questions arising under it, had resolved to defeat its operation.[76] The author of these letters may well have been Denman; he had used this form of signature in his private correspondence,[77] and in a private letter to Brougham dated 13 December 1851 he referred to 'the outrageous mutiny among the judges on [the] subject of [the] new law of evidence'.[78]

It is likely that this publicity had a chastening effect on the judges; after 1851 there were no more complaints of judicial perversity in interpreting the Act. In their Second Report the Common Law Commissioners wrote:

It is painful to contemplate the amount of injustice which must have taken place under the exclusive system of the English law, not only in cases actually brought into Court and there wrongly decided in consequence of the exclusion of evidence, but in numberless cases in which parties silently submitted to wrongs from inability to avail themselves of proof, which, though morally conclusive, was in law inadmissible. From

communicating upon the matter with some of the authorities' and the clause was dropped. When passed, the Act applied to all pending actions and proceedings in which evidence would be taken on and after 1 November 1851 (ibid., 165; 18 (1851–2), 9).
[75] *The Times*, 8 October 1851.
[76] See, in particular, the letter published on 20 December.
[77] Arnould, *Lord Denman*, vol. II, pp. 276–7.
[78] Brougham MSS No 10941.

the time, however, when the late Mr Bentham first turned the attention of the public to the defects of the English law of evidence, the system of exclusion has been crumbling away before the power of discussion and improved legislation.

As for the results of the 1851 Act, the Commissioners observed:

The new law has now been in practical operation for eighteen months; and, according to the concurrent testimony of the bench, the profession, and the public, is found to work admirably, and to contribute in an eminent degree to the administration of justice.[79]

The contributions of Denman and Brougham and of the Law Amendment Society suggest Benthamite influence on the 1851 reform. But it was, of course, still possible to reach the conclusion that parties should be competent without having been influenced by Bentham. It was not necessary to have recourse to Bentham to appreciate that abolition of the rule that prevented witnesses with an interest from giving evidence had effectively undermined the restriction on the parties.[80] Nor was the practice of allowing parties to testify a complete novelty. As early as 1830, a writer in the *Legal Observer* observed that the law should be formed to allow evidence to be given by the parties to an action, for in many instances they were the most important witnesses, if not the only ones, and 'from the commercial character of our country at the present day, the rejection of the testimony of an interested party must be most unwise'.[81] But these commercial pressures had already given rise to examination of the parties in litigation taking place outside the sphere of the superior courts of common law in arbitrations and in actions brought in the various courts of Requests. The writer in the *Law Times* who commended Lord Denman's reforms also stated that there was rarely an arbitration in which it was not expressly provided that the parties should be examined. The truth of this is confirmed by an early practitioners'

---

[79] *Second Report of H. M. Commissioners for Inquiring into the Process, Practice, and System of Pleading in the Superior Courts of Common Law* PP 1852–3 [1626] XL, p. 11.

[80] See, e.g., *Parl. Deb.*, 3rd series, lxxi, 910 (17 August 1843); *Law Times* 1 (1843), 564–5. The first edition of Taylor's *Treatise*, published in 1848, stated that 'every argument that can be urged in favour of admitting the evidence of interested witnesses in general, applies to that of parties' (*Law Review* 8 (1848), 207, 214).

[81] 'On Receiving the Evidence of Parties', *Legal Observer or Journal of Jurisprudence* 1 (1831–1), 371–3.

treatise on arbitration, published in 1845, which contained a selection of precedents. The first of these, for a simple agreement between two parties, provided that the arbitrator should be at liberty to examine the parties on oath if he saw fit.[82]

Other tribunals where the parties were heard were the Courts of Requests, or Conscience, which had been established in many places by special Acts of Parliament during the eighteenth and early nineteenth centuries.[83] The constitutions and jurisdictions of these tribunals varied. A typical Court of Requests had as judges a body of non-professional persons called commissioners, who had jurisdiction to try actions for debt in accordance with equity and good conscience (terms broadly interpreted) where the sum in dispute did not exceed 40 shillings or £5. Proceedings were informal and the parties were able to testify.[84] Similar arrangements prevailed in the old county court of Middlesex. A statute of 1750 gave authority to the suitors of the Middlesex county court and the county clerk to determine by summary procedure suits where the debt or damages amounted to less than 40 shillings. They were given power to make such orders or decrees as should seem 'just and agreeable to equity and good conscience', and 'for the better discovery of the truth, and more speedy obtaining the end of such suits' it was provided that the suitors and the county clerk could examine the parties on oath.[85]

There is controversy over whether the 1846 Act, which established the new county court system, created a new court or revived an old one.[86] In whichever way the movement from one system to another is viewed, there was nothing controversial about section 83 of the 1846 Act, which merely preserved for the parties rights to testify that had already been widely exercised. What the Act did

[82] *Law Times* 1 (1843), 564–5. See, e.g., Sidney Billing, *A Practical Treatise on the Law of Awards and Arbitrations, with Forms of Pleading, Submissions, and Awards* (London, 1845).
[83] See the lists set out in schedules (A) and (B) of the 1846 Act, which established the County Courts (9 & 10 Vict c 95).
[84] See, generally, W. H. D. Winder, 'The Courts of Requests', *Law Quarterly Review* 52 (1936), 369–94.
[85] 23 George 2 c 33 s 1. By s 3 the suitors were those qualified to serve on juries at nisi prius trials in the King's Bench, Common Pleas and Exchequer at Westminster. By s 13 the county clerks were to be barristers of at least three years' standing.
[86] Harry Smith, 'The Resurgent County Court in Victorian Britain', *American Journal of Legal History* 13 (1969), 126–7.

do was to provide, through the new and more efficient system of courts, wider opportunities for such testimony to be given, thereby emphasising still more the disadvantage of the superior courts of common law.

This was not ignored by professional opinion. In 1849, the writer of a leading article in the *Law Times* stated that the new courts had 'taught some lessons by which, if the Superior courts do not speedily profit, they will find their business continuing to decline, and if an optional jurisdiction be given to the former, that of the latter will, ere long, be reduced to the smallest span'. The exclusion of the parties and their spouses from giving evidence in the superior courts was marked out for particular disapproval: 'The consequence of this absurd and irrational exclusion is the continual failure of justice.' In the writer's opinion, it was the power to examine parties that, more than anything else, had given satisfaction in the county courts.[87]

To conclude: it is probable that some features of Bentham's critique had a part to play in achieving the extension of competency in 1851. But Bentham's was not the only influence and need not have been the main one. These reforms could also have developed naturally from existing institutions and earlier precedent: the competency of parties in tribunals outside the superior Common Law courts, and the inroad into incompetency from interest already made in 1843.

---

[87] *Law Times* 13 (1849), 148. Similar arguments appeared in *Law Times* 13 (1849), 198 and in vol. 17 (1851), 38. See also a leading article in *The Times*, 21 November 1850.

5

THE INCOMPETENCY OF THE ACCUSED

The final step in removing witness disqualifications based on interest was taken with the grant of competency to all accused persons by the Criminal Evidence Act 1898. The possibility of this reform had first been referred to in Parliament forty years before. In this chapter I describe how and why the reform was ultimately achieved. The first section examines the extent to which accused persons had a right to silence in the early nineteenth century. There follows a summary of Bentham's critique of the right to silence and of the law that made the accused incompetent as a witness. The third section outlines the various moves towards reform made during the period 1858–98, and the last section examines the factors that led to the extension of competency to the accused.

THE RIGHT TO SILENCE IN THE EARLY NINETEENTH CENTURY

Bentham's critique of the accused's right to silence was developed against a background that had two principal features. The first of these was the detachment of the accused from the proceedings at their own trial by jury. Although in the eighteenth century it had been customary for the trial judge to question the accused informally, without administering an oath, that practice had virtually disappeared by 1820 – at least in those increasingly frequent cases where the accused was defended by counsel.[1]

---

[1] See, generally, John H. Langbein, 'The Historical Origins of the Privilege against Self-Incrimination at Common Law', *Michigan Law Review* 92 (1994), 1047–85.

The second feature was the increasing official encouragement to persons accused of felony to remain silent during the pre-trial investigation before a magistrate. Magistrates were bound to examine a prisoner suspected of felony, but this duty was a creature of statute and seems to have been regarded as contrary to the spirit of the common law. The point was made in the revised edition, published in 1614, of Lambarde's *Eirenarcha*, a work dealing with the duties of justices of the peace. The writer referred to the statute of Philip and Mary,[2] which had provided that where a person arrested for felony was brought before a justice of the peace, the justice should take the examination of the prisoner and the information of those bringing them, and put the same in writing. The writer added:

Here you may see (if I be not deceived) when the examination of a Felon began first to be warranted amongst us. For at the common Law, *Nemo tenebatur prodere seipsum*, and then his fault was not to be wrong [*sic*] out of himself but rather to be discovered by other means and men.[3]

Blackstone made the same point, quoting *Eirenarcha*, in his *Commentaries.*[4] A statutory provision similar to that of the statute of Philip and Mary was enacted in a consolidating Act of 1826 that dealt with criminal law.[5] This provision was varied in 1848, but the variation was made in order to recognise what had come to be existing practice; it was not an attempt by Parliament to introduce something new.[6] The 1848 statute provided that after the examination of all the prosecution witnesses, the justice should read the depositions to the accused, and should then say to them these words, or words to the like effect:

Having heard the Evidence, do you wish to say anything in answer to the Charge? You are not obliged to say anything unless you desire to do so,

---

[2] 2 & 3 Phil & Mar c 10 (1555). A statute in the previous year had already imposed the duty on justices before bailing accused persons (1 & 2 Phil & Mar c 13). The 1555 statute extended this duty to cases where the accused was not bailed but committed (Theodore F. T. Plucknett, *A Concise History of the Common Law*, 5th edn (London, 1956), p. 432). See, generally, John H. Langbein, *Prosecuting Crime in the Renaissance: England, Germany, France* (Cambridge, Mass., 1974), pp. 5–125.

[3] William Lambarde, *Eirenarcha*, rev. edn (London, 1614), Bk. II, ch. 7.

[4] Sir William Blackstone, *Commentaries on the Laws of England*, ed. Edward Christian, 15th edn (London, 1809), vol. IV, p. 296.

[5] 7 George IV c 64 s 1.

[6] 11 & 12 Vict c 42 s 18. See the speech of Sir John Jervis AG: *Parl. Deb.*, 3rd series, xcvi, 4–7 (3 February 1848).

but whatever you say will be taken down in Writing, and may be given in Evidence against you upon your Trial.

It was clear that while the witnesses were to be examined on oath, the accused was not to be sworn.[7] One reason for this was probably to ensure the voluntariness of any statement made by the accused.[8] So strong was the prohibition against administering an oath to the accused, that even where an examination *appeared* from its preliminary form of words to have been taken on oath, it was held to be inadmissible at trial, and no evidence was permitted to prove that an oath had not in fact been administered.[9] The fact that voluntariness was thought important enough to be preserved in this way implies a corresponding belief in a right to remain silent.

The decision of Richards LCB in *R* v. *Wilson* (1817)[10] carried the protection of the accused further. In this case the prisoner had been indicted for uttering forged notes, knowing them to have been forged. The crucial question was his knowledge. The principal witness for the Crown was an accomplice. To confirm his evidence, prosecuting counsel wished to produce the examination of the prisoner by the magistrate who had committed him for trial. He argued that the examination was not tendered as a confession, 'but as containing the facts which appeared upon the prisoner's examination, confirmatory of the testimony of the accomplice'. The magistrate was questioned and said that he had held out no hopes or inducements and had employed no threats, but that he had examined the prisoner at a considerable extent, in the same manner as he was accustomed to examine a witness. No oath had been administered. Richards LCB held that the examination could not be read.

An examination of itself imposes an obligation to speak the truth. If a prisoner will confess, let him do so voluntarily. Ask him what he has to say[.] But it is irregular in a magistrate to examine a prisoner in the same manner as a witness is examined.[11]

---

[7] Richard Burn, *The Justice of the Peace and Parish Officer*, 14th edn (London, 1780), vol. I, p. 537.
[8] See the discussion below of *R* v. *Wilson* (1817) 1 Holt 597. See also Langbein, 'Privilege against Self-Incrimination', 1079, n. 142.
[9] *R* v. *Smith & Hornage* (1816) 1 Stark 242.
[10] 1 Holt 597.   [11] Ibid.

Other judges did not go so far as this. In *R* v. *Ellis* (1826),[12] counsel for the accused cited the decision of Richards LCB in support of an argument to exclude an examination that had been conducted in similar circumstances. Littledale J referred to a decision of Holroyd J to the contrary and held the evidence to be admissible in principle. But he then suggested to prosecuting counsel that, as the prisoner had been refused professional assistance before the magistrate, the case should not be further pressed. Prosecuting counsel assented and the prisoner was acquitted.

R v. *Green & Others* (1832)[13] shows clearly that well before the 1848 statute the accused had in practice a right to silence before the magistrate. The case concerned an indictment for burglary. Two of the prisoners had made statements before the committing magistrates. The magistrates' clerk stated at trial that before the prisoners had said anything they had not only been told that they must not expect any favour from confessing, but that the magistrates had actually dissuaded them from confessing. Gurney B said that they should not have been dissuaded 'because that is shutting up one of the sources of justice', but he also made the point that it ought to be left entirely to the prisoner whether to make any statement or not.

The fixed practice before the 1848 Act is shown in the first edition of Archbold's *Justice of the Peace*, published in 1840:

When the magistrate asks a prisoner whether he has any thing to say in his defence, he should in fairness, at the same time, state to him that he is not to expect any favour from confessing, but that all he says will be taken down, and read in evidence against him at his trial; also, if any threat have previously been holden out to him, the magistrate ought to caution him not to be influenced by it, after which, it should be left entirely to the prisoner's own discretion, whether he will make any statement or not; he should not be pressed to do so, nor dissuaded from doing it.[14]

In his comment on the decision in *R* v. *Ellis*,[15] the author wrote that in strictness a confession obtained by means of questions from the magistrate could be used against a prisoner at the trial, but, he added, 'such a mode of obtaining it is not very commendable, and should be avoided'.

[12] Ry & Mood 432.   [13] 5 Car & P 312.
[14] J. F. Archbold, *The Justice of the Peace, and Parish Officer* (London, 1840), vol. I, p. 233.
[15] See n. 12.

In this way the magistrate's original statutory obligation to take an examination of the accused was substantially weakened. For some decades before the 1840s, the practice surrounding the examination of a suspected felon by the justices had been reflecting a tension felt to exist between the words of the statute and the common law principle referred to by Lambarde and Blackstone. While it could not be said that a right to silence in these circumstances existed by virtue of the strict law, such a right was recognised in practice. It was therefore in a context where in practice the accused was encouraged to be silent before his trial and by law compelled to be silent during it that Bentham developed his critique.

BENTHAM'S CRITIQUE

Bentham aimed at abolition of the rule making accused persons incompetent to testify. It is clear from his writings that, once given a competent accused, he would have permitted no right to avoid questioning. The primary argument that supported Bentham's contention that the accused should be competent and compellable was based on his view of the function of procedural law. This was assisted by an argument that the existing law gave rise to various mischiefs, and by a refutation of the arguments employed by supporters of the existing law.

As has already been said, Bentham divided law into two main classes: substantive law; and adjective, or procedural, law. Adjective law he subdivided into punitory laws, which gave directions to an official to apply sanctions, and rules of adjudication. The latter included 'means of coming to the truth', of which the law of evidence was a part. The particular function of evidence law was the achieving of 'rectitude of decision'; that is to say, getting at the facts so that the substantive law could be accurately applied.[16] In order to get at the facts, a system of judicial procedure needed two aims. The first was to enable the whole of the existing stock of evidence to be presented if demanded for a judicial purpose. The

---

[16] Cf. Michael A. Menlowe, 'Bentham, Self-Incrimination and the Law of Evidence', *Law Quarterly Review* 104 (1988), 286, 287–9.

second was to ensure that such evidence should be presented in the most trustworthy shape possible.

In relation to the first of these aims, Bentham argued that:

Non-compulsion is negative exclusion. To refuse to take, at the instance of the party having need of the evidence, the steps necessary to cause its being forthcoming, is to exclude it.[17]

The implication was that an accused should be not only competent, but compellable. Bentham insisted that the advantage of interrogation was its propensity to clear up doubts.

On both sides, its property is to clear up all doubts – all doubts produced or left by other evidence – doubts which without its aid can never be cleared up. Possessing this property, it is not less favourable to innocence than adverse to delinquency. All suspected persons who are not guilty, court it; none but the guilty shrink from it.[18]

Interrogation could, for example, be used to supply the deficiencies of real evidence. Thus it could be the case that an apparently incriminating article had been placed by someone other than the accused in the place where it was found.

On this, as on all other occasions, the way to know is to inquire: a proposition that from the beginning of the world to the present day has never been a secret to any human being, unless it be to English lawyers. And of whom to inquire? Of whom, but of the one person in the world, who, if the fact be in existence, cannot fail to know of it? – the one person in the world, in comparison with whose evidence, every other imaginable species of evidence, direct or circumstantial (except in so far as this naturally best evidence happens, by the force of sinister motives, to be driven into mendacity), is a miserable makeshift.[19]

An obvious inference could be made from refusal to submit to interrogation:

From the known principles of human nature, according to a course of observation common to all mankind – according to the result of a set of observations, which it can scarce happen to a man to have arrived at man's estate without having had frequent occasion to make – between delinquency on the one hand, and silence under inquiry on the other, there is a manifest connexion; a connexion too natural not to be constant and inseparable.[20]

Bentham thought that the incompetency of the accused gave rise to a number of mischiefs. It led to the exclusion of the best

[17] *Rationale of Judicial Evidence* in *Works*, vol. VII, p. 562.
[18] Ibid., p. 39.   [19] Ibid., p. 14.   [20] Ibid., pp. 445–6.

possible evidence and made misdecision more likely; in addition, it encouraged recourse to bad evidence of various sorts to take the place of the good evidence that had been excluded. An example was the supposed confession of the accused, delivered through the medium of hearsay and without the opportunity of explanation, completion, or correction. It led to the increase of delay, vexation, and expense, because it was likely to be necessary to look to a variety of sources for supplementary evidence. Finally, the rule had a pernicious effect on 'the moral branch of the public mind'. For example, in order to punish one member of a group of malefactors it became necessary to nourish and encourage another in order to obtain his testimony against his former partner in crime.[21]

Bentham condemned the arguments used to support exclusion as 'groundless and utterly indefensible prejudices – conceits, founded not on the principle of utility, but solely on the principle of caprice'.[22] He identified five such arguments. The first consisted in assuming the propriety of the rule, so that opponents might be led to believe that their ideas were rejected by all reasonable people. Secondly, there was 'the old woman's reason', the essence of which was that it was hard upon a man to be obliged to incriminate himself. But, Bentham retorted, it was hard for a man to do anything he did not like, especially if it led to his being punished. He also pointed out that the punishment itself could be reduced if its incidence were to be made more certain by making the accused liable to examination.

The third argument, 'the fox-hunter's reason', consisted in introducing into legal procedure an idea of fairness in the sense used by sportsmen. It was only fair that a fox should have an opportunity to run a certain distance in order to provide a chance of escape, and it was not permissible to destroy the fox by the more certain method of shooting. Bentham conceded that in the sporting code these rules were rational because they were appropriate to the object of sport, namely, amusement. But, as things stood, the same principle was applied to the administration of justice. 'Every villain let loose one term, that he may bring custom the next, is a sort of bag-fox, nursed by the common hunt at Westminster ... To different persons, both a fox and a criminal

[21] Ibid., pp. 446–9.   [22] Ibid., p. 24.

have their use: the use of a fox is to be hunted; the use of a criminal is to be tried.'

Bentham also identified arguments in favour of silence, which relied for their force on confounding interrogation with torture. But he pointed out that putting a question to a defendant was no more an act of torture than if they were an ordinary witness. Finally, there were arguments that referred to unpopular institutions. These depended for their force on establishing a link between the proposed reform and earlier unpopular institutions, such as the Court of Star Chamber or the Court of High Commission. Bentham replied that it might as well be argued that no court should ever sit in a room that had stars painted on the ceiling, or that judges ought not to be appointed by a commission. Because some things done by these courts were bad, it did not follow that everything was.[23]

Bentham's critique must be assessed in its context. Pre-trial investigations in the 1820s were carried out by justices of the peace,[24] and Bentham's concern was therefore entirely with the exercise of a right to silence in proceedings that may have been informal but were always controlled by a judicial officer. In this connection, it is important to remember the reliance Bentham placed on publicity as a protection against official abuse of power. In particular, he believed that if judicial work was done in public, the judges' care for their own reputations would operate as a perpetual check on their actions.[25] The risk to an innocent person from compulsory interrogation would therefore be small, since bullying or otherwise unfair methods of questioning would be eliminated by exposure to publicity. Nevertheless, Bentham appears to have been willing that the right to silence should be abolished before the provisions he had devised for the protection of suspected or accused persons were put in place. He took the view that a balance had to be struck between the interests of innocent suspects and those of other innocents who would suffer if

---

[23] Ibid., pp. 451–5.

[24] See above, pp. 123–7, 'The Right to Silence in the Early Nineteenth Century'.

[25] *Judicial Establishment*, in *Works*, vol. IV, p. 316; *Principles of Judicial Procedure*, in *Works*, vol. II, p. 21. See also Postema, *Bentham and the Common Law Tradition*, pp. 364–73.

the legal system continued to provide ineffective remedies against crime.[26]

Because Bentham attached great importance to rectitude of decision, there was, in principle, no reason why evidence should not be excluded in pursuit of this particular utility. But it does not appear that he thought of the exclusion of evidence to avoid misdecision as a realistic possibility. Even when writing about false confessions, he could not come to terms completely with his subject. 'To a first view, nothing can be more paradoxical than the case of a man's having recourse to falsehood for the purpose of subjecting himself, perhaps to the punishment, at least to the disrepute, attached to a supposed act of delinquency which in fact he has not committed.'[27] In any case, he stated, false confessions were most rare; at least, he hoped they were. 'The case of false confession is a case which, in the present state of jurisprudence among civilized nations ... has seldom been exemplified: so at least one wishes and hopes to be able to believe, for the honour of governments and of human nature.' The only instance in which it had been in any degree frequent was in cases of witchcraft.[28]

Bentham does not appear to have looked for any safeguard against false confessions beyond a more careful interrogation. Thus, in respect of all material facts, especially the act constituting the physical part of the offence, time and place ought to be specified so that any falsity might appear when the details of the confession were set beside other inconsistent evidence. The idea that a confession based on hope or fear should be rejected was thought by Bentham to be absurd.

Accused or suspected of a crime, guilty or innocent, – what but hope or fear should induce a man to speak? Guilty, in particular, what but hope or fear should induce a man to confess? Confession without hope or fear, is an action without a motive, an effect without a cause.

Bentham emphasised that what there was of reason in the principle amounted simply to the need for a judge examining an accused to be on his guard against 'the sinister inducements, to the action of which a man in such a situation is exposed'.[29]

---

[26] Hart, 'The Demystification of the Law', in *Essays on Bentham*, p. 37 n. 52; William Twining, 'The Way of the Baffled Medic', in *Rethinking Evidence*, p. 339 n. 25.

[27] *Rationale of Judicial Evidence* in *Works*, vol. VII, p. 34.

[28] Ibid., p. 37.   [29] Ibid., pp. 36–7.

The story of how accused persons became competent witnesses in their own defence falls into three parts. The first, covering the period from 1858 to 1878, saw unsuccessful attempts to achieve this reform by Lord Brougham and by Vincent Scully, Sir Fitzroy Kelly, and Evelyn Ashley, private members of the House of Commons who had connections with the law.[30] The second period, from 1879 to 1883, saw government attempts to introduce this reform as part of a wider attempt at codification of criminal law and procedure. It soon became clear that the size of the task was too great, and in the third period, from 1884 to 1898, individual government measures to achieve competency for the accused were introduced. These were for some time unsuccessful. At first, this was because of the opposition of Irish Nationalist members; later failures resulted simply from the pressure of parliamentary time.

Private Members' bills: 1858–78

Neither the removal of interest as a bar to testifying in civil cases, nor the extension of competency to civil parties, gave rise immediately to calls for parallel reforms in criminal procedure. The question of accused persons' competency was not raised in Parliament until 1858. In March of that year, Lord Brougham referred to the subject in a debate on the county courts. Having observed that the great objection made to the 1851 Act had been that it would lead to endless perjury, Brougham reminded the House that he had denied this at the time, and claimed that subsequent experience had proved him right. He proposed that the defendant

---

[30] Vincent Scully (1810–71). Called to the Irish Bar, 1833; QC 1849. Liberal member for Cork. Described by Sir John Trelawny as 'a great oddity ... who said he never liked to have any transactions with a person who did not drink his liquor, on the ground that his head was always cool and he was sure to get the upper hand' (*Trelawny Diaries 1858–1865*, p. 215). Sir Fitzroy Kelly (1796–1880). A strong Tory who sat for a number of constituencies and ultimately for the eastern division of Suffolk (1852), which he represented until raised to the Bench. Before that he had held office as Solicitor General and Attorney General. He was an ardent law reformer. Amongst other reforms, he was an early supporter of codification and of a court of criminal appeal. Evelyn Ashley (1836–1907). Called to the Bar, 1863. Member of the Oxford circuit. Magistrate for Dorset. Liberal MP for Poole (1874–80) and the Isle of Wight (1880–5).

in a criminal suit should have the right, if he chose, of being examined on oath, though if he did so he should be subject to cross-examination by the prosecution.[31]

In the same parliamentary session Brougham introduced a bill to allow any persons on trial for treason, felony, or misdemeanour to give evidence on their own behalf. The spouse of the accused was also to be permitted to give evidence for the defence if desirous of doing so. Evidence was to be given on oath, and the accused was to be subject to cross-examination in the same way as any other witness. Clause 5, which extended to civil cases, provided that no witness should be able to refuse to answer a question 'on the Ground that his Answer may degrade him, or may show or tend to show that he has been guilty of any Offence or Misconduct, or that he has done anything which may render him liable to any Penalty, Forfeiture, or Ecclesiastical Censure'. The answer to such a question was not, however, to be admissible against the witness in any other proceedings, except in a prosecution for perjury brought in respect of that answer, and the court's power to stop a question or answer on the ground of irrelevance was affirmed.[32]

In the event, the bill was postponed in deference to the opinion of Lord Campbell, Chief Justice of the Queen's Bench, that the subject ought to be fully discussed by the profession and the public during the recess.[33] Another bill to achieve this purpose was presented by Brougham in 1859.[34] It was given a first reading, but proceeded no further for lack of time.[35] Some judges were thought to favour the adoption of Brougham's measure in a limited form, which would have allowed the accused to give evidence in all cases of misdemeanour where the real prosecutor was called as a witness.[36] In the following year, Brougham introduced a bill that granted a right to testify in cases of misdemeanour only, but it failed for lack of time.[37]

In 1865, separate bills to extend competency to accused persons

---

[31] *The Times*, 19 March 1858, p. 6.
[32] *House of Lords Sessional Papers* 1857–8 (49) IV 373.
[33] *Law Magazine* 5 (1858), 409.
[34] *House of Lords Sessional Papers* 1859, Session 1, (34) II 395.
[35] *Parl. Deb.*, 3rd series, clii, 760–6 (24 February 1859).
[36] *Law Magazine* 7 (1859), 255–6.
[37] *Parl. Deb.*, 3rd series, clix, 1084–5 (28 June 1860).

were introduced in the House of Commons by Vincent Scully and Sir Fitzroy Kelly. Scully's bill contained only two clauses. It provided that the accused and his or her spouse should be competent, but not compellable, in all criminal proceedings. It also provided that a witness taking advantage of this provision should be subject to cross-examination and then compellable to answer any question, notwithstanding that it might tend to criminate the accused.[38] Kelly's bill had similar provisions and also contained clauses affecting evidence in actions instituted in consequence of adultery and for breach of promise of marriage.[39]

In the debate on the second reading of Kelly's bill, its author accepted that the provision to make accused persons competent would produce 'a very great difference of opinion'. He asked that the bill be read a second time without opposition, because it would be necessary to discuss every clause in Committee. He also asked if Scully would be willing to postpone the second reading of his bill, since it dealt with the same subject. Scully agreed to this and Kelly's bill was read without opposition, though Sir Roundell Palmer, the Attorney General, indicated that at present the Government did not favour the proposed changes.[40] Neither bill made any further progress.

On 11 February 1876, Evelyn Ashley introduced a bill in the House of Commons to extend competency to accused persons. This was effected by clauses 3 and 4; by clause 5 such persons were made competent, though not compellable, for a co-accused. Clause 6 provided that evidence was to be on oath, or, where permitted, on affirmation, and was to be subject to cross-examination in the same way as any other evidence. The accused was not to be allowed to refuse to answer a question on the ground that the answer would tend to incriminate them. By clause 10, accused persons were made liable to prosecution for perjury, notwithstanding that they might have been acquitted on the principal charge.[41] The bill was fully debated on the motion for a second reading on 24 May and 26 July 1876. By the second occasion, however, it was clear that too little remained of the parliamentary session for the bill to have time to become law. At the end of the

---

[38] *House of Commons Parliamentary Papers* 1865 (8) I 471.
[39] *House of Commons Parliamentary Papers* 1865 (20) II 469.
[40] *Parl. Deb.*, 3rd series, clxxvii, 939–45 (1 March 1865).
[41] *House of Commons Parliamentary Papers* 1876 (61) I 511.

debate, Ashley therefore withdrew his motion for a second reading.

In 1877, Ashley introduced another bill to make defendants competent in criminal cases, but it proceeded no further than a first reading. The provisions were the same as those contained in the bill of the previous year, with the exception of an additional clause, which provided that the neglect or refusal of an accused person to give evidence should not create any presumption against them, nor should any comment be made upon any such neglect or refusal during trial.[42]

In 1878, Ashley made another attempt at this reform with an identical bill.[43] In the debate on its second reading, the Attorney General, Sir John Holker, announced that the Law Officers intended to introduce a measure on the subject of criminal law, including a code of criminal procedure for indictable offences. It was proposed that this should contain some clauses, the exact nature of which was as yet unsettled, but which would have the effect of carrying out to a great extent the desires of those favouring Ashley's bill. Holker hoped that this latter bill would be referred to a select committee, which might make an extremely valuable report that could be used by the Government when they brought in their measure. Ashley, perhaps unfortunately for the cause of reform, accepted this offer. The House by a majority of 109 voted that the bill be read a second time, and it was then sent to a select committee;[44] it proceeded no further.

Reform within a code: 1879–83

Cairns and Holker, Disraeli's Lord Chancellor and Attorney General, had been impressed by J. F. Stephen's work on a Homicide Bill (1874) and by his *Digest of Criminal Law* (1877). Therefore, it was to Stephen that they turned when they wished a draft code of criminal law to be prepared. It was intended that Stephen's completed code should subsequently be revised by a Royal Commission, of which Stephen himself was to be a member, the others being Lord Blackburn, Lord Justice Lush, and an Irish judge, Mr Justice Barry.

[42] *House of Commons Parliamentary Papers* 1877 (76) I 481.
[43] *House of Commons Parliamentary Papers* 1878 (23) II 243.
[44] *Parl. Deb.*, 3rd series, ccxxxvii, 657–88 (30 January 1878).

Section 368 of Stephen's unrevised Code[45] attempted to involve the accused more closely in the proceedings. It provided that at the close of the prosecution case the court should inform defendants that they might make any statement as to the charge against them, and that if they did so they would be questioned on it. Defendants might then either make a statement or, if defended by counsel, be examined in chief. Subsequent cross-examination was to be confined to matters in issue and was not to be directed to matters affecting a defendant's credit or character. Section 368 was silent as to the operation of the privilege against self-incrimination. Stephen may have taken the view that, since this was a witness's privilege, it could not be claimed by the defendant: the section provided that the defendant should not be sworn as a witness or be punished for making false statements.

The Royal Commission appointed to revise Stephen's code reported in 1879.[46] Section 523 of the draft code, which formed an appendix to the Report, made the accused and the accused's spouse competent witnesses for the defence. The Commissioners were divided over whether it should be enacted. They thought, however, that if the accused were to give evidence on their own behalf, they should do so on the same conditions as other witnesses, subject to some special protection in regard to cross-examination.[47] Section 523 departed significantly from the corresponding provision in Stephen's original code. After making the accused and his or her spouse competent for the defence in trials on indictment, the section provided that the prosecution should not be able to call them as witnesses, but that if they gave evidence they could be cross-examined like any other witness. They were thus potentially exposed to cross-examination as to credit, but a discretion was given to the judge to limit cross-examination to such an extent as he thought proper. Thus the Commission favoured making the accused more like an ordinary witness than had been the case in Stephen's original proposals.

On 3 April 1879, the Attorney General, Sir John Holker, moved for leave to bring in the bill prepared by the Commission.

---

[45] Contained in the Criminal Code (Indictable Offences) Bill 1878: *House of Commons Parliamentary Papers* 1878 (178) II 5.
[46] *Report of the Royal Commission Appointed to Consider the Law Relating to Indictable Offences* (1879) [C. 2345].
[47] Ibid., p. 37.

On the subject of clause 523, he said that his own mind was almost evenly balanced. He asked for full discussion, and said that he would consent to the withdrawal of the provision if feeling was adverse to its introduction.

For upwards of four hours, there followed what Sir Henry James[48] called 'a rambling discussion', which may have been caused by the size of the legislative task and the realisation that it was unlikely to be accomplished. A bill that not only consolidated but also attempted to improve a large branch of the law could not hope to get by without much debate; yet, like any ordinary bill, it had to be passed by the end of the session in which it was introduced. If it failed in this it was lost, and the whole legislative process had to be begun again in the next session. This was the fate of the 1879 bill. It was given a second reading on 5 May 1879, the general feeling being in favour of codification and of passing the bill, subject to discussion of controversial changes in committee. But in answer to a question on 30 June, the Attorney General said that, owing to the condition of public business, it might not be possible to proceed with the code in that session, and this was confirmed in his answer to another question on 3 July.[49]

Another bill to provide a criminal code[50] was introduced by the Attorney General on 6 February 1880. Clause 471 contained in substance the same provisions for making the accused competent as had clause 523 of the bill introduced in the previous session. In accordance with the government's wish, the new bill was read a second time on 23 February 1880 with only a short debate, the intention being that full consideration would be given to it by a select committee with the power to divide the measure into a number of bills, so that if time ran out at least some of the provisions might become law. Despite these intentions, however, no further progress was made. Parliament had dealt successfully with bulky legislation before; for example, the Merchant Shipping Bill of 1854. But, as Sir Henry James pointed out, that bill had

---

[48] (1828–1911). Called to the Bar, 1852. Entered Parliament as a Liberal in 1869; QC 1869; Solicitor General, October 1873; Attorney General, November 1873–February 1874, April 1880–June 1885. From 1895 to 1902, he was Chancellor of the Duchy of Lancaster, having been created 1st Baron James of Hereford.

[49] *Parl. Deb.*, 3rd series, ccxlv, 310–47 (3 April 1879); 1750–3 (5 May 1879); ccxlvii, 953 (30 June 1879); 1281 (3 July 1879).

[50] *House of Commons Parliamentary Papers* 1880 (2) II 1.

dealt with only one subject, while this bill dealt with many subjects of great political and social importance.[51]

As well as the government bill, the session also saw a bill for a criminal code introduced by private members. Brought in by William Wheelhouse, Mr Serjeant Spinks and Captain Pim, the bill contained provisions as to the accused's competency, which differed substantially from those in the government bill.[52] Clause 337 of this Criminal Code (No. 2) Bill provided that:

> Upon every trial under the provisions of this Code, every accused person shall be competent to be examined in the same manner (subject as hereinafter provided) as any ordinary person, either by or on behalf of the prosecution, or on his own behalf, or on behalf of any person jointly accused with him.

Thus the accused was to be a compellable witness for the prosecution, and perhaps also for a co-accused. Clause 338 provided that when an accused person was examined by the prosecution, the examination might be taken at any time before the close of the evidence for the prosecution. By clause 341, the accused was not in any circumstances to take the oath or affirm before being examined. The clause also gave the accused some measure of protection by providing that they should not be asked any question with a view to impeaching their credit generally. Further, the questions put were in any case to be 'such only as are reasonably calculated to elicit the whole knowledge of the accused in relation to the particular offence then being tried'. Unfortunately, there is no indication of the amount of support that the bill might have had, as it was dropped before a second reading.[53]

The next legislative move was in 1882, when several private members brought in a Criminal Law Amendment Bill, which embodied in great part the recommendations of the Royal Com-

---

[51] *Parl. Deb.*, 3rd series, ccl, 244; 1236–48.
[52] *House of Commons Parliamentary Papers* 1880 (47) II 223. Frederick Lowton Spinks (1816–99) was called to the Bar in 1843. He became a serjeant-at-law in 1862, and was a magistrate for Kent from 1866. A Conservative, he sat for Oldham 1874–80. William Wheelhouse (1821–86) was called to the Bar in 1844. He subsequently joined the Northern circuit and the West Riding and Leeds sessions. Appointed QC in 1877. A Conservative, he sat for Leeds 1868–80. Bedford Clapperton Trevelyan Pim (1826–86). After a naval career, he was called to the Bar in 1873 and became a magistrate for Middlesex. A Conservative, he sat for Gravesend 1874–80.
[53] See under 'Criminal Code (No. 2) Bill' in *Parl. Deb.*, 3rd series, ccli, general index.

mission.[54] Among its provisions was clause 106, which made the accused and the spouse competent for the defence, and followed almost exactly the wording of the corresponding clause in the 1879 bill. In the debate on the second reading, Charles Hopwood, Liberal member for Stockport and one of those who had introduced the bill, noted that in the speech from the throne at the start of the session a bill to give effect to the recommendations of the Royal Commission had been promised, but he hoped that the Attorney General would not attribute want of respect in his proceeding with a measure that, so to speak, had been 'on the stocks' for some time before that announcement.

The Attorney General, Sir Henry James, said that he did not wish to oppose the second reading, but he emphasised that the responsibility for altering the law to such an extent must rest with the Government. He said that he hoped to present a government measure before long, observing that the House had already, by a majority of considerably more than two to one, voted in favour of Evelyn Ashley's bill to allow prisoners to give evidence. He reminded the House that the Law Officer of the late government[55] had voted in support, as he himself had done; since that time he had not heard anything to alter his opinion. He thought it a proposition that would receive the acquiescence of a great majority of the House, and one that would be in accord with public opinion.[56]

The bill received a second reading but was dropped at the committee stage. It is not clear whether this was because a government bill had been promised or because time ran out. In *The Times* a leading article supported the reform, but concluded pessimistically:

Except that England is not as other countries, it might be supposed that, with judgments and parties thus united in recommending a change in the rules of evidence, the change would be at once made. In reality, it may be years before it is accomplished.[57]

In the following year, the Government introduced the Criminal Code (Indictable Offences Procedure), 1883, Bill.[58] Clause 100

[54] *House of Commons Parliamentary Papers* 1882 (15) II 1.
[55] Disraeli's second cabinet, formed in February 1874. It had been succeeded by Gladstone's second cabinet, formed in April 1880.
[56] *Parl. Deb.*, 3rd series, cclxvii, 402–40 (8 March 1882).
[57] *The Times*, 10 March 1882.
[58] *House of Commons Parliamentary Papers* 1883 (8) II 249.

provided for the competency of accused persons and their spouses in trials on indictment and was in virtually the same terms as clause 106 of the 1882 bill, save that clause 100 made no reference to the spouse as witness for someone jointly indicted with the accused.

By now, the many failures to achieve a reform for which there had been substantial support seem to have produced apathy. Edward Clarke, Conservative member for Plymouth, said that he wished he could think that the almost absolute indifference with which the House had treated the question of law reform was an augury that these measures were likely soon to pass into law. But he was afraid it simply meant that there would be a resolution of the House to delegate to committee the consideration of all questions, not only of detail but of principle, connected with the bill. The speech of Sir Henry James, the Attorney General, showed that by then government ministers recognised that it was useless to try to introduce the Code as a whole, because it contained too much material to have any chance of being passed in one session. There was general agreement that it should be introduced in parts, and since the part on procedure was relatively independent from the rest, the Government decided that it should be dealt with first.[59]

But although this bill achieved a second reading, it soon became clear that very little progress could be made in committee. On 26 June 1883, the standing committee reported that it had begun consideration of the bill on 5 June. Since then, the first eleven clauses had been considered. Notice had already been given of 390 amendments to be moved on the remaining 120 clauses. The committee reported that there was no prospect of its being able to consider the remaining clauses, or any substantial proportion of them, so as to allow the bill to be reported to the House at a time that would allow for proper consideration. The committee therefore resolved not to proceed further with its consideration of the bill.[60]

The report of the debate on the second reading shows that Irish

[59] *Parl. Deb.*, 3rd series, cclxxviii, 90–166 (12 April 1883).
[60] *Special Report and Reports on the Criminal Code (Indictable Offences Procedure) Bill, and the Court of Criminal Appeal Bill with the Proceedings of the Standing Committee on Law and Courts of Justice and Legal Procedure. House of Commons Parliamentary Papers* 1883 (225) XI 319, p. 5.

Nationalist members began to intervene and cause delays when the proceedings were about two-thirds under way. Even after the vote that the bill be read a second time it was necessary for there to be an adjourned debate on the motion to commit the bill to the standing committee.[61] It seems likely that Irish Nationalist members, possibly supported by some die-hard opponents of reform, were responsible for adopting delaying tactics in committee. The opposition of Irish Nationalist MPs at Westminster, who wished to exclude Ireland from the scope of legislation extending competency to the accused, began in 1883 and continued for about ten years. By the end of that period it had become clear to both Liberal and Conservative governments that unless Nationalist demands were met, the reform might be put off indefinitely. Attempts to extend such legislation to Ireland then ceased. The opposition of Nationalist MPs arose because they thought that the reform would expose accused persons to an even greater extent than was already the case to a prejudiced judiciary. Nationalist MPs also saw the Westminster debates as an opportunity to attack the entire administration of justice in Ireland. In addition, the proposed reforms had to face the obstructive tactics of the wider campaign by Nationalist MPs to secure home rule for Ireland.[62]

But there may well have been more general opposition to the proposed legislation. *The Times* observed that even with complete freedom from obstruction things could not have moved very fast; what some saw as obstruction might have been 'caution and deliberation which were well warranted by the magnitude and importance of the subject'.[63]

Individual government measures: 1884–98

In 1884, Lord Bramwell presented a short bill to extend competency to the accused.[64] It was passed in the House of Lords, but

---

[61] *Parl. Deb.*, 3rd series, cclxxviii, 332–49 (16 April 1883).
[62] Claire Jackson, 'Irish Political Opposition to the Passage of Criminal Evidence Reform at Westminster, 1883–98', in J. F. McEldowney and Paul O'Higgins, eds., *The Common Law Tradition: Essays in Irish Legal History* (Blackrock, Ireland, 1990), pp. 185–201.
[63] *The Times*, 23 June 1883.
[64] *House of Lords Sessional Papers* 1884 (9) IV 39.

made no further progress. Perhaps prompted by this, a government bill was introduced for this purpose in the House of Commons in 1885, but it too failed to make any progress.[65]

The subject also arose in that year when the Commons were considering the Criminal Law Amendment Bill, which dealt with certain sexual offences. At the committee stage James Picton, Liberal member for Leicester, introduced a provision that extended competence to persons charged under the proposed legislation and to their husbands or wives. In this respect, Picton was following a pattern already set by earlier legislation, which, in creating new offences, had provided that persons charged with those offences should be competent to give evidence in their own defence.[66] The Attorney General, Sir Richard Webster, said that it was right in some cases to allow the accused to give evidence; of all classes of cases, that dealt with in this bill (i.e. sex offences) was one in which the defendant should be able to do so. The clause was agreed to after a short debate.[67]

Another government bill was introduced in the Commons in 1888.[68] Based on the bill introduced in the Lords in 1884, clause 1 provided as follows:

Where a person is charged with an offence, whether solely or with others, the person charged and his wife or her husband, as the case may be, may be called as a witness at any stage of the proceedings at which witnesses may be called, other than an inquiry before a grand jury.
  Provided as follows:
  (1) The person charged shall not be called as a witness without his consent:

---

[65] *House of Commons Parliamentary Papers* 1884–5 (65) II 363.
[66] By the Master and Servant Act 1867, parties to a contract of service and their spouses were competent witnesses on the hearing of an information or complaint. The Licensing Act 1872 provided by s 51 that offences under the Act could be prosecuted in the manner provided by the Summary Jurisdiction Act 1848, s 14 of which allowed the defendant to give evidence on the hearing of an information or complaint. By s 11 of the Conspiracy and Protection of Property Act 1875, on the hearing of any indictment or information for offences involving breach of contract contained in ss 4, 5 and 6 the parties to the contract and their spouses were made competent to give evidence. The Explosives Act 1875, in certain circumstances, placed the onus of establishing a defence on the occupier of a factory and in such cases the defendant by s 87 was made a competent witness. By s 4 of the Merchant Shipping Act 1876 the onus of proving a defence on a charge of sending a ship to sea in an unseaworthy state was placed on the defendant, who was also made a competent witness.
[67] *Parl. Deb.*, 3rd series, ccc, 905–11 (3 August 1885).
[68] *House of Commons Parliamentary Papers* 1888 (132) II 407.

(2) The wife or husband of the person charged shall not be called as a witness without the consent of that person, except in any case in which such wife or husband might have been compelled to give evidence before the passing of this Act:

(3) A person called as a witness in pursuance of this Act shall not be asked, and if asked, shall not be required to answer, any question tending to show that any person charged has committed or been convicted of any offence other than that wherewith he is then charged, unless either –

(a) the proof that the person charged has committed or been convicted of that other offence is admissible evidence to show that he is guilty of the offence wherewith he is then charged; or,

(b) the person charged has given evidence of good character.

The bill was presented and read for a first time on 21 February 1888. On 22 March, the Attorney General, Sir Richard Webster, moved that it be read a second time. The report of the debate shows that the only major difficulty was the objection of Irish members to the extension of the proposed legislation to their country; in the end, their objections proved fatal. Although the bill was read a second time, its progress in committee came to a halt as the result of Irish members' amendments and it was withdrawn on 15 November 1888.[69]

In 1892, a further bill passed the House of Lords and obtained a first and second reading in the Commons. On 6 May, it was committed to the standing committee on law, but the session ended before any progress could be made.[70] Another bill was introduced in the Lords in 1893. This was passed in that House, but the difficulties it was likely to encounter in the Commons were indicated by Lord Ashbourne, who informed the Lords that there were now some Irish members in the Commons who thought that the reform should not extend to Ireland and would block any bill which contained such a provision, while other Irish members said that they would not permit a bill to pass if Ireland were omitted from it.[71] Between them, these objectors brought progress to a halt, and the bill was withdrawn before its second reading in the Commons. Further bills were introduced in 1894, and in the three

---

[69] *Parl. Deb.*, 3rd series, cccxxiv, 68–148 (22 March 1888); cccxxv, 1564–91 (7 May 1888); 1929–32 (10 May 1888); cccxxx, 1220 (15 November 1888).

[70] *Parl. Deb.*, 4th series, i, 665–9 (18 February 1892).

[71] *Parl. Deb.*, 4th series, x, 188 (16 March 1893).

following years. Because of a mixture of obstruction and lack of
time, none was successful.

The bill containing the reform that would at last become law
was introduced in the House of Lords by the Lord Chancellor, the
Earl of Halsbury, in February 1898. This bill received its second
reading in the Lords on 10 March without a division[72] and went
through the remaining stages without opposition. The bill received its first reading in the Commons on 14 March. The debate
on the second reading took place on 25 April. On a division, 230
voted in favour of a second reading and 80 against.[73] The bill
received the royal assent on 12 August 1898.

WHY WERE THE ACCUSED MADE COMPETENT?

During the latter part of the eighteenth and the early nineteenth
centuries, a system of adversary procedure became established in
criminal jury trials that minimised the part played by the accused.
The extension of competency to all accused persons modified this
system and was brought about for a number of reasons. In the first
place, it came to be realised by a substantial body of legal opinion
that the reform was necessary for the protection of the accused.
This need for protection had at first encouraged the silencing of
the accused, but was later seen to require his involvement in the
trial on terms as near as possible to those applying to ordinary
witnesses. The fear of an increase in perjury from this development would at one time have been an obstacle. But the reforms
allowing interested persons to testify in civil cases had weakened
the force of this argument by the time proposals began to be made
in relation to criminal trials and the argument lost even more
significance as the debate proceeded. Adoption of the reform
depended on convincing a majority in Parliament, and significant
numbers of the legal profession, that no radical alterations to the
criminal process were involved. Supporters of the proposal were
in time able to allay many such anxieties and to present the reform
as an extension of earlier developments rather than a departure
from traditional ways. The reform may have been more readily

[72] *Parl. Deb.*, 4th series, liv, 1170–84 (10 March 1898).
[73] *Parl. Deb.*, 4th series, lvi, 977–1082 (25 April 1898).

made because it accorded with the increased importance attached to individual responsibility that for much of the nineteenth century was a theme both in political theory and in legislation affecting criminal law. Some of the principal arguments employed in favour of the reform had affinities with arguments that Bentham had used, and Benthamite influences can be found in the work of Brougham and of the Law Amendment Society. It is also possible that Bentham's work may have had an indirect part to play through the examples set by American reforms. But any Benthamite influence there might have been was exerted in a much diluted form. The legislation ultimately passed in 1898 did nothing to further Bentham's ideal of 'domestic' or 'summary' procedure, and the accused's right to silence, which Bentham had notoriously criticised, was not only preserved but emphasised.

Competency as a feature of adversary procedure

A fully fledged model of adversary procedure has been described as one in which the decision-maker remains neutral and passive during the trial of the case, and in which the litigants are responsible for the production and quality of the proof on which the case is to be decided. This encourages the development of a class of skilled advocates, because the difficulties in finding, organising, and presenting persuasive proofs make it likely that inexperienced litigants will need assistance. Such a procedure will provide an elaborate set of rules to govern the trial and the behaviour of the advocates so as to ensure the integrity of the process and speedy resolution of cases.[74] At the beginning of the nineteenth century, the procedural features of criminal trials most closely corresponding to this model were the shift of the task of adducing evidence from judge to counsel, with the consequent relegation of the judge to a more passive role, and the elaboration of rules to govern procedure and the admissibility of evidence.

The beginnings of these developments can be seen in the early decades of the eighteenth century; afterwards there was a gradual

---

[74] Stephan Landsman, 'The Rise of the Contentious Spirit: Adversary Procedure in Eighteenth Century England', *Cornell Law Review* 75 (1990), 497, 500–1. See, generally, Mirjan R. Damaska, *The Faces of Justice and State Authority: a Comparative Approach to the Legal Process* (New Haven, Conn., and London, 1986), ch. 4.

increase, with a heightened momentum during the final decades of
the eighteenth and the early decades of the nineteenth century.[75]
Although the details of how this came about are not entirely clear,
it is now apparent that, in relation to criminal trials,

adversary procedure cannot be defended as part of our historic common
law bequest. The criminal lawyer and the complex procedures that have
grown up to serve him and to contain him are historical upstarts.[76]

In the early part of the eighteenth century, the accused, though
unsworn, took an active role in their own defence in response to
judicial questioning. Exclusionary rules of evidence were virtually
non-existent. The only exceptions were rules concerning competency and certain privileges, which did not include a privilege
against self-incrimination. Appearances by lawyers for either the
prosecution or the defence were rare, and this continued to be the
case until well after the middle of the century. Gradually,
however, from about the mid-1730s, counsel began to appear on
behalf of accused persons. They were permitted at first merely to
examine and cross-examine witnesses. The accused still played a
prominent part; indeed, counsel began by adding strength to the
defence rather than by taking it over completely, and persons
accused of felony had to wait until 1836 for a statute to abolish the
rule that prevented counsel from addressing the jury on their
behalf in a concluding speech.[77] Until that date, the degree of
participation allowed to defence counsel in felony cases had
depended on the discretion of the trial judge, which had been
exercised in a variety of ways from circuit to circuit.[78]

---

[75] John H. Langbein, 'The Criminal Trial before the Lawyers', *University of
Chicago Law Review* 45 (1978), 263–316; 'Shaping the Eighteenth-Century
Criminal Trial: a View from the Ryder Sources', *University of Chicago Law
Review* 50 (1983), 1–136; J. B. Post, 'The Admissibility of Defence Counsel in
English Criminal Procedure', *Journal of Legal History* 5 (1984), 23–32; J. M.
Beattie, 'Scales of Justice: Defence Counsel and the English Criminal Trial in
the Eighteenth and Nineteenth Centuries', *Law and History Review* 9 (1991),
221–67.

[76] Langbein, 'Criminal Trial before the Lawyers', 316.

[77] 6 & 7 Will IV c 114. Counsel had been allowed in treason cases since 1695, and
had always been allowed in cases of misdemeanour (J. H. Baker, *An Introduction
to English Legal History*, 3rd edn (London, 1990), p. 583 n. 50).

[78] J. H. Baker, 'Criminal Courts and Procedure at Common Law 1550–1800', in J.
S. Cockburn, ed., *Crime in England 1550–1800* (London, 1977), pp. 15, 37.
Hawkins justified the rule on the ground that 'it requires no manner of skill to
make a plain and honest defence, which in cases of this kind is always the best'
(William Hawkins, *A Treatise of the Pleas of the Crown; or a System of the*

Nevertheless, defendants were increasingly taking a back seat in proceedings, and so, compared with their position during much of the eighteenth century, were judges. A French visitor to this country, named Cottu, described what he had seen on a tour of the Northern Circuit in about 1820 as the guest of Bench and Bar. His impression was that the accused did so little in his own defence that 'his hat stuck on a pole might without inconvenience be his substitute at the trial'.[79] The judge, who was 'almost a stranger' to what was going on, took notes of the evidence. Sometimes the judge asked questions of a witness, but his object was 'more to obtain an explanation of the witness's depositions, than to establish any additional circumstances against the prisoner'. At the end of each deposition the prisoner was told to put to the witness whatever questions he pleased. Neither the counsel for the prosecution nor for the defence had a right to comment on the evidence. According to Cottu, prisoners were generally represented by counsel in the country, but very rarely in London.[80] In summing up, the judge commented very little and generally simply read the notes that he had made during the trial, 'without attempting to disguise their dryness by pompous reflections, applicable or not to the subject'. Cottu observed a marked difference between the position of the accused in English and French trials. In England,

[p]ublic interest is not excited by the countenance of the prisoner, who is placed with his back to the spectators; nor by the unfolding of the proofs, nor by the prisoner's resistance, nor by the judge's exertions to discover the truth. There is no contest between the plaintiff and the defendant; and the latter never offers any thing more than the spectacle of a man who seems careless about the issue of the trial, and leaves his life to be disputed between the prosecutor's counsel and his own. Neither the sound of his voice becoming more faint and tremulous with the accumulating mass of proofs against him; nor the still increasing ghastliness of his countenance, nor the sweat which stands upon his forehead, nor the convincing silence of guilt, laid bare and forced to yield, call forth the passions of the by-

---

Principal Matters Relating to that Subject, Digested under Proper Heads, ed. Thomas Leach, 7th edn (London, 1795), vol. IV, p. 365).

[79] Charles Cottu, *On the Administration of Criminal Justice in England; and the Spirit of the English Government*, trans. from the French, (London, 1822), p. 105. J. M. Beattie found that at the Old Bailey in 1800 something like seven out of ten defendants, including many on capital charges, had no counsel to assist them, and that for the whole of the eighteenth century the vast majority of prisoners at Surrey Assizes made their own defence (J. M. Beattie, *Crime and the Courts in England 1660–1800* (Oxford, 1986), p. 375).

[80] Cottu, *Administration of Criminal Justice in England*, pp. 88–9.

standers, and summon from their hearts pity, horror, vengeance, and all those vehement feelings produced by our trials. In England, all is calm and tranquil: counsel, jury, judges, the public, nay the prisoner himself, whom no one apprizes of his danger, and the overwhelming strength of the evidence.[81]

The increasing role of counsel in criminal trials was reflected in a development in law reporting, which extended to ordinary criminal trials only with the nisi prius reports of the late eighteenth century.[82]

The initial impetus towards these developments may have been judicial awareness of flaws in criminal procedure, especially those associated with the use of accomplices who had volunteered evidence for the Crown in hope of a pardon.[83] Until the middle of the nineteenth century, a system of rewards, offered by the government, local authorities, and by private organisations and individuals was the chief means of discovering and convicting offenders. Many beneficiaries were themselves criminals who took money or pardons to betray their accomplices. Inevitably, the prospect of reward led to perjury and the conviction of the innocent. But the evidence of police officers might be no more reliable than that of accomplices. Their basic pay was poor, and they were allowed to claim rewards offered for the detection and conviction of offenders. Entrapment of persons by thief-takers into the commission of crimes had been a cause of anxiety in the eighteenth century. Police officers had not at that time been involved, but they were involved in similar scandals in 1816, which revealed a regular practice of corruption. James Harmer, an attorney who specialised in miscarriages of justice in the early decades of the nineteenth century, encountered conspiracies by police to commit perjury to secure the conviction of persons obnoxious to them. Recent research has shown that all social classes used the criminal law in this period to further personal conflicts, with the result that '[it is] virtually impossible to be sure that even the plainest of cases reported in trial reports ... are not in fact successful conspiracies against innocent men and women'.[84]

[81] Ibid., pp. 105–6.
[82] Cf. Langbein, 'Criminal Trial before the Lawyers', 264.
[83] Langbein, 'Shaping the Eighteenth-Century Criminal Trial', 132–4.
[84] D. Hay and F. Snyder, eds., *Policing and Prosecution in Britain, 1750–1850* (Oxford, 1989), pp. 47–9, 344, 380–4. For Harmer, see *Dictionary of National*

But the principal reason why adversary procedure developed in criminal trials was probably a population explosion at the Bar, which led to pressure by counsel for participation in criminal trials. The *Law List* for the period 1785–1840 showed figures for practising barristers as follows:[85]

```
1785 ...  379
1790 ...  424
1800 ...  577
1810 ...  708
1820 ...  840
1830 ... 1129
1840 ... 1835
```

This had a corresponding impact on the circuits. In 1785, a total of 133 barristers belonged to the six English circuits; by 1820, there were 319, and by 1860, there were 626. In the 1850s, those attempting to practise at the Bar had increased to such an extent that there was a sharp fall in the numbers of new entrants.[86]

The expansion of the practising Bar was observed by John Payne Collier, who published under a pseudonym a series of articles about the Bench and Bar, which were re-published in collected form in 1819.[87] He noted that 'the Barristers in Westminster Hall appear to have multiplied so rapidly within the last ten or fifteen years, that in none of the Courts are the seats

---

Biography, and V. A. C. Gatrell, *The Hanging Tree: Execution and the English People 1770–1868* (Oxford, 1994), pp. 435–8.

[85] Daniel Duman, 'Pathway to Professionalism: The English Bar in the Eighteenth and Nineteenth Centuries', *Journal of Social History* (1980), 615–28. From 1841, the figures are less easy to interpret; in that year the *Law List* began to include the names of most newly called barristers, whether practising or not (ibid., 627 n. 21). [86] Ibid., 619–21.

[87] Amicus Curiae [Collier], *Criticisms on the Bar; Including Strictures on the Principal Counsel Practising in the Courts of King's Bench, Common Pleas, Chancery and Exchequer* (London, 1819). J. P. Collier (1789–1883) became a student of the Middle Temple in 1811, and for a time earned a living as a reporter of legal and parliamentary affairs, as a dramatic and literary critic, and as a writer of leading articles. He was not called to the Bar until 1829, and he soon gave up the law in favour of journalism and literature. At a later stage in his life he became involved in the production of literary forgeries, but there seems no reason to doubt the veracity of his much earlier account of life in the courts. See his entry in *Dictionary of National Biography*.

assigned to them sufficient for the purpose'.[88] He also wrote of the way in which a young barrister might develop a practice on circuit, even though he had 'hardly had the opportunity of hearing the sound of his own voice in the metropolis'. On the circuit, relatives and friends could exert influence, and this was 'one of the modern modes by which men creep into business'. He had not known one instance in recent years of a man of talent making his name in a single case. Instead,

individuals have slowly worked their way upwards, first by holding briefs as juniors to a silk gown or a coif, and subsequently by inducing an attorney, with whom they are connected, or with whom they have scraped an acquaintance, to entrust them with a leading brief.[89]

In this atmosphere young barristers would have been eager to break into work wherever they could, and criminal work is likely to have been an attractive developing market.[90]

The common law judges who allowed members of the Bar to take an increasing part in criminal trials cannot have done so in ignorance of what the result was likely to be, for they were already familiar with adversary procedure from the regular appearance of counsel before them in civil proceedings. The extent to which it was possible for counsel to control such proceedings by the early decades of the nineteenth century can be seen from Collier's account. He complained that there were 'few abuses at the Bar more crying at the present moment than the mode in which the examination of witnesses is sometimes conducted', and he referred to 'the manner in which Counsel are permitted to overstep all the bounds of decorum and propriety in their interrogatories'. Female delicacy, he alleged, had been outraged by unfeeling wantonness; innocent witnesses had been bewildered by rapid and purposely complicated questions, and trapped into falsehood.

A clear example of the way in which counsel were taking over the conduct of trials can be found in the career of Sir William

---

[88] Amicus Curiae, *Criticisms on the Bar*, p. 297.
[89] Ibid., p. 136.
[90] Cf. the debates on extending competency to the accused that took place later in the century. On several occasions it was remarked that criminal work, and prosecution work in particular, was often entrusted to young and inexperienced counsel.

Garrow before his appointment to the Bench. Collier referred to Garrow's 'penetrating sagacity' in cross-examination, adding,

and though true it is that he was seldom very scrupulous as to the mode in which he extracted or confounded truth, and though he had as much coarseness and as little feeling as any man who ever practised, yet he seldom without some cause or other broke through the ordinary rules of decorum and politeness . . .

According to Collier, during the time when Garrow had been in practice at the Bar,

he was justly considered unrivalled in this respect, and few men, not even those of the highest rank, ventured to put themselves in competition; but since his elevation to the Bench there is scarcely a single Counsel, however young and inexperienced, who does not think himself warranted in going all lengths, and this frequently without any instructions to warrant an attack upon the character and demeanour of the witness: all flatter themselves that they are peculiarly gifted, and take every opportunity of shewing how much they are deceived in their self-conceited estimate.[91]

The development of adversary procedure in criminal trials accorded with a perceived need for a fairer, more efficient, and so more generally acceptable system of criminal justice. This perception can be seen in the parliamentary debates during the early decades of the nineteenth century on the punishment for felony and on whether persons accused of felony should be allowed to make their defence by counsel.

Evidence given before Sir James Mackintosh's committee, set up in 1819 to consider the punishment for felony, showed the existence of concern, especially in the legal and commercial worlds, about the unfairness and inefficiency of existing laws in failing to maintain proportionality between offences and punishment.[92] The perception of criminal procedure as unfair and inefficient was referred to in a debate in 1826 on a motion for leave to bring in a bill to allow persons prosecuted for felony to make their defence by counsel. James Scarlett remarked that the vast number of acquittals was one of the greatest defects of the law, and that they were frequently caused by the prosecutor's feeling for the unprotected state of the criminal, as a result of which he

---

[91] Amicus Curiae, *Criticisms on the Bar*, pp. 109–12. See also Thomas Hague, *A Letter to William Garrow* (London, ?1810).
[92] *Parl. Deb.*, first series, xl, 1527–33 (6 July 1819).

allowed the accused to escape. Another cause, he said, was the disproportion of punishment to crime. He thought that the introduction of counsel for the defence 'would have a tendency to produce more convictions, and more just and satisfactory convictions, than the present system'. Peel objected that the reform was not publicly called for, but Thomas Denman replied that it was to avoid popular discontent that the measure was suggested.[93]

The evidence to Mackintosh's committee and the speeches in the 1826 debate had highlighted the unfairness of the existing system of criminal law and procedure, its inefficiency, and the need to make the system more generally acceptable so as to secure property and avoid popular discontent. The evidence and the debate also showed the existence of some support from the legal profession for making the criminal system fairer and more efficient, and judges who had the conduct of criminal trials may have shared these views. It was the judges who, in the previous century, had in their discretion allowed counsel some part in criminal trials to ensure a fairer basis for dealing with the evidence of informers.[94] Even if their successors in the early nineteenth century were not prepared to support a statutory basis for the participation of counsel, they may nevertheless have been prepared to use their own discretion to permit counsel to conduct defences in individual cases.

What was needed to make the competency of the accused acceptable was a conviction that it would involve no essential change in the balance of power that had already been struck between judge, counsel, and the accused in a criminal trial. For this reason, the roles of all three were the subject of considerable debate from the 1850s onwards. Initially, the strong opposition that the proposal for reform encountered was based on the fear that it would lead to oppressive conduct on the part of prosecuting counsel and, worse still, to increased and oppressive participation by the judge. The latter fear was made more vivid by the example of what were regarded throughout the nineteenth century as the oppressive judicial practices in continental systems of criminal justice, particularly in the French system.

In 1802, Romilly observed on a visit to France that

---

[93] *Parl. Deb.*, New Series, xv, 589, 622–32 (24 April 1826).
[94] See n. 82.

the judges often endeavour to show their ability and to gain the admiration of the audience by their mode of cross-examining the prisoners. This necessarily makes them, as it were, parties, and gives them an interest to convict. They become advocates against the prisoners; a prisoner who should foil the judge by his mode of answering his questions, particularly if by that means he should raise a laugh from the audience, would have little chance of obtaining a judgment from him in his favour.[95]

Romilly had already noted that if the great object of all trials was to discover the truth, the examination of the accused was an indispensable part of the proceedings; his reference to the behaviour of French judges had been no more than a caveat. But, in 1848, a broader disapproval was shown in a leading article in the *Law Review*. 'We have more than once or twice had occasion to remark', the editor wrote, 'upon the singular want of sound views on the all-important subject of evidence which the proceedings of the French courts hardly ever fail to exhibit'.[96]

What that 'want of sound views' might lead to was described in a leading article in *The Times* in 1856, which commented on the conduct of English criminal trials at quarter sessions and assizes. The writer stated:

There is none of that unseemly and passionate invective which is so copiously displayed on the part of foreign tribunals – none of that unfair and injudicial bullying which betrays an innocent prisoner into self-accusation – none of that boisterous and arrogant inquisition which prides itself on assuming that the imputation and the verification of guilt are the same thing.[97]

In the debate on the bill introduced by Brougham in 1859, Lord Campbell said that what was proposed was 'an utter subversion of the mode in which criminal justice had hitherto been administered in this country'. It would, he claimed, introduce into England a system that worked lamentably in a neighbouring country. He added that he had read of trials in France 'in which the accused parties had been put to a species of moral torture, and had been driven to tell lies in their own defence', although they were innocent of the crimes with which they had been charged.[98]

---

[95] *Memoirs of the Life of Sir Samuel Romilly, Written by Himself; with a Selection from His Correspondence, Edited by His Sons*. (London, 1840; repr. Shannon, 1971), vol. II, pp. 83–4.

[96] *Law Review and Quarterly Journal of British and Foreign Jurisprudence* 9 (1848–9), 149.

[97] *The Times*, 23 August 1856. Cf. the comments of Cottu: n. 81 and text.

[98] *Parl. Deb.*, 3rd series, clii, 762–3 (24 February 1859).

In 1862, a leading article in *The Times* referred to the feeling that the old maxim that no one was bound to criminate himself was in spirit opposed to the examination and cross-examination of the accused. The writer continued:

[T]here is often in the settled usages of England a wisdom which, though it may be foolishness to logicians and theorists, seldom fails to recommend itself to society at large. While the deficiencies of our English system are probably overrated, it is impossible to overrate the evils that might arise from transplanting the French criminal procedure to our own country.

He described how the French judge

often passes bounds which the most unscrupulous English barrister would respect in cross-examining a hostile witness. He browbeats the prisoner, he taunts him, he sneers at him, be reproaches him in a voice trembling with suppressed anger, he distorts his answers, he insinuates motives, he glances at the jury and addresses stage 'asides' to them; he makes claptrap moral observations; in short, he does everything that is least in accordance with our ideal of the English Judge.[99]

The oppression argument could also be employed without any reference to continental practices. For example, when Francis Worsley published a pamphlet in 1861 in response to a paper by J. Pitt Taylor advocating the reform, he said nothing of France but argued that the principle of excluding nothing that could aid the discovery of truth was one that his readers' own ancestors would have used to justify the infliction of torture. He added that Taylor proposed to substitute mental for physical torture. Cross-examination of the prisoner was 'the pressing of a man expressly to confound and convict him when you have him in a dock, a prisoner under charge, and in peril, *in such a situation of body and mind that it is a wrong to your fellow man to examine him adversely at all*'.[100]

---

[99] *The Times*, 29 November 1862. See also *The Times*, 22 November 1862, p. 10; leading article in the *Solicitors' Journal and Reporter* 9 (25 March 1865), 427–8; *Parl. Deb.*, 3rd series, cclxxviii, 93–4: 12 April 1883. It is likely that English criticism was justified: a historian of criminal justice in France recently concluded that 'there is substantial evidence that the meaning and process of criminal justice were debased in nineteenth- and twentieth-century France' (Benjamin F. Martin, *Crime and Criminal Justice under the Third Republic: the Shame of Marianne* (Baton Rouge, La., and London, 1990), p. 273). The defects that were generally perceived in both English and French criminal procedure at about the middle of the century appear vividly in the comic sketch reproduced in the Appendix.

[100] Francis Worsley, *An Examination of Mr Pitt Taylor's Thesis 'On the Expediency*

As late as 1879, the writer of an essay in the *Edinburgh Review* argued that the simplest of all questions that could be put in cross-examination would be one going directly to the guilt of the prisoner. If prisoners denied what was put to them by counsel for the Crown and were later convicted, they could, the writer presumed, be tried for perjury. It was argued that the result of this would be to apply a species of terrorism to the accused to extort a confession. The writer continued:

But, even without putting so crucial a question, counsel in cross-examining will certainly try to entrap the prisoner into difficulties. Sir James Stephen himself somewhere speaks of cross-examination as being almost necessarily unfair, and when applied to such ignorant and terrified persons as most prisoners on their trial prove themselves, though it will perhaps be effective in ensuring convictions, it will be at a sacrifice of that appearance of fair play which has so maintained the public estimation of our criminal courts.[101]

Fears of increased judicial intervention were implicit in criticism of continental practices, and were also the subject of explicit discussion. In 1862, the writer of a leading article in *The Times* thought that if competency were extended to the accused, 'we should soon find a great change in the temper of our judicial functionaries, not excepting even the highest'. Mr Serjeant Simon, in a parliamentary debate in 1876, expressed the fear that scenes of wrangling would develop between judges and prisoners, which would become a public scandal, leading to a lessening of the dignity of the Bench and of public confidence in judicial impartiality.[102] In the same debate, the Attorney General, Sir John Holker, said that confidence in the criminal law could be shaken because a prisoner giving evidence might be examined by the judge. But,

[t]he moment a Judge descended from the calm, serene atmosphere with which he ought to be surrounded, to the region of turmoil and advocacy, that moment he would lose the fairness and impartiality which ought to distinguish all who held the high office of a Judge. It might be that he would do so unconsciously; but, even without desiring to do so, he could

of Passing an Act to Permit Defendants in Criminal Courts and their Wives or Husbands to Testify on Oath' (London, 1861), pp. 3, 7. (Emphasis original.)
[101] [Arthur Elliot] 'The Code of Criminal Law', *Edinburgh Review* 150 (1879), 524, 549–50.
[102] *The Times*, 29 November 1862; *Parl. Deb.*, 3rd series, ccxxx, 1929 (26 July 1876).

not help entering into a contest with the prisoner which would, at least, have the effect of shaking confidence in his perfect impartiality.[103]

There was a fear that some judges might be all too ready to descend into the arena. The bulk of criminal business was not conducted at assizes, and Alfred Wills QC wondered if the public in general realised the atmosphere that prevailed in many courts of quarter sessions. The subject, he said, was a delicate one, and he did not mean to say that there were not such courts where justice was fairly and temperately administered. He continued:

> But I am very sure that there are such courts, of which nothing of the kind can honestly be said; where the prevailing tone is that of a sturdy conviction, perhaps unconsciously but none the less vigorously entertained and acted upon, that the man who appears in the dock must be guilty of the offence charged; where an unhesitating credence is given to all policemen in general and to certain 'active and intelligent' sergeants or inspectors in particular; and where an undefended man, against whom anything like a *prima facie* case is made, has no more chance of escape than a blown fox has with the hounds in full cry at his heels, and all the earth stopped for miles around.[104]

Another fear was that if the law were changed, judges themselves would often have to cross-examine prisoners. Most prosecutions were conducted by inexperienced counsel, in many cases by young men just called to the Bar, while the defence was almost invariably conducted by able and experienced counsel. In a case where prosecuting counsel was at a disadvantage for this reason, a judge would feel bound to intervene in the interests of justice and take over cross-examination where it was being inefficiently carried out.[105]

The difficulties already being experienced by some judges in cases where the prisoner could give evidence were emphasised by Sir Herbert Stephen, the Clerk of Assize for the Northern Circuit. In the 1890s, he wrote that one judge of high eminence in the criminal courts had confessed to him that he was absolutely

---

[103] *Parl. Deb.*, 3rd series, ccxxx, 1937–8.

[104] Alfred Wills QC, 'Should Prisoners Be Examined?', *Nineteenth Century* 3 (1878), 169, 175.

[105] *Parl. Deb.*, 4th series, xlviii, 791–2 (8 April 1897). The experience of Collins LJ in prosecutions under the Criminal Law Amendment Act 1885 had shown him that they were frequently conducted by inexperienced young counsel, and that a crucial question had often to be put by the judge to a prisoner who was giving evidence. See the speech of Alfred Lyttelton: *Parl. Deb.*, 4th series, lvi, 1015 (25 April 1898).

unable to retain impartiality when he 'cross-examined' a prisoner and received answers that were evasive, indirect, or seemingly untruthful.[106] Another judicial opponent of extending competency was the Chairman of Middlesex Quarter Sessions, who wrote that a change in the law that allowed the accused to give evidence would 'throttle and imperil the impartial and even friendly attitude of the English Bench to prisoners'.[107]

While fears of this kind can be found even in the debates immediately preceding the passing of the Criminal Evidence Act, there can also be found from the 1850s onwards a conviction that the English 'tradition' of fairness to the accused was too firmly entrenched to be upset by the proposed change. For example, in 1865, the writer of a leading article in the *Law Times* thought it unlikely that an innocent person would get entangled under cross-examination, as occurred sometimes under the French system of interrogation, because examination by counsel according to English rules of evidence, enforced by the prisoner's counsel under the eye of an English judge, was a very different thing from 'the judicial vivisection by which the Bench displays its cleverness and zeal in France'.[108] Immediately after the passing of the Criminal Evidence Act, Roscoe considered the possibility of excessive judicial questioning in the *Edinburgh Review*, and concluded that, 'the traditions of English justice are so contrary to anything like the continental systems, and the sense of the country is so pronounced on the point, that we are confident that these two factors will prevent any injustice being done to prisoners'.[109]

Another fear was that the balance of power in the criminal trial would be shifted to the detriment of the accused by effectively forcing them to testify, and that this would somehow lead to an

---

[106] Sir Herbert Stephen, *Prisoners on Oath: Present and Future* (London, 1898), pp. 24–6. Stephen also confirmed that criminal business was often entrusted to inexperienced counsel, who frequently omitted to put questions that clearly ought to have been put.

[107] See the speech of Llewellyn Atherley-Jones, quoting the Chairman: *Parl. Deb.*, 4th series, lvi, 1034 (25 April 1898).

[108] *Law Times* 40 (4 March 1865), 213–14.

[109] [E. S. Roscoe] 'The Reform of the Law of Evidence', *Edinburgh Review* 189 (1899), 194, 208. See also *Solicitors' Journal* 2 (1857–8), 430–1; *Parl. Deb.*, 3rd series, clii, 763 (24 February 1859); J. F. Stephen, *A General View of the Criminal Law of England* (London, 1863), pp. 199–200; 'Suggestions as to the Reform of the Criminal Law', *Nineteenth Century* 2 (1877), 756–7.

alteration in the standard, or even the burden, of proof.[110] As with the fear concerning the roles of prosecuting counsel and judge, this was never wholly dispelled before the 1898 legislation. The argument merely became less convincing, either because it was thought that sufficient safeguards could be developed, or because the fears were felt to be outweighed by the need for change in order to remove anomalies and encourage rectitude of decision.

There were some proposals that the accused should be compelled to testify; for example, Brougham suggested this in 1859.[111] In 1872, the Attorney General, Sir John Coleridge, said that if defendants were to be competent, they had to be compellable also. Coleridge asserted that he 'could never be a party to a half-hearted change of the law, which should allow a clever, unscrupulous, cool and practised man to call himself as a witness and tell his story, while in another case a person would not be called whose examination would probably tend to the real investigation of truth'.[112] In 1877, J. F. Stephen expressed the view that prisoners ought in every case to be called upon to tell their own story and to be questioned as to its truth,[113] and the private members' bill presented in 1880 provided for the compulsory examination of the accused.[114]

There was never any chance that these proposals would be acceptable. But some feared that if accused persons were to be made competent, the practical effect would be to compel them to give evidence, because adverse inferences would be drawn from

---

[110] Cf. modern arguments about the interpretation of the Criminal Justice and Public Order Act 1994, s 35; e.g., *per* Mansfield QC, *arg.*, in *R* v. *Cowan* [1995] 3 WLR 881.

[111] *Parl. Deb.*, 3rd series, clii, 761 (24 February 1859).

[112] Coleridge was speaking at the annual congress of the National Association for the Promotion of Social Science (*Law Magazine and Review* (New Series) 1 (1872), 823). This society resulted from the convergence in the mid-1850s of a number of reform movements, one of which was the Law Amendment Society. See, generally, Lawrence Goldman, 'The Social Science Association, 1857–1886: a Context for Mid-Victorian Liberalism', *English Historical Review* 101 (1986), 95–134.

[113] J. F. Stephen, 'Suggestions as to the Reform of the Criminal Law', *Nineteenth Century* 2 (1877), 736, 755.

[114] See n. 52 and text. See also E. D. Lewis, *On the Codification of the Criminal Law of England* (London, 1878); K. J. M. Smith and Stephen White, 'An Episode in Criminal Law Reform through Private Initiative', in Peter Birks, ed., *The Life of the Law*, Proceedings of the Tenth British Legal History Conference Oxford 1991, (London, 1993), pp. 235–56.

their silence. Some reformers had indeed thought it reasonable to draw adverse inferences from silence. In 1858, Brougham said that in the majority of cases where prisoners chose not to give evidence, the reason for silence would be the consciousness of their inability to withstand cross-examination, and in such a case he could see no very great hardship in drawing such an inference.[115] A few years, later J. Pitt Taylor was prepared to have silence interpreted as evidence of guilt on the basis that the law did not favour the prisoner *as a criminal*, but as a person who might *not* be a criminal.[116] In 1898, William Ambrose, Conservative member for the Harrow division of Middlesex, thought that people might be deterred from committing crime by the knowledge that they might be called upon to explain their actions, and that if they failed to respond an inference of guilt could be made against them.[117]

By contrast, there were no doubt many others who felt, as did Lord Campbell in 1859, that what was proposed was 'an utter subversion of the mode in which criminal justice had hitherto been administered in this country', and that if competency were to be extended, prisoners who chose not to give evidence would unjustly be held to 'afford the strongest presumption of their guilt'.[118] Others thought that a compromise might be possible. A

---

[115] *The Times*, 19 March 1858, p. 6. Brougham was not the only person to dismiss the objection as a minor difficulty. The Dublin correspondent of the *Solicitors' Journal* acknowledged that there was some weight in the objection, but added: 'It is to be remembered that prosecutions are generally managed in a somewhat perfunctory manner. Counsel (in crown cases) very humanely and properly forego the use of those minor tricks of advocacy which their professional zeal induces them to make use of so constantly at nisi prius' (*Solicitors' Journal and Reporter* 2 (1857–8), 564–5). A leading article in the *Solicitors' Journal* at about the same time said that the accused need not give evidence if not desirous of doing so, but that there was 'no principle of law or of justice which would entitle him to protection from the natural consequences of a pregnant silence' (*Solicitors' Journal and Reporter* 4 (1859–60), 696–7).

[116] J. Pitt Taylor, 'On the Expediency of Passing an Act to Permit Defendants in Criminal Courts, and their Wives or Husbands, to Testify on Oath', *Solicitors' Journal and Reporter* 5 (1860–1), 363–4. The paper had originally been read at a meeting of the Society for Promoting the Amendment of the Law. See also *Edinburgh Review* 121 (1865), 109, 132–3; *Law Times* 40 (4 March 1865), 213–14; *Parl. Deb.*, 3rd series, ccxxx, 1976 (26 July 1876).

[117] *Parl. Deb.*, 4th series, lvi, 1042 (25 April 1898).

[118] *Parl. Deb.*, 3rd series, clii, 762 (24 February 1859). See also Francis Worsley (n. 100 and text); *The Times* 11 May 1863 (leading article); the speech of Morgan Lloyd (*Parl. Deb.*, 3rd series, cclxxviii, 93–4: 12 April 1883).

judicial warning to the jury was discussed as early as 1862; but the writer of a leading article in *The Times* that discussed this device was not sure that it would remove the danger.[119] In 1876, Russell Gurney, the Recorder of London, allowed that the objection based on inferences that could be drawn from a failure to give evidence was 'a somewhat strong point', but thought that it might to some extent be obviated by obliging the judge to follow the American practice of warning the jury not to draw any inference from an accused's failure to testify.[120]

Any suggestion that the accused should be put under an obligation to testify was likely to arouse fears of some alteration in either the standard or the burden of proof; sometimes the language used in argument clearly suggested that a change would follow. For example, J. F. Stephen wrote in an essay in *Nineteenth Century* that the accused should not be examined as witnesses, but in order, if they should be innocent, to give them an opportunity of proving their innocence by explaining matters apparently suspicious; or, if guilty, in order to prove their guilt by showing that they were unable to provide such explanations.[121]

One of the most persuasive presentations of the argument that extending competency would involve a change in the burden of proof appeared in a leading article in the *Solicitor's Journal* that commented on Sir Fitzroy Kelly's bill.[122] The writer stated that at present an accused person could put before the jury, either through his counsel or in his own unsworn statement, any story he pleased. Unless the sworn evidence contradicted that story, or the story was in itself so absurd as to be unworthy of belief, the judge would direct an acquittal, for it was the duty of the prosecution to disprove with evidence every hypothesis consistent with the innocence of the accused.[123] If the accused stated the truth, the prosecution evidence, unless perjured, would not be inconsistent with what he stated. This put the accused in a better position than if he had been allowed to give evidence without cross-examination.

---

[119] *The Times*, 4 November 1862.
[120] *Parl. Deb.*, 3rd series, ccxxx, 1932–3 (26 July 1876).
[121] Stephen, 'Reform of the Criminal Law', 754.
[122] *Solicitors' Journal and Reporter* 9 (1864–5), 427–8.
[123] The writer may have had in mind the direction of Baron Alderson to the jury in *R* v. *Hodge* (1838) 2 Lew CC 227, 228. For a modern discussion of this way of expressing the standard of proof, see A. A. S. Zuckerman, *The Principles of Criminal Evidence* (Oxford, 1989), pp. 134–40.

An accused person or his counsel might suggest half a dozen inconsistent stories; if any one of these was consistent with the prosecution evidence, the accused would have to be acquitted. However, 'if he were bound to select and swear to any of them, and was to fail in his proof of that, he would be, practically if not theoretically, bound to stand or fall by his own story, and might be convicted . . . not because it was proved that he had committed the offence, but because he had been shown to have told a lie about it'.[124]

Three principal arguments were relied on by reformers in favour of extending competency to all accused persons: it was said that the change was necessary for the discovery of truth; to safeguard the innocent; and to remove obvious anomalies.

When Brougham introduced his bill in 1858, the preamble recited its purpose as being: 'For the better Administration of Justice in Criminal Matters, both as regards the Conviction of Offenders and the Acquittal of Persons not Guilty'.[125] In this way he emphasised the function of the reform as a means of discovering truth. This object was supported by the *Solicitors' Journal*, which commented that, 'our ordinary practice in criminal cases evinces a somewhat puerile timidity, and an almost morbid tendency to strain technicalities to the exclusion of truth, for the protection of delinquents'.[126] Ashley's bill, in 1876, had a very similar preamble,[127] and the value of the reform as a means of discovering truth was a common theme of debates inside and outside Parliament between 1858 and 1898.[128]

---

[124] Thirty years later, Sir Herbert Stephen argued that in cases where the accused could not give evidence the jury asked the correct question: 'Has the Crown proved that he did it?'. But where the accused could give evidence they asked instead: 'Did he do it?' (Sir Herbert Stephen, *Prisoners on Oath: Present and Future* (London, 1898), pp. 16–17). See also the speech of John Lloyd Morgan: *Parl. Deb.*, 4th series, xlviii, 785–7 (8 April 1897).

[125] *House of Lords Sessional Papers* 1857–8 (49) IV 373,

[126] *Solicitors' Journal and Reporter* 2 (1857–8), 430.

[127] The preamble recited that, 'it is expedient for the better administration of justice in criminal proceedings, both as regards the conviction of offenders and the acquittal of innocent persons, to make prisoners or defendants and their wives or husbands competent to give evidence' (*House of Commons Parliamentary Papers* 1876 (61) I 511).

[128] For example, in 1861, J. Pitt Taylor, denying that the admission of the accused's testimony would mislead juries, argued that: 'In investigating questions of fact, men are far more likely to err by being forced to grope their way to a conclusion in the twilight or in the dark, than by having their mental vision

It was sometimes said that the fullest examination of the evidence would always be of advantage to an innocent accused.[129] But other, more particular, arguments were often put forward. One of these was that the unsworn statement that the accused was allowed to make did not have the weight of evidence on oath. Thus, in 1858, Brougham argued that because the statement that the accused could make was not on oath and not subject to cross-examination, it had no more weight than the speech of their counsel or their plea of 'not guilty'.[130] In March 1859, it was argued, in a leading article in the *Solicitors' Journal*, that the accused, though allowed to make an unsworn statement from the dock, was not permitted to speak in the only way in which their speaking could be recognised as effectual.[131]

The argument most frequently used was that, without the opportunity to give evidence, an accused stood in danger of wrongful conviction. For example, in 1861, J. Pitt Taylor argued that the existing law failed to show sufficient forbearance towards prisoners, for it closed their mouths and permitted them to be convicted on evidence that they might be able to disprove, or at least explain, if they were to give evidence. He asked whether it was just or wise that the innocent should be exposed to the danger of a wrongful conviction in order that the guilty should have no temptation to utter falsehood.[132]

On several occasions it was argued that the reform would enable undefended prisoners to present their case more effectively, because they could readily have their attention drawn to the relevant prosecution evidence and would not have to rely solely on their own inexpert cross-examination of prosecution witnesses.

---

dazzled by excess of light.' In the following year, Charles Dickens, in an editorial article in the magazine *All the Year Round*, said that examining the prisoner would increase the likelihood that the guilty would be convicted and the innocent acquitted (*Solicitors' Journal and Reporter* 5 (1860–1), 363; 'Examine the Prisoner', *All the Year Round* 7 (7 June 1862), 306–8. See also *The Times*, 29 November 1862; *Parl. Deb.*, 3rd series, ccxxxvii, 668: 30 January 1878).

[129] See, e.g., *Law Magazine and Law Review* 7 (1859), 255; Stephen, 'Reform of the Criminal Law', 752.

[130] *The Times*, 19 March 1858, p. 6.

[131] *Solicitors' Journal and Reporter* 4 (1859–60), 696.

[132] *Solicitors' Journal and Reporter* 5 (1860–1), 384. See also *Parl. Deb.*, 3rd series, cxcv, 1813 (28 April 1869); *The Times*, 17 February 1865; *Law Times* 40 (4 March 1865), 573.

For instance, Robert Lowe said in 1865 that he could see no reason why a culprit should not be called on to explain those circumstances that seemed to bear most hardly on them. He thought that such a rule might be of advantage to prisoners, many of whom were poor, uneducated, bewildered, and confused; therefore, if innocent, they would benefit from having their attention drawn to the most incriminating parts of the evidence.[133] In 1875, similar arguments were used by L. A. Goodeve, the writer of an article in the *Law Magazine and Review*, who proposed examination of the accused by the court on the lines permitted in India. The attention of the accused would be directed by the examination to the points bearing against him, so that he would have an opportunity of answering and explaining these points. If undefended, the accused would 'learn on what matters to cross-examine or to call witnesses, instead of blundering in confusion, and so bringing about his own conviction'.[134] In 1878, Ashley argued that the reform was particularly necessary for the protection of a prisoner who was undefended. He pointed out that such a man was forbidden to deal with the prosecution evidence

in the only way which his low education usually permitted; but was perplexed and baffled by being called upon to lay the foundation for a skilled address to the jury by questions which he was told to put to the witness, but which invariably took the form of statements in which he was constantly being checked by the Court.[135]

There were also suggestions that the reform was desirable because only if prisoners were allowed to give evidence could they hope to deal effectively with testimony given by the police. In his article in the *Law Magazine and Review*, Goodeve accepted that evidence of what a defendant had said in answer to police questions was often admitted; but this, he argued, was insufficient to put the defence case properly before the jury. Police testimony, 'unconsciously perhaps', was not altogether independent, and the court was more likely to arrive at the truth by examining the accused himself than by hearing what he had said at second hand from the police.[136] The problem of police evidence was raised in

[133] [Robert Lowe] 'Criminal Law Reform', *Edinburgh Review* 121 (1865), 132.
[134] L. A. Goodeve, 'The Examination of Accused Persons', *Law Magazine and Review*, 4th series, 1 (1875–6), 643–4.
[135] *Parl. Deb.*, 3rd series, ccxxxvii, 660 (30 January 1878).
[136] Goodeve, 'Examination of Accused Persons', 645–6.

1876 by George Whalley, Liberal member for Peterborough, who contended that the existing system left accused persons almost entirely at the mercy of the police, 'who frequently perjured themselves and conspired together to secure convictions'. He declared that there was a great and growing dissatisfaction in many places with the conduct of the police; in some cases policemen were continued in their office who ought to have been removed. Whalley's speech brought cries of protest and his arguments were not adopted by other speakers in the debate, but Goodeve's earlier comment indicates that the objections might have been to Whalley's extreme language rather than to the suggestion of police bias.[137]

Whatever the reasons, it was recognised in 1882 by a member of the Government that innocent persons had been and were at risk as a result of the existing state of the law. In a parliamentary debate in that year, the Home Secretary, Sir William Harcourt, said that he did not believe it possible for anyone to occupy the position that he himself held without being satisfied that in those cases where a miscarriage of justice had occurred and innocent persons had been convicted, the miscarriage might have been prevented if the accused had been able to tell their own story.[138]

Supporters of the reform naturally believed that innocent defendants would wish to be able to testify, even if this meant that they would have to undergo cross-examination.[139] It was not difficult to move from talking about the wishes of innocent defendants to talking about their rights. J. Pitt Taylor wrote of the innocent man's 'natural right of asserting his innocence in the most solemn manner'.[140] Evelyn Ashley, on the motion for the second reading of his bill in 1876, declared that he took for his motto the words of Bentham: 'Innocence claims the right of speaking, as guilt invokes the privilege of silence.' He said that he based his appeal for reform not on the ground that it would make

[137] *Parl. Deb.*, 3rd series, ccxxx, 1938 (26 July 1876).
[138] *Parl. Deb.*, 3rd series, cclxvii, 431 (8 March 1882). In 1896, the editor of the *Solicitors' Journal* gave his opinion in favour of changing the law, saying, 'every month which Parliament delays to bring about this reform sees many an innocent man running a grave risk which he ought not to be compelled to run' (*Solicitors' Journal and Reporter* 40 (1895–6), 561–2).
[139] *Parl. Deb.*, 3rd series, clii, 763 (24 February 1859); *Law Times* 40 (1864–5), 213–14.
[140] *Solicitors' Journal and Reporter* 5 (1860–1), 364.

the conviction of the guilty more certain, 'but on the right that every innocent person had to state his own case and tell his own story under all the sanctions which law and custom made necessary, if the Court and jury were to pay proper attention to the statements – namely, under oath and subject to cross-examination'.[141]

When Brougham raised the question of the accused's competence in 1858, one of his main arguments in favour of reform was that it would remove anomalies. He pointed out that in ninety-nine cases out of a hundred there was a private prosecutor who could be examined on oath and cross-examined, while the mouth of the accused was stopped. Moreover, conspiracies, frauds, and acts of violence could be the subject of civil actions, and then the defendant was able to give evidence. In bankruptcy cases, he added, persons were examined whether they wished it or not, despite the fact that they might incriminate themselves.[142] Another anomaly was that the rule excluding the accused from testifying was an example of exclusion on the ground of interest, a principle already largely discredited by the time Brougham raised the question in 1858.[143]

When Evelyn Ashley proposed his bill in 1876, the argument based on anomalies had become considerably stronger. Several statutes had recently created new criminal offences and allowed those charged under them to give evidence in their defence.[144] Ashley also argued by analogy with bankruptcy law, as Brougham had done, and with divorce law. Respondents and co-respondents were by then allowed to give evidence, and Ashley argued that these proceedings were of a quasi-penal character.[145] The Criminal Law Amendment Act 1885 produced particularly blatant

---

[141] *Parl. Deb.*, 3rd series, ccxxix, 1182 (24 May 1876). See also *Parl. Deb.*, 3rd series, ccxxxvii, 669 (30 January 1878); 4th series, i, 667 (18 February 1892); xlvii, 812 (8 April 1897).

[142] *The Times*, 19 March 1858, p. 6. From the reign of Elizabeth I, successive statutes had been passed to prevent frauds in bankruptcy. They had provided that bankrupts, when called upon to answer any questions concerning their estate and effects, should not be allowed to avail themselves of the common law maxim, 'Nemo tenetur seipsum accusare' ('No one is bound to accuse himself/herself'). If bankrupts refused to answer they would be liable to committal for contempt, as upon a refusal to answer any other lawful question (see the judgment of Lord Campbell CJ in *R* v. *Scott* (1856) 25 LJMC 128).

[143] See ch. 4.   [144] See n. 66 and text.

[145] *Parl. Deb.*, 3rd series, ccxxix, 1183 (24 May 1876).

anomalies. For example, it created a number of sexual offences, mainly against women. A person who was charged with any of these was allowed by the statute to give evidence in his defence; but a person charged with rape, a common law offence, was incompetent to testify.[146] In 1888, the Attorney General, Sir Richard Webster, acknowledged that the first great reason for reforming the law was the creation in the previous twenty years of some ten or fifteen new offences in which the accused or his wife could give evidence.[147]

Few opponents of the proposed reform attempted to meet the challenge presented by the arguments based on anomalies. Two who did were Edward Pickersgill, Liberal member for South West Bethnal Green, and Sir Herbert Stephen, the Clerk of Assize for the Northern Circuit. Pickersgill in effect denied that there were any anomalies, and argued that Acts allowing the accused to testify were, with one or two exceptions, concerned with offences far more analogous to torts than to crime.[148] In some cases this may have been true. However, one of the exceptions was the Criminal Law Amendment Act, and, as this accounted for many of the prosecutions where the accused was able to testify, Pickersgill's argument cannot have seemed convincing. Sir Herbert Stephen accepted that anomalies had been allowed to develop, and he regarded these as the sole reason why innocent persons were convicted; his proposed solution was to abolish most, if not all, of these.[149]

Two further arguments, though not frequently used, may have added weight to the reformers' case. One was that the extension of competency to the accused would lead to more open justice. For example, in 1858, the Dublin correspondent of the *Solicitors' Journal* pointed out that frequently,

the defence which our law will not allow to be put forward during the trial, is afterwards in effect transmitted in writing by the friends of the prisoner to the Home Secretary – or rather to one of his subordinates,

---

[146] See the speech of Mr Serjeant Simon: *Parl. Deb.*, 3rd series, ccc, 911 (3 August 1885).

[147] *Parl. Deb.*, 3rd series, cccxxiv, 68 (22 March 1888). See also the letter from Sir Harry Poland in *The Times*, 12 November 1896, p. 4. Poland had been Treasury Counsel at the Central Criminal Court and adviser to the Home Office in criminal matters for an unequalled period of twenty-three years.

[148] *Parl. Deb.*, 4rd series, xlviii, 788 (8 April 1897).

[149] Stephen, *Prisoners on Oath*, p. 64.

who in private, irresponsibly, without any personal knowledge or observation of the matter, in point of fact reviews the decisions of judge and jury. Not the least of the arguments for the change is, that, could all sources of testimony be resorted to, the criminal justice of the country would be dispensed more in open courts of justice, and less in the Home Secretary's office.[150]

A similar account was given in 1876 by Russell Gurney, Conservative member for Southampton and Recorder of London. His experience was that very often the only person who could prove a man's innocence was his wife, especially as to events alleged to have occurred at night. But under existing law the prisoner's wife could not be heard in his defence although, paradoxically, his mistress could. From the account given by Gurney of cases he had tried, it appears that in practice a wife, after her husband's conviction, might swear an affidavit establishing an alibi for him. An application, supported by the affidavit, would then be made to the Home Office for the prisoner's release. Usually, the trial judge would be asked for his opinion and in due course a pardon might be granted. Gurney observed that it was very difficult to decide against granting a pardon if the wife could not be examined in court.[151]

The other argument was noted by J. Pitt Taylor, who drew attention to the fact that prosecutors could and did exploit the rule that made accused persons incompetent so as to deprive the defence of witnesses. There was a 'very mischievous and oppressive practice' whereby in prosecutions for conspiracy, riot, and similar offences some persons were improperly included in the indictment to ensure that they were unable to testify on behalf of those who had been properly prosecuted.[152]

The decline of the perjury argument

A traditional argument against change had been that extending competency to interested parties would lead to an increase in perjury. Respect for truth was regarded as a social cement, and at least in this matter Bentham was at one with less radical thinkers. In *The Rationale of Reward*, published in 1825, he wrote:

[150] *Solicitors' Journal and Reporter* 2 (1857–8), 565.
[151] *Parl. Deb.*, 3rd series, ccxxx, 1930–1 (26 July 1876).
[152] *Solicitors' Journal and Reporter* 5 (1860–1), 384.

Veracity is one of the most important bases of human society. The due administration of justice absolutely depends upon it; whatever tends to weaken it, saps the foundations of morality, security, and happiness.[153]

Truth-telling could also be supported on a strictly non-consequentialist basis by Christians, especially those supporters of 'godliness and good learning', such as Thomas Arnold, who were leaders of the movement for educational reform in the 1830s and 1850s. David Newsome has described their position in this way:

It was in defence of truthfulness, then, that the advocates of 'godliness and good learning' most delighted to stand. It was the link which bound the two principles together. Truthfulness was as essential an attribute of godliness as the quest for truth was the object of good learning. To inculcate a love of truth was, then, the primary duty of the teacher. In their passionate conviction of the duty to extirpate falsehood, and the inclination towards falsehood, the Victorian moralists may seem at times brutal. Innumerable cautionary tales were manufactured for the edification of the young. For the liar no fate was too terrible.[154]

Sometimes religious principles were combined with consequentialism. A good example can be found in a sermon on 'The Sin of Lying', preached by the Rev. C. J. Vaughan, a disciple of Thomas Arnold and Head Master of Harrow, which was published in 1847. In his view,

any approach to direct falsehood, however it might veil itself, would be spoken of in just terms of reprobation by a large majority of the higher classes of society. There are multitudes of persons who, even without any strong feeling of religion, would forfeit anything, or suffer anything, rather than sully the truthfulness of their word.[155]

Although the perjury argument was used against the legislation proposed in 1843 to extend competency to interested non-parties to a suit, the legal profession and members of parliament alike discounted the dangers and the bill became law with very little

---

[153] *Works*, vol. II, p. 210. See also *Works*, vol. VI, p. 264.

[154] David Newsome, *Godliness and Good Learning: Four Studies on a Victorian Ideal* (London, 1961), pp. 47–8.

[155] Charles John Vaughan, *Sermons Preached in the Chapel of Harrow School* (London, 1847), p. 244. Later, he gave a clearer idea of what might be involved in 'any approach to direct falsehood, however it might veil itself'. He explained that 'lying is wherever deceit is: wherever there is a purpose to deceive another, whoever that other may be, and by whatever means the deception may be practised; whether by dishonest concealment, or by taking unfair advantages, or by equivocation . . . or by doing that behind another's back which we know that he will give us credit for not doing; or whether it be by more positive or deliberate falsehood' (ibid., p. 249).

opposition. The perjury argument was again unsuccessful when it was used in 1851 to oppose the extension of competency to parties. It is significant that on that occasion the survey of county court judges conducted by the Law Amendment Society showed that although some thought that there had been an increase in perjury, they also thought that this was outweighed by the benefits of admitting such evidence.[156]

Nevertheless, in 1861, the perjury argument was one of the most important contained in a pamphlet written by Francis Worsley, a barrister of the Middle Temple, to oppose a paper in favour of extending competency to the accused, which had been published earlier that year by J. Pitt Taylor. Taylor had been dismissive of the perjury argument, pointing out that it had been used in 1851 but that Lord Brougham's Act had nevertheless been passed. While conceding that the reform might have led to a slight increase in perjury, Taylor had claimed that this evil could not be regarded as very alarming, and that it faded into insignificance when contrasted with the benefits that had resulted from the 1851 Act.[157] In this, as has been shown, his opinion matched that of the county court judges on the effects of extending competency to parties in their courts. Nonetheless Worsley thought that Taylor had not taken the risk of perjury seriously enough:

Society, as constituted, inevitably leads thousands of our poorer fellow men and women into a daily violation of our criminal law; but that the legislature, whose duty it is to rectify and abate this tendency by preventive and reformatory laws, should deliberately enact temptations to the perjury they punish, is an idea which will not bear Mr Taylor's reconsideration.[158]

This was not merely the idiosyncratic view of a private member of the Bar. In 1876, the perjury argument was relied on in Parliament by the Common Serjeant, Sir Thomas Chambers, and the Attorney General, Sir John Holker. The former argued that it would be immoral in the highest degree for the House to legislate for the admission of witnesses who would get into the witness-box under influences that would make it impossible for them to tell the truth. The latter emphasised the gravity of perjury, saying that it was a crime far more serious than most of those with which

---

[156] See ch. 4, n. 69 and text.
[157] *Solicitors' Journal and Reporter* 5 (1860–1), 363–4.
[158] Worsley, *Examination of Mr Pitt Taylor's Thesis*, pp. 5–6.

prisoners were charged, because through its commission men might lose their estates, reputation, and liberty.[159]

By 1897, however, the significance given to this argument had declined, and it played at best only a minor part in the speeches of those opposed to reform.[160] Two matters probably led to its reduced significance. The first was the government's apparently rapid change of view. In 1876, the Attorney General, Sir John Holker, was insisting on the gravity of perjury in his opposition to Evelyn Ashley's bill. Two years later, he was promising a government bill that would put into effect much of what Ashley had originally wanted. To many it must then have seemed, if it had not done so before, that the perjury argument was useful only to the extent that it was able to support a decision already reached on pragmatic grounds. When the Government was in doubt about the expediency of reform, it was content to use the fear of perjury as a weapon traditionally employed to defeat that sort of proposal. When the Government decided that it was more expedient to take up the reformers' line, it tacitly acknowledged the obsolescence of the weapon that it had used only a short while before.

The second matter that finally brought about the decline of the perjury argument was the unacceptable nature of any compromise that would allow the accused to give evidence without being sworn. For example, Charles Dickens argued that any force to be derived from a prisoner's statement would have to be derived from its own natural probability and from any supporting evidence that there might be. No force could be derived from the credit of the prisoner, 'which would be sadly impeached by his situation', so it would be inappropriate to administer the oath.[161] A similar argument was used in the *Solicitors' Journal* in a discussion of Evelyn Ashley's 1878 bill. The writer thought that a prisoner giving evidence should not do so on oath because, 'it is

---

[159] *Parl. Deb.*, 3rd series, ccxxx, 1933–4, 1938 (26 July 1876). In 1883, Morgan Lloyd, Liberal member for Beaumaris, emphasised the public significance of perjury when he said that where a prisoner had given evidence in his own defence but had been convicted, the choice would have to be made between trying and punishing the prisoner for perjury also, or publicly allowing his perjury to go unpunished (*Parl. Deb.*, 3rd series, cclxxviii, 93: 12 April 1883).

[160] See, e.g., the speeches of John Lloyd Morgan and Edward Pickersgill: *Parl. Deb.*, 4th series, xlviii, 785–92 (8 April 1897).

[161] Charles Dickens, 'Examine the Prisoner', *All the Year Round* 7 (7 June 1862), 307.

not in reason to be expected of criminal human nature that the truth will be spoken by a criminal on his trial'.[162] J. F. Stephen proposed that only ordinary witnesses should testify on oath in a criminal trial, because persons who were on trial had so much to lose that their testimony, considered merely as testimony, was valueless. Belief in what the accused stated ought, therefore, to depend only upon such matters as its inherent probability, and the way in which it fitted into and explained matters stated by others.[163]

The Royal Commission that revised Stephen's code made the accused much more like an ordinary witness. In particular, it rejected Stephen's provision that the accused should not be sworn as a witness.[164] It is likely that the reason for this was the realisation that such a distinction between the testimony of prosecution witnesses and that of the accused would place the latter at a disadvantage that it might be impossible to overcome. The distinction would also have been likely to produce an adverse effect on the presumption of innocence in favour of the accused. The insecurity of this presumption was illustrated by Charles Dickens, who expressed the view that,

so perfect are the arrangements, so accurate the investigations, which precede a trial, that, practically speaking, an innocent person is very rarely placed in the dock.[165]

He took the robust view that if innocent persons did find themselves in the dock, it was likely to be their own fault.

There is never any fear, in an English trial, of the process of the court pressing too severely on an accused. It deals with him too tenderly. After all, even in the case of an innocent man finding himself in the dock, there must be present, if not guilt, a certain laches or carelessness, or indirect culpability of some sort, which has brought him there; and for this he must pay a little penalty. Thus if he complain of severe cross-examination, it is his own act in some degree that has brought it on him.[166]

An image of continuity

For competency to be extended to the accused it was important that the reform should not be thought to entail any radical change

---

[162] *Solicitors' Journal and Reporter* 22 (1877–8), 277–8.
[163] Stephen, 'Reform of the Criminal Law', 753–4.   [164] See n. 46 and text.
[165] Dickens, 'Examine the Prisoner', 306.   [166] Ibid., 307–8.

in the balance of power in criminal trials. It is clear from the frequency of arguments based on analogies with existing law that those taking part in the various debates thought that any change should appear to be a natural development of existing practices. It is likely that from the late 1870s a majority in Parliament, and perhaps in the legal profession, judged most of the proposals to have passed this test. Ashley's bill in 1878 might well have been passed if the Government had not promised its own bill. Any of the Government's proposals after 1878 could probably have been passed had they not been linked to a criminal code or become the subject of Irish Nationalist obstruction.[167]

No doubt a little breathing space was required after the extension of competency to parties in civil actions before the implications of that reform could be recognised. On 19 December 1851, a leading article appeared in *The Times* on the subject of evidence in criminal cases. This was prompted not by the Law of Evidence Amendment Act, but by a recent case of mistaken identity in which a wrongful conviction had only by chance been avoided. The writer, after some general reflections on the nature of evidence, concluded: 'How easy it is, despite of all our administrative machinery, all our scientific rules, and with no evil intent, to swear away the life or liberty of an innocent person!' Nowhere did he make the point that the risk of wrongful conviction might be reduced if persons accused in criminal cases were themselves able to testify. The subject of criminal law and procedure was considered again in a leading article in 1853, in which the writer argued for a number of procedural reforms, including improved methods of reviewing decisions. No direct reference was made to the incompetency of the accused, but the writer did ask: 'Why should the means of ascertaining truth and guarding against error which are found efficient for civil cases be wholly unfit for criminal?'[168]

When Brougham raised the question in Parliament in 1858, the writer of a leading article in the *Solicitors' Journal* argued that what seemed at first sight 'a startling innovation' was 'but a logical carrying out of the principle originally applied, with some timidity and hesitation, in Lord Denman's Evidence Act, and afterwards

[167] See nn. 51 and 62 and text.   [168] *The Times*, 3 June 1853.

more boldly developed in the County Courts Acts'.[169] In 1861, J. Pitt Taylor, arguing in support of the reform, stated that, so far as was practicable, the rules of evidence ought to be the same in civil and criminal proceedings.[170] In *The Times* on 4 November 1862, the writer of a leading article asserted that any arguments there might have been against allowing the accused to give evidence foundered on the fact that the law had been changed to allow the parties in civil actions to do so. In addition, once Parliament began to pass statutes allowing the accused to give evidence when charged with some offences, it became possible to argue that a general extension would only be taking existing rules of criminal procedure to their logical conclusion. The argument based on analogy thus became another way of presenting the argument based on anomaly.[171]

Competency and individual responsibility

The extension of competency to all accused persons may have been more readily achieved because this reform was consistent with the emphasis placed on individual responsibility by much nineteenth-century political theory. Between the paternalistic relationships of the eighteenth-century state and the administrative state, which was largely in place by the 1870s, came a period in which individualism was valued in social and political reform.[172]

Atiyah has suggested that individualism as a social or intellectual force may have reached its apogee with the publication of

---

[169] *Solicitors' Journal and Reporter* 2 (1857–8), 430.
[170] *Solicitors' Journal and Reporter* 5 (1860–1), 363.
[171] See nn. 66 and 147 and text.
[172] P. S. Atiyah, *The Rise and Fall of Freedom of Contract* (Oxford, 1979), pp. 256–60. However, Atiyah acknowledged the dangers of over-simplification; in particular, that of failing to appreciate the diversity of views existing in the nineteenth century and of assuming that changes in intellectual or moral movements occurred cleanly at given moments of time. He saw clear signs, for example, that the waning of what he referred to as the older, pre-nineteenth-century, type of paternalism was a protracted affair, especially in the law (ibid., pp. 262–3). It is hardly surprising that in such an essentially conservative profession pockets of paternalism should have survived, or that they should have manifested themselves in opposition to extending competency to the accused.

John Stuart Mill's *On Liberty* in 1859.[173] Even if this is true, there
was certainly no rapid decline from that point. The dominant
philosopher in late-Victorian England was T. H. Green, and
individualism was central to his philosophy also. Green's emphasis on the development of individual character appeared in
discussions of what he called 'freedom in the positive sense', by
which he meant not merely 'freedom to do as we like irrespectively
of what it is that we like', but rather, 'the greater power on the
part of the citizens as a body to make the most and best of
themselves'.[174] Self-realisation was at the basis of political obligation:

[T]he claim or right of the individual to have certain powers secured to
him by society, and the counter-claim of society to exercise certain powers
over the individual, alike rest on the fact that these powers are necessary
to the fulfilment of man's vocation as a moral being, to an effectual self-
devotion to the work of developing the perfect character in himself and
others.[175]

A doctrine of self-realisation was also involved in Green's ethics.
He argued that persons realised themselves, first, by being conscious of having a 'higher' (or 'better', or 'possible') self; and
secondly, by trying to make their actual character identical with
the idea they had of their 'higher' self.[176] Such theories of self-
realisation placed a strong emphasis on individual responsibility:

No-one can convey a good character to another. Every one must make his
own character for himself. All that one man can do to make another better
is to remove obstacles, and supply conditions favourable to the formation
of a good character.[177]

Extension of competency to the accused accorded well with a
political theory based on individual responsibility. A legal system
that values individual responsibility is likely to have as its central
purpose a process of argument and communication with the
defendant closely related to moral criticism; both express a proper

[173] Atiyah, *Rise and Fall*, p. 260.
[174] T. H. Green, *Lecture on Liberal Legislation and Freedom of Contract*, in *Works of Thomas Hill Green*, ed. R. L. Nettleship, 3rd edn (London, 1891), vol. III, pp. 370–1.
[175] T. H. Green, *Lecture on the Principles of Political Obligation*, in *Works of T. H. Green*, vol. II, p. 347.
[176] Melvin Richter, *The Politics of Conscience: T. H. Green and His Age* (London, 1964; repr. Lanham, Maryland, 1983), p. 204.
[177] T. H. Green, *Prolegomena to Ethics* (1883), sect. 332.

respect for the accused as a rational and responsible agent. If the criminal trial is seen in this way, rather than as a purely instrumental process for achieving a correct decision about facts, it follows that an accused will have a right to be heard, because the absence of that right would entail a refusal by the court to recognise the accused's status as a participant in the trial.

This is bound to call into question the accused's right of silence at trial, for if the accused are to be treated as rational and responsible agents they cannot deny that status by refusing to participate in their trial. In short, the accused's status carries duties as well as rights, and these include the duty to give evidence and to submit to questioning by counsel for the prosecution.[178] It has been shown earlier that the right to silence at trial was a constantly recurring subject of discussion in proposals for legislation and in debates inside and outside Parliament, from Brougham's proposals of 1858 to the passing of the Criminal Evidence Act 1898. Frequently, there were suggestions that it would be unobjectionable to infer guilt from silence, and there were even proposals that would have obliged the accused to submit to questioning. While it is true that the latter were rejected, and that comment on the silence of an accused at trial was substantially limited, both in the wording of the 1898 Act and in subsequent interpretation, the fact that these proposals were made at all shows that the legislation was debated in an intellectual climate that recognised the principle of individual responsibility. This in itself was favourable to the extension of competency. The fact that the debates ended in a compromise does not diminish the importance accorded to the principle.

The question of Bentham's influence

Any influence that Bentham had on the general extension of competency to accused persons was almost certainly indirect and slight. Bentham had advocated a compulsory examination of the accused, possibly by the judge, and ideally without a jury. The jury was a feature of 'regular' or 'technical' procedure, which was rule based and to be contrasted with 'natural', 'domestic', or

---

[178] See, generally, R. A. Duff, *Trials and Punishments* (Cambridge, 1986), especially pp. 129–35.

'summary' procedure.[179] When reform finally came, it was within the framework of an adversarial system that was becoming more, rather than less, rule based, in which the right to silence had become more firmly established than at the time when Bentham was developing his critique. With this substantial reservation, it is possible to see two ways in which Bentham's critique may have played a part in preparing the way for the extension of competency to the accused. First, some of Bentham's ideas may have been mediated through Brougham and the Law Amendment Society. In addition, similar reforms in the United States of America appear to have been stimulated in part by Bentham's work, and the American experience may have done something to make the reform more acceptable in England.

It has already been suggested that three principal arguments were relied on by supporters of this reform: it was necessary for discovering truth; for safeguarding the innocent; and for removing anomalies. Bentham frequently argued that extension of competency would aid the discovery of truth and safeguard the innocent.[180] In addition, the argument that the reform would do away with the need to do justice in the Home Secretary's office rather than in open court may have been influenced by the importance attached by Bentham to publicity and accountability in the administration of justice.[181] These were hardly original arguments, however, and the fact that a Member of Parliament used an argument that Bentham also had used does not establish that he followed Bentham in his own use of it.[182] We are on firmer ground in suggesting that the influence of Bentham may have been mediated through the efforts of Brougham and the Law Amendment Society, and thereby have made some contribution to the reform finally achieved. Brougham initiated legislation in 1858, 1859, and 1860. In 1844, he had formed the Law Amendment Society,[183] and that society, with its quarterly journal, the *Law*

---

[179] See ch. 3, n. 24 and text.
[180] See, e.g., *Rationale of Judicial Evidence* in *Works*, vol. VII, pp. 44, 338–9, 368, 386–7, 599.
[181] See, e.g., *Draught of a New Plan for the Organisation of the Judicial Establishment in France*, in *Works*, vol. IV, p. 316; *Principles of Judicial Procedure* in *Works*, vol. II, p. 32. See also Postema, *Bentham and the Common Law Tradition*, pp. 364–73. For justice in the Home Secretary's office, see n. 150 and text.
[182] See ch. 1, nn. 29–31 and text.   [183] Stewart, *Brougham*, p. 348.

Review, kept the issue before the eyes of the legal profession for several decades. For example, it had been at the invitation of the Law Amendment Society that J. Pitt Taylor, the evidence scholar, read a paper in 1861 in support of the reform. The Society itself campaigned for the reform, and as part of its activities sent questionnaires to the Chief Justice and Attorney General of each of the United States of America and of the provinces of the Dominion of Canada in the hope of getting the most recent information on the subject from the most experienced sources.[184] In 1857, Brougham formed a committee to establish a National Association for the Promotion of Social Science, and until 1865 he was its president.[185] The latter organisation also discussed the question from time to time.[186]

In 1866, the year after Vincent Scully and Sir Fitzroy Kelly had introduced legislation to make the accused competent, the *Law Times* and the *Law Magazine and Law Review* drew attention to the way in which the law concerning the competency of the accused was developing in America. In March 1864, a law had been passed in Maine to allow the accused to testify in criminal cases. This development had been largely due to the efforts of Chief Justice Appleton, who in his own writings had acknowledged his debt to Bentham.[187] Similar legislation had followed in other states. The writer in the *Law Times* referred to these developments but suggested that such reforms were more readily made in a country where all was comparatively new than in one where all had 'grown and hung together undisturbed during the progress of many centuries of national existence'.[188]

The writer in the *Law Magazine and Law Review* had more polemical aims. He noted that a bill to enable accused persons to give evidence was currently likely to pass in Massachusetts, and stated that the subject was of sufficient interest to English readers to reproduce in full the report that had been made on the Massachusetts bill by the Committee on the Judiciary of that state.[189] This report supported the reform with a number of

---

[184] Goodeve, 'Examination of Accused Persons', 630.
[185] Stewart, *Brougham*, pp. 358–9.
[186] *Law Magazine and Law Review* 24 (1868), 167, 274.
[187] See ch. 1, nn. 24–6 and text.   [188] *Law Times* 41 (1865–6), 843–4.
[189] *Law Magazine and Law Review* 21 (1866), 339–47. The report stated that the views contained in it were not fully concurred with by every member of the

arguments that, without acknowledging him as their source, clearly had affinities with arguments that Bentham had employed. The writers of the report acknowledged the contribution that the reform would make to the discovery of truth by pointing out the accused's position as 'the most important witness'. They also alleged that no innocent person would wish to be excluded: 'It is the interest and the wish of every innocent man suspected of crime to explain at once inculpating circumstances, and from no source can such satisfactory explanations be obtained'.[190]

The writers of the report also argued that if the rule of exclusion had been designed to save culprits from a fancied hardship of seeing themselves condemned out of their own mouths, it had failed to achieve this, because any writing or speech of the accused could be given in evidence against them. Such second-hand evidence, however, was almost certain to be deceptively incomplete because the witness might have misheard, misunderstood, or have wilfully or negligently misreported.[191] Yet the only person who could complete the incompleteness or explain the incorrectness had to suffer in silence. 'In daily life we follow no such rule. What father so inquires into the alleged misconduct of his children, or what employer thus verifies suspicions of his agents?' This argument based on an analogy with daily life was one of the fundamental arguments used by Bentham to advocate a 'natural' rather than a 'technical' system of procedure.[192]

The report also considered two of the principal objections to the reform: the problem of the inferences that would be drawn from silence; and the perjury argument. The 'inference from silence' argument received a plainly Benthamite response:

May you not now show every act of the prisoner, from the time of the alleged crime and before it, and urge that the natural inference from each or any is the guilt of the man who under the circumstances would act as he acted? And can the deduction which you would urge have any other ultimate foundation than the collective experience of human nature in all time, teaching every man of common sense that under given circumstances, in a vast majority of cases, an innocent man acts in one way and a guilty man in quite a different way?

Why is the voluntary silence of a man labouring under a grievous

Committee, and that the bill was not a measure that had the unanimous support of the Committee.
[190] Cf. nn. 18 and 19 and text.   [191] Cf. n. 21 and text.
[192] *Rationale of Judicial Evidence* in *Works*, vol. VII, pp. 197–8.

suspicion assumed by all men to be evidence of guilt? Simply, because the invariable experience of mankind has demonstrated that the innocent hastens to tell his story, conscious that in full disclosure is his defence. Why should not this necessary inference of universal experience, springing from the very nature of man, be used against the guilty who dares not trust to a tissue of lies, and will not tell the truth? Does it bear hard upon the guilty? In what way? Nay, even if it did so, wherefore not? Is criminal law intended to relieve the guilty? Is not the sure conviction of crime desired?[193]

In reply to the objection that such a change would encourage perjury, the report argued that this applied equally to allowing parties in civil actions to give evidence. It had not been thought a sufficient argument when that reform had been under consideration, nor should it be thought so now.

The Committee appended to the report a letter from Chief Justice Appleton, which dealt with the practical workings of the proposed reform, and which the *Law Magazine and Law Review* also published. Appleton stated that he had had no doubt that the change should be made in his own state of Maine, and that nothing had since occurred to weaken his opinion. 'I have tried criminal cases in which the accused being innocent owed his honourable acquittal in no slight degree to his own testimony, and the clear and frank manner in which it was delivered.'[194] Erroneous verdicts would occasionally be rendered, whether the accused was admitted to testify or not, so long as juries were composed of fallible men. He also emphasised the benefits of reform: increased openness in the administration of justice and a reduced danger of misdecision.

All the evidence attainable and needed for a full understanding of the case should be forthcoming, unless the evils of delay, vexation and expense consequent upon its procurement should exceed those arising from possible misdecision.

The exclusion of evidence is the exclusion of the means of correct decision. The greater the mass of evidence excluded, the less the chances of such decision, until, if all evidence be excluded, resort must be had only to lot.[195]

---

[193] *Law Magazine and Law Review* 21 (1866), 341–2. Cf. n. 20 and text.
[194] *Law Magazine and Law Review* 21 (1866), 343. Appleton did not deal directly with the problem presented by the innocent defendant who gave evidence badly. His opinion that, 'being innocent, he would not resort to falsehood to establish such innocence' (ibid., 344) is, in addition, at variance with the experience of English judges and barristers recorded throughout the century in debates on this subject.
[195] *Law Magazine and Law Review* 21 (1866), 343.

Appleton's debt must have been obvious to anyone familiar with Bentham's writings. For the benefit of those who were not, he concluded by referring to the more elaborate examination of the question 'in the masterly work of Bentham on the law of evidence, where the reasons for the proposed change are stated with a cogency of argumentation unanswered and unanswerable'.

6

CONCLUSION

In the first chapter of this book I indicated that the traditional story, which had assigned to Bentham a leading place in the nineteenth-century development of evidence law and had been supported amongst others by Brougham, Maine, Dicey, Holds-worth, and Hart, was in need of revision. I suggested two main lines of inquiry: first, into the workings of the common law; second, into what other factors should be taken into account when considering the statutory reforms. The common law in particular was ripe for investigation because writers who accorded Bentham his leading position invariably did so on the basis of his supposed influence on the statutory reforms of the period under considera-tion, while they were silent on any influence he might have had on common law development. This in itself suggests that Bentham's part in the development of evidence law may have been over-rated, because if we look at the law reports and at the textbooks on evidence published during this period we can observe, at least in civil as opposed to criminal evidence, increasing activity on the part of judges, writers, and law reporters.

Supporters of 'Bentham's immense influence' on the law of evidence neglected their hero's radical critique of the common law, in which he had condemned alike judge-made law and rules of evidence of all kinds, but in particular exclusionary rules. Bentham's critique had no effect on evidence *case* law during the nineteenth century; but, if Bentham was supposed to have ex-ercised such a considerable influence, was it not curious that it should have been confined to *statutory* reforms? Was there such a division between what went on in Parliament and what went on within the legal profession that this was likely?

In fact, an examination of what went on in Parliament often shows strong links between the legal profession and those advo-

cating statutory reforms, not least because a significant number of
lawyers or others with legal connections sat in Parliament, and
because governments that supported reforming legislation took
good care to ensure that their measures were broadly supported
within the profession. In relation to at least this area of law
reform, governments followed rather than led opinion. We therefore need to look for factors other than Bentham's work in the
history of these legislative reforms. When we look, we see a more
complex story than that traditionally told, in which Bentham had
indeed a part to play, but not the only or even the main part.

At each of the two stages when a general extension of the right
to affirm instead of taking the oath was being considered – first,
when the proposal was to extend such a right to all who had
religious scruples against taking an oath, and afterwards, when the
proposal was to extend the right further to include those who had
no religious beliefs – the movement for reform was assisted to a
very large extent by two factors: one was the growth of religious
scepticism; the other, an increasing sense of social stability. Of the
two factors, the latter was almost certainly the more important.
Increasing social stability made religion less necessary as a social
cement. This led to more open scepticism and to a decrease in the
significance of those religious rituals, such as the oath in courts of
law, which had hitherto reinforced the links between Church and
state. The significance of social stability in the debates about
compulsory oath-taking can be seen in the arguments of both
proponents and opponents of reform; it was by far the weightiest
consideration on each side.

In these debates – and they took place mainly in Parliament –
the figure of Bentham is remote. His critique of the laws making
witnesses incompetent by reason of their opinions on religion had
received its most extensive publicity two decades before the first
general extension of the right to affirm in 1854, and over forty
years before the final removal of restrictions in 1869. In the
decades after Bentham's death, in 1832, supporters of his opinions
had been able to organise effectively in many instances so as to
influence administrative reforms. However, this sort of organisation was far less easy to achieve where statutory reforms were
concerned. There were two main reasons for this. The first was
that the membership of the House of Commons and of the House
of Lords was too large to be susceptible to the sort of manoeuvres

that worked well in the much smaller units of administrative responsibility. The second was that government support was crucial to the success of reforming legislation, because the requirement that legislation be passed in a single parliamentary session placed a strict limit on the period of time available for effective persuasion and manipulation.

It is not, of course, surprising to find that some supporters of proposed statutory reforms used arguments that had been employed earlier by Bentham; but it does not follow from this that they took their arguments from him. Indeed, Bentham's own arguments had not always been original. More important is the fact that underlying Bentham's proposals was his radical critique, which saw oaths as the instruments of sinister interest, not only of 'Judge & Co' but of the established Church. This highly idiosyncratic feature was adopted only rarely by writers supporting reform outside Parliament, and never by supporters of reform in Parliament.

Of the statutes removing incompetency by reason of infamy or interest, the first of significance in this period was Lord Denman's Act of 1843. This abolished the last instances of incompetency by reason of criminal conviction as well as those rules affecting the competency of non-parties who had an interest in the outcome of litigation. These were reforms that Bentham had advocated and that came about as a result of the efforts of Lord Denman. But, although his thinking on law reform had been influenced by Bentham's work, Denman was far from being a convinced Benthamite. At this stage, for example, he was unprepared to extend competency to the parties themselves in civil actions. Further, Denman could not have been successful without the support of the profession, particularly that of the common law judges and the Attorney General.

The Law of Evidence Amendment Act 1851, which made competent the parties to civil litigation, is probably the most likely product of Benthamite influence among Victorian statutes dealing with evidence. While the contributions of Denman, Brougham, and the Law Amendment Society suggest that this was so, support for the reform can also be explained on the basis of an extension of the principle embodied in the 1843 Act, and the experience of existing practices of dispute resolution in the old courts of requests, the new county courts, and in arbitrations.

Incompetency based on interest was not completely abolished until the passing of the Criminal Evidence Act 1898. Bentham had been concerned to remove the prohibition on testimony from the accused at trial. However, he had also wanted to compel the accused to submit to questioning and would have allowed a court to infer guilt from failure to respond. By contrast, at the time when Bentham was developing this critique, the judges, relying on what they regarded as common law tradition, were encouraging the recognition of a right to silence at the pre-trial hearing before a magistrate. Judges were also allowing the accused to adopt a far more passive role at trial than had been usual during much of the eighteenth century, when accused persons had been expected to respond to judicial questioning.

This isolation of the accused was brought about as counsel began to be increasingly involved in the conduct of criminal trials. However, the pressure that had made the incursion of counsel an acceptable development – the need to provide a fairer hearing to protect defendants more effectively against perjured testimony of self-interested prosecution witnesses – was also likely to lead in time to an increasing demand that all appropriate measures should be taken in the search for truth, including the reception of testimony from the accused. To make accused persons competent could benefit the defence, because it would allow the persons often best qualified to do so to explain what had happened and to have their explanations put on the same level as the testimony of other witnesses. But such a move could also benefit the prosecution by exposing the accused to cross-examination, and it is clear that some, such as Lord Bramwell,[1] supported reform in the hope of redressing the balance in criminal trials, which, in their view, had tipped too far in favour of the defence. The move to allow accused persons to testify is best seen as the final stage in the working-out of the adversarial process, which in the early decades of the nineteenth century had removed the accused from the arena where less formal eighteenth-century procedure had placed him.[2]

---

[1] *Parl. Deb.*, 3rd series, ccciii, 1470–1 (1886).
[2] See also Joel N. Bodansky, 'The Abolition of the Party-Witness Disqualification: an Historical Survey', *Kentucky Law Journal* 70 (1981–2), 129; Graham Parker, 'The Prisoner in the Box – the Making of the Criminal Evidence Act, 1898', in J. A. Guy and H. G. Beale, eds., *Law and Social Change in British History: Papers Presented to the British Legal History Conference, 14–17 July 1981*, Royal

The debates on this reform, though they appear to have interested a wider public than those concerning earlier reforms, were still largely conducted in Parliament and by members who had some connection with the legal profession.[3] The key to success was to persuade a majority in the profession, and then in the Government of the day, that, although some adjustment might be necessary, there would be no radical alteration in the existing balance of power in criminal trials between judge, counsel and the accused. This is shown by the importance attached in debates to the fear that a change in the law would lead to more direct judicial intervention in the proceedings, or that the position of the accused would be weakened, either by their being forced to testify or because the burden or standard of proof would be affected. Although such fears can be found until 1898, the more entrenched the existing adversarial system became, the less the danger appeared to be.

As on earlier occasions, some of the arguments urged in favour of reform had affinities with arguments deployed by Bentham, and Benthamite ideas can be found in the work of Brougham and of the Law Amendment Society. It is also possible that Bentham's critique played an indirect part in the reform through examples set in America, where similar reforms can be traced more directly to Bentham through the endeavours of Chief Justice Appleton. But the legislation passed in 1898 protected the accused to a large extent from a comprehensive cross-examination and thereby limited the search for truth, which had been the declared aim of Bentham's recommendation to extend competency to the accused. The accused's right to silence, which Bentham had notoriously criticised, was recognised by statute in 1848 in relation to pre-trial proceedings. It was preserved by the 1898 legislation, and the right to comment on its exercise was limited.

Because of the lack of an effective criminal appellate system before 1907, such development of the common law of evidence as

Historical Society Studies in History Series No. 40 (London and New Jersey, 1984), pp. 156–75.
[3] It has already been observed that issues involving criminal procedure arising during the nineteenth century were mostly discussed in legal circles: see W. R. Cornish, 'Criminal Justice and Punishment', in *Crime and Law in Nineteenth Century Britain*, ed. W. R. Cornish *et al.* (Dublin, 1978), p. 57. However, in relation to the competency of accused persons there was more division and less conservatism than this essay suggests.

took place tended to be in the civil courts. But that development was diametrically opposed to the line proposed by Bentham. What emerged was a system of law that became increasingly rule based, whereas Bentham had denied the possibility of making effective rules to govern the reception of evidence. Evidence law also became increasingly exclusionary, whereas Bentham had advocated freedom of proof, insisting that matters affecting weight should not be allowed to affect admissibility. After the creation of the Court of Criminal Appeal in 1907, criminal evidence followed the same rule-based, exclusionary pattern as its civil counterpart.

The story I have suggested as a replacement for that of 'Bentham's immense influence' is one that is more complex. It shows at all stages of legislation the power of a legal profession that had for the greater part to be convinced before a reform could succeed. The power of the profession emerges again when we consider the part played in legal development by the working-out of a new, adversarial way of conducting criminal trials. This seems to have begun on an ad hoc basis, perhaps stimulated by little more than the need for young barristers to extend their opportunities for practice in an overcrowded profession. The new story shows a more flexible approach to oaths in an apparently more stable society, in which religion seemed less vital as a social cement. Another part of the story involves a new way of looking at the common law by setting greater store on rule-based certainty than on flexibility and discretion. In the end, the story is not one of evidence law as a self-contained system, influenced primarily by the work of a great jurisprudent, but of evidence law as a part of the Victorian world to which it belonged – influenced by a variety of social, political, and intellectual pressures.

APPENDIX

[See ch. 5, n. 99.]

The following comic sketch, described as coming from 'an old number of a well-known periodical', was reproduced by a correspondent on the subject of a bill to make accused persons competent witnesses in 1865. (*Solicitors' Journal and Reporter* 9 (1864–5), 500–1).

TWO CRIMINAL TRIALS

Scene – *An English court of justice*

The Law. Prisoner, don't plead guilty. How do you know whether a case can be made out against you?

Prisoner. Thank you, my lord, but as I did it –

The Law. Be silent, my good man. How do you know you did it – did what your offence is said to be?

Witness. My Lord, he did take –

The Law. Be very careful, sir. Remember your oath. How do you know that it was this man?

Witness. I have known him, I should think, for –

The Law. Never mind what you think. Did you see him take the thing?

Witness. I was walking –

The Law. Who asked whether you were walking, or riding, or flying, or crawling on your stomach? Answer the question. Did you see him?

Witness. Yes, my lord.

The Law. Was it at night or in the day?

Witness. At night.

The Law. Can you see in the dark?

Witness. There was a moon, my lord.

The Law. Of course there was; but did it shine?

Witness. Very brightly.

The Law. You can swear that it was he, and no one else?

Witness. Yes, my lord.

The Law. Do you know that he has a brother very like him?

Witness. It wasn't his brother, my lord.

The Law. Answer the question, or you'll get into trouble. Do you know the fact that his brother is very like him?

Witness. He is not so very like, my lord.

The Law. How dare you say that? It is only your opinion. Will you swear that there was light enough to enable you to be certain that this was the man?

Witness. I know the fellow well enough, my lord.

The Law. How dare you call him names? You dislike him evidently, and the jury will be cautious in accepting your evidence. Be careful, sir!

Prisoner. He tells the truth, my lord. I did –

The Law. Hold your tongue, my poor man.

Prisoner. But it is true that I took –

The Law. Keep him silent, gaoler. Go down, you sir, and feel ashamed of having shown animosity in that sacred box. Gentleman of the jury – Such charges are easily made, but disproved with difficulty. The witness had evidently an animus. The prisoner has borne a good character, at least nothing has been proved against him, and his readiness to admit everything is creditable to him. Still, it is for you to say guilty or not guilty.

Jury. Guilty, my lord!

The Law. As the jury has found you guilty of stealing these sovereigns, prisoner, I have only to pass sentence, which I shall make very light. You will be imprisoned, without hard labour, for a month.

Prisoner. I can do that on my head, my lord.

[*Flings his nailed shoe at the foreman, and exit shouting.*]

Scene – *A French court of justice*

The Law. Prisoner, I am afraid you are an awful scoundrel. Why don't you confess, and make reparation to society?

Prisoner. Because I am innocent.

The Law. You say that with a certain impudence which proves you hardened in crime. How came you to rob your master?

Prisoner. I never did.

The Law. This reiteration of a plea which is clearly false is disrespectful to the Court, and will aggravate your punishment. Are you fond of the theatre?

Prisoner. Yes.

The Law. That denotes a love of pleasure which is frequently found united with dishonesty. Do you smoke?

Prisoner. A good deal.

The Law. Doubtless, to stupify the reproaches of a menacing conscience. Do you go to mass?

Prisoner. At regular times.

The Law. That shows you to be a hypocrite. Now witness, is he not guilty?

Witness. No, my lord.

The Law. How dare you say that? Did you commit the crime yourself?

Witness. Certainly not.

The Law. Don't answer in that petulant way. What is your character? Are you fond of the theatre?

Witness. No.

The Law. Just so. A dark and gloomy nature cannot enjoy innocent recreation. Do you smoke?

Witness. Very little.

The Law. You fear to be traced by the smell of your clothes. You know that tobacco increases our revenue, and you wilfully abstain in order to injure your country. Do you go to mass?

Witness. Seldom.

The Law. You feel your evil character unfits you for the solemnities of the Church. Go down. The next. Now, what have you to say, woman?

Witness. The accused is an excellent husband –

The Law. Are you his wife?

Witness. No, my lord, but his wife's friend, and I know –

The Law. Then the less you have to say in the future to the wife of an accused person the better. Perhaps you are in love with him?

Witness. My lord, I have a husband whom I love, and children whom I adore, and because any of them might be charged falsely, as the prisoner is, I came to say what I can for justice.

The Law. That theatrical sentiment you have learned from some play, and your reciting it here is most indecent. Go down. Gentlemen of the jury, – It is quite clear that this scoundrel is guilty. His insolent denials, the class of witnesses, atheists, profligates, frequenters of theatres, gloomy conspirators, and the like make his guilt evident; besides which a gaoler heard him say *Mon Dieu* in sleep, which showed temporary remorse. Finally, I happen to know that he is guilty, for I knew his father in his youth, and he was a vile assassin. Gentlemen, you have only to say Guilty.

The Jury. Not guilty.

The Law. You are a contumacious set of rebellious and illogical pigs, and I shall see whether the Procureur of his Majesty cannot deal with you as conspirators. Meanwhile, abandon the box you have disgraced.

[*Exeunt the jurymen, confirmed in Imperialism.*]

BIBLIOGRAPHY

PRIMARY SOURCES
Manuscript sources

Bentham Papers at University College London. ['UCL' followed by box and page numbers.]

Brougham Papers at University College London. ['Brougham MSS' followed by number.]

Parliamentary papers

Parliamentary Debates, New Series, 3rd series, and 4th series.

Bills in House of Commons and House of Lords Sessional Papers. [References to the latter are those in the British Library catalogue.]

Second Report of H. M. Commissioners for Inquiring into the Process, Practice, and System of Pleading in the Superior Courts of Common Law. PP 1852–3 [1626] XL.

Report of the Royal Commission appointed to consider the Law Relating to Indictable Offences. (1879) [C. 2345].

Special Report and Reports on the Criminal Code (Indictable Offences Procedure) Bill, and the Court of Criminal Appeal Bill with the Proceedings of the Standing Committee on Law and Courts of Justice and Legal Procedure. House of Commons Parliamentary Papers 1883 (225) XI 319.

Newspapers and periodicals

All the Year Round

Annual Register

Edinburgh Review

Jurist, or Quarterly Journal of Jurisprudence and Legislation

Law Magazine, or Quarterly Review of Jurisprudence [1828–56]

Law Magazine and Law Review or Quarterly Journal of Jurisprudence [1856–71]

Law Magazine and Review (New Series) [1872–5]

Law Magazine and Review (4th Series) [1876–98]

Law Review and Quarterly Journal of British and Foreign Jurisprudence [1844–56]
Law Times
Legal Observer or Journal of Jurisprudence
National Review
Nineteenth Century
Solicitors' Journal and Reporter
The Times
Westminster Review

Books, pamphlets, and articles

Appleton, John. *The Rules of Evidence Stated and Discussed.* Philadelphia, Penn., 1860.
Archbold, J. F. *The Justice of the Peace, and Parish Officer.* London, 1840.
Bacon, Francis. *The Works of Francis Bacon.* Edited by J. Spedding, R. Ellis, and D. Heath. London, 1857–74.
Bentham, Jeremy. *The Works of Jeremy Bentham, Published under the Superintendence of his Executor, John Bowring,* 11 vols. Edinburgh, 1838–43. ['*Works*']
 '*Swear not at All*': *Containing an Exposure of the Inutility and Mischievousness . . . of the Ceremony of an Oath.* London, 1813.
 Traité des preuves judiciaires, Ouvrage extrait des MSS de M Jeremie Bentham, jurisconsulte anglais, par Et Dumont. Paris, 1823.
 A Treatise on Judicial Evidence, Extracted from the MSS of Jeremy Bentham by M. Dumont, Translated into English. London, 1825.
 Rationale of Judicial Evidence, Specially Applied to English Practice, from the MSS of Jeremy Bentham. London, 1827.
Best, William Draper. *The Substance of a Charge Delivered to the Grand Jury of Wiltshire at the Summer Assizes 1827, by the Lord Chief Justice Best.* London, 1827.
Best, William Mawdesley. *A Treatise on the Principles of Evidence and Practice as to Proofs in Courts of Common Law; with Elementary Rules for Conducting the Examination and Cross-Examination of Witnesses.* London, 1849, and subsequent edns. ['Best, *Treatise*']
Billing, Sidney. *A Practical Treatise on the Law of Awards and Arbitrations, with Forms of Pleadings, Submissions and Awards.* London, 1845.
Blackstone, Sir William. *Commentaries on the Laws of England.* Edited by Edward Christian. 15th edn. London, 1809.
Bowen, Edward. 'Bishop Colenso on the Pentateuch'. *The National Review* 16 (January and April 1863), pp. 1–27.
Brougham, Henry. *A Speech on the Present State of the Law of the Country; Delivered in the House of Commons, on Thursday, February 7, 1828.* 2nd edn. London, 1828.
 Speeches of Henry Lord Brougham upon Questions Relating to Public Rights, Duties & Interests; with Historical Introductions, and a

Critical Dissertation upon the Eloquence of the Ancients. Edinburgh, 1838.

Burn, Richard. *The Justice of the Peace and Parish Officer.* 14th edn. London, 1780.

Cobbett's Complete Collection of State Trials and Proceedings for High Treason and other Crimes and Misdemeanours from the Earliest Period to the Present Time. Edited by T. B. Howell. London, 1809.

Coke, Sir Edward. *The First Part of the Institutes of the Laws of England; or, a Commentary upon Littleton.* Edited by Francis Hargreave and Charles Butler. 19th edn. London, 1832.

[Collier, John Payne]. *Criticisms on the Bar; Including Strictures on the Principal Counsel Practising in the Courts of King's Bench, Common Pleas, Chancery and Exchequer.* London, 1819.

Cottu, Charles. *On the Administration of Criminal Justice in England; and the spirit of the English Government.* Translated from the French. London, 1822.

Dickens, Charles. 'Examine the Prisoner.' *All the Year Round* 7 (7 June 1862), 306–8.

Gilbert, Sir Jeffrey. *The Law of Evidence.* 3rd edn. London, 1769.

Gisborne, Thomas. *An Enquiry into the Duties of Men in the Higher and Middle Classes of Society in Great Britain.* 2nd edn. London, 1795.

Green, T. H. *Works of Thomas Hill Green.* Edited by R. L. Nettleship. 3rd edn. London, 1891.

Hague, Thomas. *A Letter to William Garrow . . .* London, ?1810.

Hale, Sir Matthew. *The History of the Pleas of the Crown.* Edited by George Wilson. London, 1778.

Hawkins, William. *A Treatise of the Pleas of the Crown; or a System of the Principal Matters Relating to that Subject, Digested under Proper Heads.* Edited by Thomas Leach. 6th edn, London, 1787; 7th edn, London, 1795.

Hooker, Richard. *Of the Laws of Ecclesiastical Polity.* Everyman's Library edn. London, 1907.

Lambarde, William. *Eirenarcha.* Rev. edn, London, 1614.

Lamoine, Georges (ed.). *Charges to the Grand Jury 1689–1803.* Camden Fourth Series, vol. XXXXIII. London, 1992.

Lewis, E. D. *On the Codification of the Criminal Law of England.* London, 1878.

Locke, John. *An Essay Concerning Human Understanding.* Edited with a foreword by Peter H. Nidditch. Oxford, 1975.

Longley, Charles Thomas. *A Charge Addressed to the Clergy of Ripon at the Triennial Visitation in September 1844.* 1844.

Lowndes, John J. *A Few Brief Remarks on Lord Denman's Bill for Improving the Law of Evidence.* London, 1843.

Mill, J. S. *Collected Works of John Stuart Mill.* Edited by John M. Robson and Jack Stillinger. Toronto, 1963–91.

More, Hannah. *The Works of Hannah More.* London, 1853.

Morley, John. (Viscount Morley). *Critical Miscellanies.* London, 1886.

Paley, William. *The Principles of Moral and Political Philosophy*. London, 1785 and subsequent edns.

Phillipps, Samuel March. *A Treatise on the Law of Evidence*. London, 1814, and subsequent edns. ['Phillipps, *Treatise*']

Politics for the People (Anon.) London, 1848.

Pothier, R. J. *A Treatise on the Law of Obligations, or Contracts. Translated from the French, with an Introduction, Appendix, and Notes, Illustrative of the English Law on the Subject by William Davie Evans, Esq Barrister at Law*. London, 1806.

Pretyman, George; afterwards Tomline. *A Sermon Preached before the Lords Spiritual and Temporal in the Abbey Church at Westminster, on Friday, January 30, 1789*. London, 1789.

Romilly, Sir Samuel. *Memoirs of the Life of Sir Samuel Romilly, Written by Himself; with a Selection from His Correspondence. Edited by his Sons*. London, 1840; repr. Shannon, 1971.

Starkie, Thomas. *A Practical Treatise of the Law of Evidence, and Digest of Proofs in Civil and Criminal Proceedings*. London, 1824 and subsequent edns. ['Starkie, *Treatise*']

Stephen, Sir Herbert. *Prisoners on Oath: Present and Future*. London, 1898.

Stephen, Sir James Fitzjames. *A General View of the Criminal Law of England*. London, 1863.

'Suggestions as to the Reform of the Criminal Law.' *Nineteenth Century* 2 (1877).

The Indian Evidence Act with an Introduction on the Principles of Judicial Evidence. Calcutta, 1872.

A Digest of the Law of Evidence. 2nd edn. London, 1876.

Taylor, J. Pitt. *Treatise on the Law of Evidence*. London, 1848 and subsequent edns. ['Taylor, *Treatise*']

'On the Expediency of Passing an Act to Permit Defendants in Criminal Courts, and their Wives or Husbands, to Testify on Oath.' *Solicitors' Journal and Reporter* 5 (1861–1), 363–4.

Trelawny, Sir John. *The Parliamentary Diaries of Sir John Trelawny, 1858–1865*. Edited by T. A. Jenkins. Camden Fourth Series, vol. XXXX. London, 1990.

The Parliamentary Diaries of Sir John Trelawny, 1868–73. Edited by T. A. Jenkins. *Camden Miscellany* XXXII, Camden Fifth Series, vol. III. London, 1994.

Vaughan, Charles John. *Sermons Preached in the Chapel of Harrow School*. London, 1847.

Wilmot, Sir John E. Eardley. *Lord Brougham's Acts and Bills, from 1811 to the Present Time, now first Collected and Arranged, with an Analytical Review Shewing their Results upon the Amendment of the Law*. London, 1857.

Worsley, Francis. *An Examination of Mr Pitt Taylor's Thesis 'On the Expediency of Passing an Act to Permit Defendants in Criminal Courts and their Wives or Husbands to Testify on Oath'*. London, 1861.

194   *Bibliography*

SECONDARY WORKS

Allen, Sir Carleton Kemp. *Law in the Making*. 7th edn. Oxford, 1964.

Arnould, Sir Joseph. *Memoir of Thomas, First Lord Denman*. London, 1873.

Atiyah, P. S. *The Rise and Fall of Freedom of Contract*. Oxford, 1979.

Bagehot, Walter. *Biographical Studies*. Edited by R. H. Hutton. New edn. London, 1907.

Baker, J. H. 'Criminal Courts and Procedure at Common Law 1550–1800.' In J. S. Cockburn, ed., *Crime in England 1550–1800*, pp. 15–48. London, 1977.

An Introduction to English Legal History. 3rd edn. London, 1990.

Beattie, J. M. *Crime and the Courts in England 1660–1800*. Oxford, 1986.

'Scales of Justice: Defence Counsel and the English Criminal Trial in the Eighteenth and Nineteenth Centuries.' *Law and History Review* 9 (1991), 221–67.

Bodansky, Joel N. 'The Abolition of the Party-Witness Disqualification: an Historical Survey.' *Kentucky Law Journal* 70 (1981–2), 91–130.

Briggs, Asa. *The Age of Improvement: 1783–1867*. Rev. edn. London, 1979.

Burn, W. L. *The Age of Equipoise: a Study of the Mid-Victorian Generation*. London, 1968.

Chadwick, Owen. *The Secularization of the European Mind in the Nineteenth Century*. Canto edn. Cambridge, 1990.

Clark, J. C. D. *English Society 1688–1832*. Cambridge, 1985.

Coleridge, Ernest Hartley. *Life & Correspondence of John Duke Lord Coleridge Lord Chief Justice of England*. London, 1904.

Conway, Stephen. 'Bentham and the Nineteenth-Century Revolution in Government.' In Richard Bellamy, ed., *Victorian Liberalism: Nineteenth-Century Political Thought and Practice*, pp. 71–90. London, 1990.

Cornish, W. R. 'Criminal Justice and Punishment.' In W. R. Cornish *et al.*, eds., *Crime and Law in Nineteenth Century Britain*, pp. 7–65. Dublin, 1978.

Cornish, W. R. and G. de N. Clark. *Law and Society in England 1750–1950*. London, 1989.

Crimmins, James E. *Secular Utilitarianism: Social Science and the Critique of Religion in the Thought of Jeremy Bentham*. Oxford, 1990.

Cross, J. W. *George Eliot's Life as Related in her Letters and Journals*. Edinburgh and London, 1885.

Damaska, Mirjan R. *The Faces of Justice and State Authority: a Comparative Approach to the Legal Process*. New Haven, Conn. and London, 1986.

Daniel, W. T. S. *The History and Origin of the Law Reports*. London, n.d.

Dicey, A. V. *Lectures on the Relation between Law and Public Opinion in England during the Nineteenth Century*. London, 1905; 2nd edn., 1914.

Dillon, John Forrest. 'Bentham's Influence in the Reforms of the Nineteenth Century.' In *Select Essays in Anglo-American Legal History*, compiled and edited by a committee of the Association of American Law Schools, vol. I, pp. 492–515. Cambridge, 1907.

Dinwiddy, John. *Bentham*. Oxford, 1989.

Duff, R. A. *Trials and Punishments*. Cambridge, 1986.

Duman, Daniel. 'Pathway to Professionalism: the English Bar in the Eighteenth and Nineteenth Centuries.' *Journal of Social History* (1980), 615–28.

Evans, Jim. 'Change in the Doctrine of Precedent during the Nineteenth Century.' In Laurence Goldstein, ed., *Precedent in Law*, pp. 35–72. Oxford, 1987.

Fay, C. R. *Palace of Industry, 1851: a Study of the Great Exhibition and its Fruits*. Cambridge, 1951.

Finer, S. E. 'The Transmission of Benthamite Ideas 1820–50.' In Gillian Sutherland, ed., *Studies in the Growth of Nineteenth-Century Government*, pp. 11–32. London, 1972.

Froude, James Anthony. *Thomas Carlyle: a History of his Life in London, 1834–1881*. New impression. London, 1919.

Gatrell, V. A. C. *The Hanging Tree: Execution and the English People 1770–1868*. Oxford, 1994.

Gold, David M. *The Shaping of Nineteenth-Century Law: John Appleton and Responsible Individualism*. New York, 1990.

Goldman, Lawrence. 'The Social Science Association, 1857–1886: a Context for Mid-Victorian Liberalism.' *English Historical Review* 101 (1986), 95–134.

Green, V. H. H. *Oxford Common Room: a Study of Lincoln College and Mark Pattison*. London, 1957.

Guest, Stephen. 'The Scope of the Hearsay Rule.' *Law Quarterly Review* 101 (1985), 385–404.

Halévy, Elie. *The Growth of Philosophic Radicalism*. Trans. Mary Morris. London, 1928.

A History of the English People in the Nineteenth Century. Trans. E. I. Watkin. 2nd edn. London, 1949.

Harrison, Ross. *Bentham*. London, 1983.

Hart, H. L. A. 'The Demystification of the Law.' In *Essays on Bentham: Studies in Jurisprudence and Political Theory*, pp. 21–39. Oxford, 1982.

Hay, D. and F. Snyder (eds.). *Policing and Prosecution in Britain, 1750–1850*. Oxford, 1989.

Hinchcliff, Peter. *Benjamin Jowett and the Christian Religion*. Oxford, 1987.

Holdsworth, Sir William. *A History of English Law*. London, 1922–66.

Hole, Robert. *Pulpits, Politics and Public Order in England, 1760–1832*. Cambridge, 1989.

Howson, C. and Peter Urbach. *Scientific Reasoning: the Bayesian Approach*. La Salle, Ill., 1989.

Jackson, Claire. 'Irish Political Opposition to the Passage of Criminal Evidence Reform at Westminster, 1883–98.' In J. F. McEldowney and Paul O'Higgins, eds., *The Common Law Tradition: Essays in Irish Legal History*, pp. 185–201. Blackrock, 1990.

Keeton, G. W. and O. R. Marshall. 'Bentham's Influence on the Law of Evidence.' In G. W. Keeton and G. Schwarzenberger, eds., *Jeremy Bentham and the Law*, pp. 49–101. London, 1948.

Kelley, Donald R. 'History, English Law and the Renaissance.' *Past and Present* 65 (1974), 24–51; 72 (1976), 143–6.

Landsman, Stephan. 'The Rise of the Contentious Spirit: Adversary Procedure in Eighteenth Century England.' *Cornell Law Review* 75 (1990), 497–609.

'From Gilbert to Bentham: the Reconceptualization of Evidence Theory.' *Wayne Law Review* 36 (1990), 1149–86.

Langbein, John H. *Prosecuting Crime in the Renaissance: England, Germany, France.* Cambridge, Mass., 1974.

'The Criminal Trial before the Lawyers.' *University of Chicago Law Review* 45 (1978), 263–316.

'Shaping the Eighteenth-Century Criminal Trial: a View from the Ryder Sources.' *University of Chicago Law Review* 50 (1983), 1–136.

'The Historical Origins of the Privilege against Self-Incrimination at Common Law.' *Michigan Law Review* 92 (1994), 1047–85.

Lewis, A. D. E. 'Bentham's View of the Right to Silence.' In Roger Rideout and Bob Hepple, eds., *Current Legal Problems 1990*, pp. 135–57. London, 1990.

'The Background to Bentham on Evidence.' *Utilitas* 2 (1990), 195–219.

Lieberman, David. *The Province of Legislation Determined: Legal Theory in Eighteenth-Century Britain.* Cambridge, 1989.

Lobban, Michael. *The Common Law and English Jurisprudence 1760–1850.* Oxford, 1991.

Macaulay, Thomas Babington, 1st Baron Macaulay. *The History of England from the Accession of James II.* Repr. London, 1880.

Maine, Sir Henry Sumner. *Ancient Law.* New edn. with notes by Sir Frederick Pollock. London, 1930.

Manchester, A. H. *A Modern Legal History of England and Wales 1750–1950.* London, 1980.

Martin, Benjamin F. *Crime and Criminal Justice under the Third Republic: the Shame of Marianne.* Baton Rouge, La. and London, 1990.

Menlowe, Michael A. 'Bentham, Self-Incrimination and the Law of Evidence.' *Law Quarterly Review* 104 (1988), 286–307.

Midgley, T. S. 'The Role of Legal History.' *British Journal of Law and Society* 2 (1975), 153–65.

Nance, Dale A. 'The Best Evidence Principle.' *Iowa Law Review* 73 (1988): 227–97.

Newsome, David. *Godliness and Good Learning: Four Studies on a Victorian Ideal.* London, 1961.

Parker, Graham. 'The Prisoner in the Box – the Making of the Criminal Evidence Act, 1898.' In J. A. Guy and H. G. Beale, eds., *Law and Social Change in British History: Papers Presented to the Bristol Legal*

History Conference, 14–17 July 1981, pp. 156–75. Royal Historical Society Studies in History Series No. 40. London, 1984.

Plucknett, Theodore F. T. *A Concise History of the Common Law*. 5th edn. London, 1956.

Pocock, J. G. A. *The Ancient Constitution and the Feudal Law: a Study of English Historical Thought in the Seventeenth Century*. Reissue with retrospect. Cambridge, 1987.

Post, J. B. 'The Admissibility of Defence Counsel in English Criminal Procedure.' *Journal of Legal History* 5 (1984), 23–32.

Postema, Gerald J. *Bentham and the Common Law Tradition*. Oxford, 1986.

Radzinowicz, Sir Leon. *A History of English Criminal Law and its Administration from 1750*. London, 1948–86. ['Radzinowicz, *History of English Criminal Law*']

Sir James Fitzjames Stephen (1829–1894) and his Contribution to the Development of Criminal Law. Selden Society Lecture. London, 1957.

Richter, Melvin. *The Politics of Conscience: T. H. Green and His Age*. London, 1964; repr. Lanham, 1983.

Royle, Edward. *Victorian Infidels: the Origins of the British Secularist Movement 1791–1866*. Manchester, 1974.

Shannon, Richard. *The Crisis of Imperialism 1865–1915*. Paladin edn. London, 1976.

Shapin, Steven. *A Social History of Truth: Civility and Science in Seventeenth-Century England*. Chicago, Ill., 1994.

Shapiro, Barbara J. 'Law Reform in Seventeenth Century England.' *American Journal of Legal History* 19 (1975), 280–312.

'Sir Francis Bacon and the Mid-Seventeenth Century Movement for Law Reform.' *American Journal of Legal History* 24 (1980), 331–62.

Sidgwick, A. and E. M. Sidgwick. *Henry Sidgwick: a Memoir*. London, 1906.

Silving, Helen. 'The Oath: I.' *Yale Law Journal* 68 (1959), 1329–90.

Simpson, A. W. B. 'The Rise and Fall of the Legal Treatise: Legal Principles and the Forms of Legal Literature.' *University of Chicago Law Review* 48 (1981), 632–79.

(ed.). *Biographical Dictionary of the Common Law*. London, 1984.

Smith, Harry. 'The Resurgent County Court in Victorian Britain.' *American Journal of Legal History* 13 (1969), 126–38.

Smith, K. J. M. *James Fitzjames Stephen: Portrait of a Victorian Rationalist*. Cambridge, 1988.

and Stephen White. 'An Episode in Criminal Law Reform through Private Initiative.' In Peter Birks, ed., *The Life of the Law*, pp. 235–56. Proceedings of the Tenth British Legal History Conference Oxford 1991. London, 1993.

Stevenson, John. *Popular Disturbances in England 1700–1870*. London, 1979.

Stewart, Robert. *Henry Brougham 1778–1868: His Public Career*. London, 1986.

Stone, Julius and W. A. N. Wells. *Evidence: its History and Policies.* Sydney, 1991.

Sugarman, David. 'Legal Theory, the Common Law Mind and the Making of the Textbook Tradition.' In William Twining, ed., *Legal Theory and Common Law*, pp. 26–61. Oxford, 1986.

Thayer, James B. *A Preliminary Treatise on Evidence at the Common Law.* Boston, Mass., 1898.

Thomas, William. *The Philosophic Radicals: Nine Studies in Theory and Practice 1817–1841.* Oxford, 1979.

Twining, William. *Theories of Evidence: Bentham and Wigmore.* London, 1985.

'1836 and All That: Laws in the University of London 1836–1986.' In B. Hepple, ed., *Current Legal Problems 1987.* London, 1987.

Rethinking Evidence: Exploratory Essays. Evanston, Ill., 1990.

Waddams, S. M. *Law, Politics and the Church of England: the Career of Stephen Lushington 1782–1873.* Cambridge, 1992.

Wiener, Martin J. *Reconstructing the Criminal: Culture, Law, and Policy in England, 1830–1914.* Cambridge, 1990.

Wigmore, J. H. *A Treatise on the System of Evidence in Trials at Common Law.* Edited by Peter Tillers. Boston, Mass., 1983.

Wilson, Sir Roland K. *The History of Modern English Law.* London, 1875.

Winder, W. H. D. 'The Courts of Requests.' *Law Quarterly Review* 52 (1936), 369–94.

Woodward, Sir Llewellyn. *The Age of Reform 1815–1870.* 2nd edn. Oxford, 1962.

Zuckerman, A. A. S. *The Principles of Criminal Evidence.* Oxford, 1989.

INDEX

privilege (*cont.*)
  private members' bills 133, 134, 135, 136
  Stephen's code 136
  see also right to silence
procedural law
  Bentham's views 9–10, 20, 54, 127–8
  family as model 9–10
public opinion 52
publicity 130
punitory laws 127

Quakers 52, 56–7
  influences on reforms 65–7

reforms
  affirmation 56–8, 60–1, 65–7
  incompetency of accused
    criminal law codes 135–41
    government measures 142–4
    private members' bills 132–5
  incompetency from infamy 100–1
  incompetency from interest 100–4
  religious incompetency
    Baptists 58
    Moravians 56–7, 65–7
    non-believers 58, 60–1
    objectors to oaths 57–60
    Separatists 57
relatives of parties 98
relevancy 28
religion
  Bentham's views 54–5
  relation with truth 168
  social function 62, 71–4, 76, 83
religious incompetency
  Bentham's views 52–6
    criticisms 89, 90–1
  common law 50–2
  competency examinations 51–2
  influences on reforms 182–3
    absurdity 85, 93
    Bentham 66–7, 88–94, 182–3
    Catholic emancipation 66
    double standard of truth 85–6, 93
    individual rights 87–8
    just convictions 76–7
    perjury 86–7, 93
    public safety 65–6
    religious scepticism 61–2, 67–72, 84–5, 93
    security of property 77–8, 93
    social stability 61–2, 72–6, 84, 93

justification 50–1
opposition to reforms 79–84
reforms
  Baptists 58
  Moravians 56–7, 65–7
  non-believers 58, 60–1
  objectors to oaths 57–60
  Quakers 52, 56–7, 65–7
  Separatists 57
religious scepticism 61–2, 67–72, 84–5, 93
  attitudes to 63–5
reports of cases 25, 148
representation of accused 145–51
rewards for evidence 148
right to affirm *see* affirmation
right to silence 123–7, 142–3
  Bentham's views 127–31
  inference of guilt 128, 159–61, 175
    Bentham's views 178–9
  proposed reforms 158–9, 175
  see also incompetency of accused
Royal Commission on Law Relating to Indictable Offences 136
rules of adjudication 127
rules of evidence *see* exclusionary rules of evidence

sanctions of truth 50–1, 86–7, 92–3
Scully, Vincent 132, 134
secularism 68, 70
  see also religious scepticism
self-realisation 174
Separatists 57
sexual offences 166
silence *see* right to silence
Social Science Association 86, 177
social stability
  function of religion 72–4, 76, 83
  influences on reforms 61–2, 72–6, 84, 93
  opposition to reforms 79–84
  relation with oaths 72
speeches of counsel 146
Spinks, Frederick Lowton 138
spouses
  affidavits 167
  compellability
    civil cases 103, 104
    criminal cases 133, 134, 143
  competency
    civil cases 98, 102, 103–4, 105
    criminal cases 133, 134, 136, 143, 167

divorce cases 165
examination 98, 102, 103, 103–4, 105
stability *see* social stability
standard of proof 158–61
Starkie's *Treatise*
  accomplice evidence 46–7
  declarations against interest 37
  incompetency from infamy 95–6
  incompetency from interest 96
  justification of exclusionary rules 20–3
Stephen, Sir Herbert 156, 161*n*
Stephen, Sir James Fitzjames
  codification
    criminal law 135–6
    evidence law 27–8
    relevancy principle 28
  views
    common law 28
    incompetency of accused 160, 171
    religion 68
    religious incompetency 84–5
subornation of perjury 113
substantive law 2
  Bentham's views 8
suscitation (Bentham's views) 11
sworn evidence *see* oaths

technical procedure 9, 10, 54
textbooks *see* treatises
Tractarianism 68
treatises 2
  accomplice evidence 43, 44, 46–7
  declarations in course of business 34

development of exclusionary rules 17–18
justification 20–4
exposition of exclusionary rules of evidence 2
influence 14–15
trials
  France contrasted 147–8, 152–4, 187–9
  roles
    accused 3, 123, 146–8
    counsel 145–7, 150–1
    judges 3, 146–7, 155–7
truth
  double standard 12, 52–3, 85–6
  relation with religion 168
  sanctions 50–1, 86–7, 92–3
  value 168

United States 10–11, 177–8
utilitarianism 5–6
  calculation of utility 9, 98

Wheelhouse, William 138
Wills, Alfred 156
Wilson, Sir Richard K. 4–5
witnesses
  compellability 109
  sanctions of truth 50–1, 86–7, 92–3
  see also accused; examination of witnesses; incompetency of accused; incompetency from infamy; incompetency from interest; religious incompetency
wives *see* spouses
written evidence 17–18